USING THE WEB TO COMPETE IN A GLOBAL MARKETPLACE

BROWNING ROCKWELL

WILEY COMPUTER PUBLISHING

JOHN WILEY & SONS

New York • Chichester • Weinheim • Brisba

CW00969892

Publisher: Robert Ipsen
Editor: Cary Sullivan
Assistant Editor: Kathryn A. Malm
Managing Editor: Brian Snapp
Electronic Products, Associate Editor: Michael Sosa
Text Design & Composition: Pronto Design & Production, Inc.

Designations used by companies to distinguish their products are often claimed as trademarks. In all instances where John Wiley & Sons, Inc., is aware of a claim, the product names appear in initial capital or ALL CAPITAL LETTERS. Readers, however, should contact the appropriate companies for more complete information regarding trademarks and registration.

This book is printed on acid-free paper. ∞

This publication is designed to provide accurate and authoritative information in regard to the subject matter covered. It is sold with the understanding that the pub-lisher is not engaged in rendering professional services. If professional advice or other expert assistance is required, the services of a competent professional per-son should be sought.

Internet World, Web Week, Web Developer, Internet Shopper, and Mecklermedia are the exclusive trademarks of Mecklermedia Corporation and are used with permission.

Library of Congress Cataloging-in-Publication Data:
Rockwell, Browning, 1955–
    Using the Web to compete in a global marketplace / Browning Rockwell.
        p.   cm.
    Includes index.
    ISBN 0-471-25262-X (pbk./online:alk.paper)
    1. Business enterprises—computer networks. 2. Industrial management—Computer network resources. 3. Internet advertising. 4. World Wide Web (Informa-tion retrieval system) 5. Electronic commerce.   I. Title.
    HD30.37.R63   1998
    658'.054678--dc21   98-24483
                                                                    CIP

Printed in the United States of America.

10 9 8 7 6 5 4 3 2 1

CONTENTS

DEDICATION

This book is dedicated to my patient and loving family—my wife Linda and my children Bailey, Johnny, Sydney, and Hayden—for their support, strength and sense of humor. I get such pleasure in exploring the world and all its webs with them—real, virtual, and otherwise.

Browning Rockwell
April, 1998

ACKNOWLEDGMENTS

Running a busy international trading company—Horizon Trading Company (www.horizoninc.com)—and not one but *two* global Web sites—Trade Compass (www.tradecompass.com) and the Global Information Network (www.ginfo.net)—each day leaves little spare time to do anything but sleep. So when I got a call from Cary Sullivan, the insightful editor from Wiley who asked me to write this book, I almost said no. It's not that I haven't wanted to do a book all these years. It's just that I was afraid I might never see my family again.

Fortunately, however, we worked out an arrangement that gave me some help. I owe a great debt to each of the contributing authors in this project—Tunga Kiyak, Jim Kessler, Tina Duong, Jennifer Albert, John Fontaine, Brian Eckert, Garrett Wasny, and Patricia Steele. As the principal contributor to this book, Garrett deserves special mention for sharing his considerable expertise concerning trade and the Internet in Chapters 9 through 12.

I would also like to thank David Cutler, who is responsible for bringing this project to life. David kept us all on track—begging, prodding, and pleading with all of us to make our contributions to the cause. In addition, I would like to thank

Diane Crain for her continued support and assistance in all my efforts during the past 14 years. I am grateful for their help.

At Wiley, both the aforementioned Cary Sullivan and Kathryn A. Malm, our guiding light, exhibited remarkable grace, patience, and good humor as we extended every deadline beyond reason. Without their enormous help, this book would never have been completed.

Finally, I'd like to thank three people who gave me help and advice along the way. To Rodney Basil, I thank you for introducing me to the world of international business. To my father, Fred Rockwell, I thank you for your support and for being a living example, as you continue to work by my side each day. And to Jeff Dearth, who introduced me to the wonders of the Internet, I thank you for your friendship, guidance, and your continued interest in my Internet career.

If this book helps you expand your global business using the Web, it's because of the talents of everyone mentioned here. Comments (even criticisms) are encouraged. Let me know what you think at either www.ginfo.net or www.wiley.com/compbooks/rockwell.

I hope you enjoy going global online and tapping the vast resources of the World Wide Web as much as I have.

ABOUT THE AUTHORS

Browning Rockwell is founder and president of Trade Compass (http://www.tradecompass.com). Mr. Rockwell began development of Trade Compass in November of 1994, and launched the service on the World Wide Web in May 1995. Since then, Trade Compass has been twice voted one of the top 50 sites on the Internet by *CIO Web Business* magazine and received the 1997 CommerceNet VIP award for providing "very innovative services" in global commerce solutions.

Trade Compass is a Microsoft Value Chain Initiative partner, an Oracle Alliance Partner, and a member of the AT&T Creative Alliance Program. The company is working closely with the Microsoft Corporation, Sterling Commerce and Oracle Corporation to integrate Internet applications for global trade and logistics. At present, Trade Compass is the Internet's top address for electronic products and services that facilitate international commerce.

In October, 1997, Mr. Rockwell founded the Global Information Network (http://www.ginfo.net), an Internet-based search engine and directory for global trade professionals. The Network also serves as the companion Web site for this book.

Mr. Rockwell is also president of Horizon Trading Company (http://www .horizoninc.com), an export trading and export management company which he founded in 1980. During the past 17 years, Horizon Trading Company has transacted more than $300 million in sales of products such as computer hardware, medical and laboratory equipment, furniture, and agricultural products. Mr. Rockwell is a specialist in export finance and international marketing strategy. He is a graduate of the College of William and Mary.

Contributing Authors

Chapter 2: Understanding Global Trade Using the Internet

Tunga Kiyak heads development for the Web site at Michigan State University's Center for International Business Education and Research (MSU-CIBER). Within that site, he also maintains the award-winning *International Business Resources on the WWW* index. Currently a Research Associate at MSU-CIBER, Kiyak plays a very active role in development of several decision support systems software for international business offered by the Center. He has given numerous speeches about conducting international research on the Internet to professional and academic communities.

Tunga Kiyak holds a BS in electrical and electronics engineering from Bogazici University in Istanbul, Turkey, as well as an MBA from Michigan State University. He is currently earning a doctorate in marketing and international business at Michigan State University.

Chapter 3: Selling Online to the World

James F. Kessler, III is director of Global Electronic Commerce/AMPeMerce at AMP Incorporated (http://www.amp.com). He joined AMP in 1994 to lead the corporation's strategic initiatives for global electronic commerce.

Before joining AMP, Kessler served as senior vice president and chief operating officer for Dallas-based IRG Technologies. Before that, he was vice president for sales and marketing in the data communications division of Northern Telecom. He spent 18 years with IBM and served as director of industry marketing. He holds degrees in physics and mathematics from Indiana University of Pennsylvania.

Chapter 4: Act Locally, Think Globally

Tina Duong is Marketing Manager at Direct Language Communications, Inc. (http://www.dlc.com), a multilingual communications firm based in San Francisco, California. She contributes to DLC's ongoing vision of providing comprehensive services for the "globalization" of business communications, either in print, digitally, or, more specifically, over the Internet.

Ms. Duong is currently responsible for managing a marketing program aimed at strategic growth, through raising awareness of the multilingual communications service industry and by careful positioning. She graduated from the University of Washington, School of Business, where she sat on an advisory board charged with instituting the first Center for International Studies in Business at the University. She subsequently graduated from the charter class of that program, with a concentration in International Marketing.

Chapter 5: Legal Factors

Jennifer Albert is a partner in the intellectual property group of the law firm of Arent Fox Kintner Plotkin & Kahn (http://www.arentfox.com). She is licensed to practice before the U.S. Patent and Trademark Office, as well as before numerous state and federal district and appellate courts.

Ms. Albert's practice includes counseling clients on issues involving cyberspace law and on-line information services, computer software, as well as negotiation and preparation of various types of computer-related agreements. She has chaired and spoken at many conferences on cyberspace law and has written several articles in this area.

Chapter 6: Technical & Security Factors

John Fontaine is an Interactive Team Leader at Arnold Communications DC, a full service advertising, public relations and new media communications agency. Prior to working at Arnold, he was the principal Internet architect for Trade Compass, having built many of Trade Compass' electronic commerce and decision-support applications. Trade Compass is a recognized leader in information systems for international commerce.

Mr. Fontaine holds a degree in Middle Eastern Studies from George Washington University. He speaks Arabic, Hebrew, and German, in addition to being fluent in the programming languages of Java, Perl, C++, SQL, and Visual Basic.

Chapter 7: Building Worldwide Virtual Communities Using Internet Resources

Brian Eckert directs corporate positioning and marketing direction for Proxicom (http://www.proxicom.com), a leading provider of Internet-based business solutions to leadership companies around the world. Prior joining Proxicom, Mr. Eckert served in executive positions for several companies, where he managed operations, strategy, marketing and sales efforts.

Brian's experience includes operational responsibility as director for the Government & Special Systems division of Fortune 500 leader Equifax Corporation. He also handled marketing and sales responsibilities as director for Information,

Inc., a custom online system and information provider for Access Teleconferencing, Intl., an international teleconferencing enterprise.

Throughout his career, Brian has demonstrated a diverse background, gained hands-on work in the communication technology arena, and maintained interactions with customers employing innovative Internet strategies to produce business value.

Chapters 9–12:
Global Internet Markets
Creating a Trade Resource Center on Your Desktop
Developing Global Business Leads Using the Internet
Going on Virtual Trade Missions

Garrett Wasny, CMC (Certified Management Consultant) is an award-winning international trade columnist, author, Webmaster and speaker based in Vancouver, Canada. His monthly column, *NAFTA North*, appears in *World Trade* magazine. He is Webmaster of the *Garrett Wasny Trade Page* (http://mypage.direct.ca/g/gwasny), an online trade intelligence center for North American businesspeople.

Mr. Wasny's informative and entertaining multimedia presentation—*How to Conquer the World: Using the Internet to Develop International Business*—has been delivered to leading international trade organizations in dozens of cities across North America and Europe, including New York, Los Angeles, Chicago, Washington, D.C., Atlanta, Dallas, Toronto, and Oslo.

Chapter 13: The Evolution to E-Commerce on the Internet

Patricia Steele is Vice President and Associate Publisher at Trade Communications, Inc. (TCI), which publishes *Export Today* magazine and *Export Today Online* (http://exporttoday.com). During her tenure at TCI, she has focused on the decade's unparalleled growth in global business and the impact of technology on trade.

Her publishing career includes working on three monthly magazines, and, more recently, using various forms of Internet publishing. Ms. Steele is a graduate of the Medill School of Journalism at Northwestern University.

INTRODUCTION

O n the Internet, distance is irrelevant, and borders and time zones are meaningless. The information for the entire world is literally at your fingertips . . . as it is happening and in real time. For business, this has an astonishing implication and opens enormous opportunities. On the Web, you will find yourself gravitating toward global markets and international trade whether you plan to or not. And, if your Web site becomes extraordinarily successful, those global markets will eventually begin to gravitate toward you.

Running a large Web site is like managing a huge global open house. You're never quite sure who will be visiting, how many people they will bring, or exactly where they are from. Users from around the world either seek out, stumble across, are linked to, or somehow hear about your site. If your offering intrigues them, they'll send you an email and request more information. If they really like your product or service, they'll order right then and there. In any case, physical proximity is never an issue. For you, this may mean a stream of unsolicited and unexpected international inquiries and sales. The stream may trickle at first, but it can quickly build to a gush as the good news spreads about your online presence.

The same applies when you run a global search online. If you spot a valuable product or service that cuts costs or boosts your business, you can use the Internet to source and import from around the globe. As long as your supplier can deliver on time and on budget, his or her location is no longer important. As countries the world over expand and deepen their Internet presence, the number of these cross-border e-connections and e-transactions will grow at an exponential rate.

For online businesses, going global is not a choice. It is an inevitable necessity. To survive and thrive in the electronic marketplace, organizations of all sizes—from the tiniest one-person basement operation to the largest multinational conglomerate—must become adept at operating in a real-time global market. This involves researching international business opportunities on line, building Web sites that attract customers from around the world, working with businesspeople and customers from other cultures, and processing orders in real-time. Some of these orders will be expected, and some will be pleasant surprises. More and more of them will come from distant lands.

About This Book

Using the Web to Compete in a Global Marketplace will show you how to prepare and position your company for the coming global boom on the Internet and how you can use Web technology to develop and enhance a wealth of international business opportunities . . . right here, right now.

Written by a team of international trade specialists and Internet technology experts, the book covers everything from understanding global trade using the Internet and how to develop international business leads online to going on virtual trade missions. You'll learn how to globalize your company Web site by taking into account language, legal, technical, security, and design issues and where to find the latest and hottest Web-based international trade databases and applications related to cargo tracking, trade finance, trade leads, trade statistics, travel reservations, translation, market research, global news, international employment, and more. What's more, you'll learn how to use these tools to help you and your organization do business around the world easier, faster, and far less expensively than you might think.

Collectively, we've endeavored to provide you with the most complete source of information for doing global business online. And all this comes at a time when trade and business opportunities around the world have never been more abundant or more lucrative.

Who Should Read This Book

If you are a businessperson who is serious about using the Internet to seek new customers, suppliers, and partners around the world, this book is for you.

If you're already directly involved in international trade and business–either as a manufacturer, distributor, exporter, importer, customs broker, freight forwarder, trade financier, trade promoter, diplomat, or cross-border air/ocean/road carrier–then this book is definitely for you. You'll learn how best to use the Internet to maximize your global marketing efforts online.

If you're indirectly involved in international trade—perhaps as a lawyer, management consultant, trade show organizer, site developer, business school professor, executive educator, or someone who advises international companies—this book is also for you. You'll learn new Web design techniques and intelligence that will not only help you better serve your existing clients who export or import but also how you may gain new offshore clients and revenue using the Internet.

Even if you're a complete novice at international trade and you've been contemplating expanding your business opportunities to wider markets, you can still use this book. During the next century, sooner or later you and your computer will receive through your modem an unsolicited offer from someone in another country. Perhaps you will read about or discover a prime opportunity outside your own country that merits a quick email. This book will show you how to respond and provide an easy-to-follow global business game plan, even if you're totally new to the Internet and international trade.

How This Book Is Structured

This book opens with general information about the Internet and its profound relationship to the global business community, especially in the Digital Age. In Chapters 4–8, we discuss specific ways to build a worldwide community of users by globalizing your Web site. In Chapters 9–12, we've identified a number of resources and markets you can use to greatly enhance your global business profile online. Finally, in Chapter 13, we discuss a number of specific issues related to what many are calling e-commerce as well as what lies ahead.

Another easy way to understand this book's structure is to look at the annotated outline we used in putting it together:

Section 1: Global Business in a Digital Age

Chapter 1: Global WebTrade. Written by Browning Rockwell, this chapter discusses the convergence of global trade and technology and the rise of the virtual company through global webtrade, a new means of conducting business using the Internet that is taking the Web by storm. Because the Web is such an efficient delivery medium, much of the cost of reaching and retaining customers has been reduced. At the same time, however, customers are quite rightly demanding lower prices and very high levels of reliability and service. This part of the Web equation is now putting tremendous pressure on company margins, thereby accelerating the need to expand global markets.

Chapter 2: Understanding Global Trade Using the Net. This chapter, written by Tunga Kiyak of Michigan State University, discusses how to assess the global trade potential of your product or service through Internet research. The author identifies a variety of Internet sites that provide useful training and tutorials on the exporting process. In many cases, these sites also monitor and update information about the changing landscape of global business, helping companies stay ahead of new regulations, legislation, and logistics concerns.

Chapter 3: Selling Online to the World: A Case Study. Jim Kessler of AMP Global Communications provides a behind-the-scenes look at how AMP sells its products to a global customer base using the Web, starting with the company's award-winning Web site and extending to other aspects of online trading. He reveals how the Web site was developed, what features have been added to make it user-friendly for an international business audience, and some of the unique challenges of selling and promoting goods online.

Section 2: Globalizing Your Web Site

Chapter 4: Think Locally, Act Globally. In this chapter, Tina Duong of Direct Language Communications, covers the various issues related to displaying a Web site in multiple languages, including translation requirements and selecting the preferred languages to highlight in various industry sectors. She also uses various case studies to illustrate solutions her company has provided to enhance the global availability of various clients online.

Chapter 5: Legal Factors. Jennifer Albert of Arent, Fox, Kinter, Plotkin & Kahn, covers the various legal issues related to creating a successful international Web site in this chapter, including copyright, protection of proprietary material, claims, liability and other considerations. She demonstrates how the unique nature of the Web creates inherent legal issues that must be carefully weighed when making final decisions about globalizing your Web site.

Chapter 6: Technical and Security Factors: Globalizing Your Web Site. This chapter, written by John Fontaine of Arnold Advertising, covers various technical and security issues related to creating a successful international Web site, including encryption, server selection, and software selection. Going global on the Web poses a number of technical and security risks that must be considered to protect your investment and preserve the integrity of your company's Web presence.

Chapter 7: Expanding Relationships through Worldwide Internet Communities. Brian Eckert of Proxicom, Inc., discusses various strategies for building worldwide virtual communities of users who will be interested in returning to your Web site again and again. As a business strategy, creating a worldwide virtual community is based on an equation in which the social needs that compel individuals to participate with each other using your Web site intersect with the value proposition that meets your organization's economic objectives. The author presents some dynamic case histories of various successful worldwide virtual communities and identifies various Web resources for ensuring success.

Chapter 8: The Role of Intranets and Extranets in a Global Marketplace. Using intranets, some companies have been very successful in encouraging their employees to generate new international business. Browning Rockwell examines the logistics involved in setting up these kinds of systems and how the content can be developed or acquired. The chapter also examines the logistics of establishing successful extranets with suppliers in other countries and the pros and cons of using extranets in this way.

Section 3: Resources and Markets

Chapter 9: Global Internet Markets Survey: Statistical Data. International trade writer and certified management consultant Garrett Wasny measures the digital "market access" of countries around the world, according to how easy or difficult it is to reach a particular market online. Data is provided for six regions and 233 countries around the world, and it reveals that the Internet is booming globally but not in a uniform manner. The quantity and quality of electronic connections vary widely by region, by country, and even within countries. The chapter also ranks the top twenty Internet markets by number of hosts, spotlights ten cyber-markets to watch, and provides 1998-2000 forecasts on the Internet and on international trade opportunities in these digital hot spots.

Chapter 10: Creating a Trade Resource Center on Your Desktop. In this chapter, Garrett Wasny reveals how to globalize your desktop and transform your computer into an international trade command post using a simple yet effective online scanning and processing system. You'll learn how to get online, create your own virtual trade library and resource center, and set up a world business filing system using only a few simple techniques and bookmarks. You'll discover the best search engines to use, along with how to organize and use Geographic Cyber-Ports—Web sites that provide geographic information about trade opportunities in a particular country and area.

Chapter 11: Developing Global Business Leads Using the Internet.
Garret Wasny explains how a simple technique—the preparation of
cyber-profiles—can help you cut through all the cyber-junk and zero in
on prime prospects online. This chapter spotlights some time-saving
search techniques that will help you take full advantage of the hyperlinked, speed-of-light medium called the Internet so you can use the Web
as a highly effective buying and selling channel. It also documents more
than sixty of the best places online to find business contacts in other
countries, each of which is updated daily and provides hundreds, if not
thousands, of fresh cross-border opportunities every week.

Chapter 12: Going on Virtual Trade Missions. In this chapter, Garrett
Wasny demonstrates how to leverage the Internet from your desktop to
achieve everything you might otherwise be able to get done only during
an overseas trade mission. You'll learn what to pack for your "trip," and
how to prepare top-notch marketing materials that can be digitally transmitted in a flash to prospects around the world. It reveals a few zero-cost
procedures that will turbocharge your browser and email. These will
boost your profile and name recognition online, organize your Internet
contacts, and allow you to translate messages for free.

Section 4: E-commerce and Beyond

Chapter 13: The Evolution to E-commerce on the Internet. This
chapter looks at how advances in digital technology and EDI are changing the face of electronic commerce and transforming the way we conduct business worldwide. Patricia Steele of Trade Communications, Inc.,
traces the evolution of e-commerce and its technology infrastructure
from EDI to the Web and speculates about the future of Internet commerce as we enter the new millennium. Strategic considerations for
global companies' sales and marketing, distribution, and customer service programs are highlighted.

Collectively, we've tried to show you how to take the necessary steps to digitally
position your company within the most exciting medium on Earth. Get ready–you'll
be doing business around the world at the speed of light.

The Companion Web Sites

Using the latest in Web technology and resources, this book's companion Web sites
(http://www.wiley.com.compbooks/rockwell and http://www.ginfo.net) exemplify many of

the ideas presented in Chapter 7 for building a worldwide community of users. When you visit the Global Information Network (GIN), you will find a wealth of information, links, current news, and handy tips for conducting business on a global scale by using the Internet.

Designed as an online gateway destination providing free information and access to more than sixteen hundred Web sites from every continent, GIN offers the convenience of a single Web address for locating the most comprehensive world business and global trade information now available over the Internet.Supported entirely by advertisers, GIN also tracks daily business news and information from around the world in the following content areas:

World Regions

- North America
- South America
- Asia
- Europe
- Middle East/Africa
- Oceania and Australia

Business Segments

- Logistics/transportation
- Economic Development/Site Selection
- Trade Technology/Software
- Finance and Banking
- Insurance/Credit Risk
- International Law

Resources

- Trade Centers/Chambers
- Trade Associations
- Education
- Visa and Travel
- Career Opportunities

Trade Information

- Research/Intelligence

- Publications
- Directories
- Exhibitions/Conferences

Through GIN, you are just one click away from today's trade news, a wealth of global trade leads, and all the latest currency rates. The site also contains listings of country codes, world time zones, and daily updates on world weather conditions in most of the world's major cities. Each day, GIN features breaking news stories from a broad range of world regions and business subjects, including logistics/transportation, finance, risk management, technology, site selection, global trade, international commerce, business travel, and more.

In addition, GIN is now equipped with a powerful advanced search engine from Alta Vista that allows searches across multiple sites throughout the network, across more than fifteen hundred links in GIN's new Tradelinks database, or across the entire World Wide Web. For advertisers, GIN currently delivers more than six hundred thousand impressions on a monthly basis, offering a wide range of rotating and "permanent" banner options, listings, and sponsored sections, including twenty-seven unique search engine pages that provide positions for banner advertising. All advertising placement includes real-time reporting through the state-of-the-art Accipiter (http://www.accipiter.com) advertising management software program, which means advertisers can easily track the results of multiple banner campaigns.

When you visit the GIN Web site, you'll also find an extensive area devoted to providing more detailed information about the material presented in this book. Here we've included tips, strategies, and ideas from many of the authors who contributed to this book, along with some rather extensive appendix information that didn't fit into the printed version.

On behalf of everyone who worked on this project, let me wish you success in your online business adventures. We welcome any email (browningr@ tradecompass.com) about your triumphs and the lessons you've learned.

GLOBAL WEBTRADE

A s novelist William Gibson once observed, "You know, the future has already arrived. It's just not evenly distributed yet." This same notion also holds true for the Internet and the World Wide Web. The future of international commerce is currently rolling out in small communities throughout the Web. Every time the Web becomes easier or cheaper to use, another business population shifts its energies and resources toward using the Web to get the job done.

Before the Internet and the liberalization of global trade, international trade was expensive, complex, time consuming, and largely for big players only. Today, cross-border commerce is low cost, simple, instant, and accessible to virtually any business, no matter how small.

In cyberspace, technology and trade are converging and intersecting. Virtually all steps in the business chain and export and import process—from market research to production to transportation to final sale—can be shrunk, improved, monitored, or expedited using Web-based tools. Knowledge is now the new currency of the global economy, and cyberspace is the new Federal Reserve and Fort Knox of intellectual capital.

Given these global changes, the time has come to coin a new term that adequately describes what businesses are accomplishing on a global scale using the Internet. These days, companies of every size have started to embrace a new way of doing business that might be called *global Webtrade*—the efficient leveraging of the Internet and the World Wide Web to conduct commerce, trade, and business on an unprecedented global scale.

What Is Global Webtrade?

Global Webtrade goes well beyond the mere adoption or embracing of Internet-based technologies to compete in today's global marketplace. And it is not simply a matter of becoming proficient in e-commerce or e-business. It also involves redefining business models, reinventing business processes, changing corporate cultures, and raising relationships with customers and suppliers to new levels of excellence.

Within the ever-widening reaches of cyberspace, sales channels will begin delivering what customers have always wanted—timeliness, accuracy, and dramatically lower costs. Stronger commercial links, more efficient trade routes, and faster information flow are now the foundations of the new global marketplace. As you might expect, the entrepreneur is the most important player in helping to build and shape the new global economy. Even larger multinational companies are starting to decentralize and reconstitute themselves as networks of entrepreneurs. The bigger the world economy, the more powerful its smallest players will become.

Fortune 500 companies now account for less than 10 percent of the total jobs within the American economy, down from 20 percent in 1970. This means that 90 percent of the U.S. economy is now made up of small- and medium-size companies, all of which are interested in using the new tools of global business to help reinvent the global economy.

As this reinvention occurs, the new global economy will emerge as an internetworked enterprise. Borders and languages will no longer limit the ability of business to expand internationally. Individual employees or work groups can assert their value and worth to large enterprises independently, regardless of physical location.

In this environment, global Webtrade can be seen as helping to redefine time and space for employees and businesses. Work can be performed from home, the office, or while on the road. Networks of business clusters spread around the world now can cooperate globally to achieve local or regional business objectives. Using the Internet, traditional hierarchical business organizations are now giving way to the team-based approach. The focus shifts away from the individual being responsible to the manager to a team that functions as a service unit within the larger whole.

Implications

Consider for a moment the implications of the trends that have produced global Webtrade. Competitive advantage in location and access to raw and finished materials no longer solely determines the distribution of wealth or the distribution of economic activities that will lead the world in the next century. This means that the avenue of wealth creation will be different in the coming century. For this reason, companies need to prepare themselves to deal with an entirely different set of operating parameters. Unless established corporations learn to reinvent themselves and their industries, newcomers will create much of the wealth. And, as we all know, in computing as well as over the Internet, newcomers are rapidly changing the rules of the game.

Much of the recent success of the direct-sale computer companies Dell and Gateway 2000 is the result of innovation in business practice rather than simply technology. They introduced build-to-order techniques that extended the supply chain backward into the supplier base and out into the sales channel through Internet-based order systems. They exemplify the kinds of companies that are using global Webtrade to their fullest advantage.

Taking risks, breaking rules, and being an agent of change is becoming more important than ever. We live in a world where digitization, deregulation, and globalization are profoundly reshaping the landscape. This will undoubtedly drive a tremendous amount of wealth creation in the coming years, just as the transition from an agrarian economy to an industrialized one created tremendous wealth in the last century. Global Webtrade will consist of real-time enterprises in which information is continuously updated and adjusted to changing business conditions. And knowledge will be the currency of the new global economy.

To stay ahead, it is my belief that companies will need to adopt global attitudes. Companies cannot continue to rely on occasional visits to customers in new international markets and still call themselves global businesses. They will need to understand the values and needs of their customers in other countries through real-time research.

But there's some good news here. There was a time when companies had to maintain large offices and staffs in many countries to qualify as a global enterprise. The Internet is challenging this requirement by allowing companies to operate effectively and interact with customers anywhere in the world, seven days a week and twenty-four hours a day.

Yet let's be clear. While technology will permit virtual business trips to key markets, I do not mean to suggest that it can ever substitute for the human interactions required to cultivate and extend successful international business relationships. In the global arena, companies will need to balance the virtual business world with the traditional business world.

Benefits

Now in its infancy, global Webtrade will begin to evolve from email (today's basic desktop "killer application") to full-blown electronic business in a very short time. How soon this occurs will be a function of how quickly businesses adopt and integrate these new business tools into the daily work process.

One thing is certain—it is not a function of how or why but when. Much as the fax replaced telex as a basic communications tool for global business in the early 1980s, the Internet and its supporting technologies will quickly be absorbed into the fundamentals of any business operation. The Italian Renaissance took centuries to spread across Europe, but businesses today are wasting no time finding ways to use information technology on the Internet to exploit the benefits of doing business electronically.

Chief among these benefits are the following:

Unlimited global reach and large potential customer base. Geographic boundaries become irrelevant, and operating hours are limited only by choices related to the software and hardware that runs the Web site.

Increased revenues. Merchants can leverage the tremendous geographical coverage and sheer volume of Web users to establish a global market presence at a very low cost.

Reduced costs. Some businesses on the Internet today hold no inventory but instead offer a range of products from several manufacturers and then link their sites directly with the order entry and fulfillment systems of key manufacturers.

Faster time to market. Internet commerce enables businesses to bring products to market much faster than with traditional techniques. New products, price changes, and catalog descriptions can immediately be changed on the Web.

Better customer relations. Online commerce enables merchants to form interactive personal relationships with their customers.

Faster customer response time. With twenty-four-hour access seven days a week, customers can find responses to their questions by going directly to up-to-the-minute, centrally maintained information. Customers can receive service, check order status, or track shipments at any time of the day or night.

Self-service. The Internet can save time and money while improving the accuracy of any business transaction by eliminating unnecessary intermediaries in the business chain between buyers and sellers.

At the same time, these benefits will also be challenged by the new demands that global customers will place on suppliers to deliver products and services cheaper and faster than ever before. No longer will the pricing discovery process be a mystery. Using global Webtrade, buyers will soon be able to source what they are looking for on a global basis at little or no cost. As companies develop electronic links to streamline the flow of goods and services around the world, enterprise applications are compressing the supply chains and cementing trading relationships. Interactive transaction-based applications are coming online as business-to-business technology links grow progressively more sophisticated.

Perhaps the most striking characteristic of the Internet is its rapid rate of growth. To its credit, the Internet has quickly become ubiquitous because of an open standard that is compatible with every major computer operating system. The number of Internet users is estimated to have doubled every year in the past five years and is projected to continue increasing by more than 50 percent per year until the end of the decade. A *conservative* estimate of the number of Internet users in 1997 ranges between 46 and 57 million people in 194 countries, and this is predicted to reach 157 million by the year 2000. More than three thousand commercial enterprises are joining the Internet every day, adding more than one hundred thousand new sites to the network on a monthly basis.

The near doubling of worldwide PC users by the end of the decade is expected to generate a seventeenfold increase in Internet usage. Nearly sixty million PCs have been shipped as Internet-ready, and this number is projected to grow to 265 million by the year 2000. Three years from now, more than 82 percent of the world's corporations expect to support fully connected internal networks.

With an estimated 25 million people online in 1997, the United States is by far the leading market for Internet-based services. The United States accounts for more than one-half of the world's Internet connections, and we now maintain 58 percent of the estimated 16.1 million host sites in the world. However, the U.S. share of global Internet usage is expected to decline as Internet use gains momentum in many parts of Europe and Asia. As of this writing, construction has begun on significant Asia-Pacific regional Internet backbones to handle increased Internet traffic flows within that region.

Any company embracing all this technology and trying to get a clear picture of the Internet and global Webtrade today is challenged by the lack of a clear understanding of how global e-commerce will reshape traditional enterprise and industry models. Even without a clear business case, companies are migrating to the use of the Web simply because they feel they have no choice if they are to survive.

The good news is that these early adopters are willing to suspend traditional business solutions in favor of other models. Many are starting to rethink their enterprises and determine what solutions might be needed to adapt to next-generation business models. Standards for technology, business processes, and business models are being sought across the globe, mostly over the Internet. These will undoubtedly evolve as a result of industry collaboration or through individual market leadership.

Trends in the Global Marketplace

To better understand what's happening in global Webtrade on the Internet, it makes sense to place this phenomenon in the context of what's happening in the larger arena of world business.

Just ten years ago, intense protectionism and dissension plagued the international trading system. Developed countries made extensive use of quantitative restrictions and other trade-distorting measures to block imports. Developing countries used high tariffs and quotas to impede international competition. The economies of Central and Eastern European countries were centrally planned and driven not by market forces but by bureaucrats.

Thanks to a variety of revolutionary political developments and trade pacts in the past decade, the world is a much different place today. Communism collapsed in Eastern Europe. The Uruguay Round of the General Agreement on Tariffs and Trade (GATT) talks replaced GATT with the World Trade Organization (WTO), a new global trade authority that has established a number of significant and binding trade rules in more than 100 countries.

In 1996, more than 120 countries signed new treaties on copyright and performances in sound recordings as part of the World Intellectual Property Organization. In February 1997, 69 countries reached a new trade deal in telecommunications services. In March 1997, a new WTO agreement eliminated tariffs on information products, including computers, software, semiconductors, and telecom equipment. The telecom and computer initiatives alone liberalized more than a trillion U.S. dollars in trade, nearly twice the size of the Canadian economy, in just two months!

In December 1997, 102 countries committed to a new WTO financial services agreement that will liberalize trillions more U.S. dollars in banking, securities, insurance, and financial data services. Also in December 1997, U.S. and European

Union officials reached agreement on guidelines for future work on trade in global e-commerce that includes a commitment to duty-free cyberspace, one not constricted by the duties, tariffs, and customs requirements that apply to the import or exort of goods. This is an exciting concept that we all understand in theory, but it still needs to be completely defined.

Regionally, countries around the globe have been forming blocs or regional trade alliances. Since 1948, at least seventy-six free trade areas or customs unions have been established around the world. Of these, more than half have been implemented in the 1990s. These include the North American Free Trade Agreement (NAFTA), the Southern Cone Common Market, which includes Argentina and Brazil, the South Asian Preferential Trade Arrangement between India and Pakistan (SAPTA), and the Common Market for Eastern and Southern Africa (COMESA).

As a result, nations around the world are embracing open markets, global trade, and private investment. Developed countries are slashing, if not completely eliminating, tariffs; removing quantitative restrictions on industrial products; and reforming the agricultural sector. Developing countries are lowering trade barriers and trimming distorting domestic and export subsidies. Their commitment to economic and trade reform has not only brought them fully into the trading system, but it has made them leading players in the global economy.

Ten emerging countries, for example, will account for more than 40 percent of all global imports by 2015. These are Argentina, Brazil, Mexico, China, Indonesia, India, Poland, South Korea, South Africa, and Turkey. All are dramatically increasing living standards and transforming rather quickly into consumer-oriented societies. These developments have also ignited a trade boom: As a share of world output, global trade was estimated at 25 percent in 1997, up from 17 percent in 1986.

Continuing trade liberalization at both the global and regional levels is expected to further boost global business and push its 25 percent share of world output even higher in the coming years. By the year 2000, new WTO trade talks are scheduled in agriculture, services, foreign investment, competition policy, labor standards, and other areas. In the Western Hemisphere, the United States and Canada are now in discussions with some thirty other countries in the region to establish the Free Trade Area of the Americas, or FTAA, which is envisioned to become a hemisphere-wide trade pact by 2005.

In Europe, the European Union recently invited Poland, the Czech Republic, Hungary, Estonia, and Slovenia to begin entry talks to join the European Union (EU) during 1998. In Asia, Asia-Pacific Economic Cooperation (APEC) is committed to achieving the goal of free and open trade and investment for APEC's industrialized economies by 2010 and for its developing economies by 2020. Work is also now underway to implement the holy grail of international trade: the entry of China into the WTO. Trade negotiators predict that Chinese accession into the WTO alone would have an impact close to that of the entire Tokyo Round, the famous seventh round of multilateral trade negotiations under GATT that yielded substantial reductions in trade barriers around the world.

All of these substantial global economic initiatives—combined with hyperspeed advancements in new Internet tools and systems—have triggered a fundamental and irreversible sea change in global business.

Start Making Plans Now

The question is no longer whether the Internet has practical commercial applications but rather how your organization should make the best use of this extraordinary business platform for global trade and investment. While some marginal producers may not be able to compete in the tough new world of global markets, operations of all sizes willing and able to change have the potential to reap enormous benefits.

The convergence of trade and technology during the past decade has created the foundation for global Webtrade. Much as rapid advances in technology, such as the steamboat, the telegraph, and the railroad, drove rapid expansion into the Wild West, the same is true of the new engines of growth and expansion at the beginning of the twenty-first century: the Internet, wireless communications, satellite technology, and network computing. Using these powerful tools, we now have the capability to provide global, instantaneous infrastructure that will be equally available to consumers everywhere, whether they live in developing countries or industrialized nations.

At the same time, virtually any intellectual property (such as documents and computer software) can also be digitized and delivered instead of being physically transported by hand. The revolution in information and communications technology is fundamentally redefining the way business is conducted. For this reason, businesses in the new inter-networked economy would do well to provide customized products and marketing campaigns to engage their global customers. They must also be prepared to develop carefully devised internal and external action plans.

Internal Plan of Action

A good place for a business to start creating a successful global presence on the Internet is to devise and implement an internal Web strategy that focuses on customer needs. Companies must create a customer-centric approach to global business on their Web sites by remembering that they will be communicating with people from around the world. The Internet will impact this approach in several ways. Internet technology offers businesses the ability to gain an in-depth understanding of their customers' needs, from product development through marketing lead development, sales, and support.

Using this information, mass marketing begins to give way to one-to-one marketing relationships with individual customers. If allowed, customer information can also be shared across corporate networks through the Internet and intranets. Web-enabled technology is allowing customers to have quick in-depth interactions with vendors. With a web browser and a few mouse clicks customers can ask questions and open a direct line of communications to a company representative.

Given these imperatives, companies should start educating their staffs on the operations of the new virtual corporation. The fact is that more and more employees (full-time, part-time, and contract) of a given company will be accessing headquarters through well-designed Web sites. And more and more customers will begin interacting with employees who do not necessarily live close by.

Many of the tools that are available through the emerging Internet technologies will only be successful if companies can integrate them into their daily work processes. Again, early adopters have successfully started using simple tools like email to increase productivity and cut costs. Many, however, have not yet tackled the complexities of integrating the Internet into their entire business process.

There is much to be done. For instance, companies need to start training staff in the global aspects of Web marketing, such as advertising and promotional issues, Web site operations, and virtual customer service. These technologies are only as good as the implementing organizations make them. In many cases, companies make the mistake of creating a Web site with a build-it-and-they-will-come attitude. But the Web now allows companies to leapfrog entire stages, transitioning from domestic to international to global in one big hop.

Another good approach is to develop a virtual business strategy just for Internet-based transactions. Just like a traditional business strategy, a company's Web strategy will require planning, education, execution, and analysis to be successful. Because of the Internet's very nature as an immature medium, companies should attempt to resolve some inherent conflicts the Internet brings forth:

Conflict 1: Opportunity versus risk. Before marching blindly forward, companies would be well advised to separate good opportunities from bad risks by focusing on cost savings first. It is important to concentrate on using Internet technologies to lower current costs, not to increase overhead.

Conflict 2: Customer needs versus company needs. Think of your customers' needs first, and worry about revenue enhancement later. Too often, companies think of using the Internet as a "get-rich-quick" solution and build Web sites that nobody visits more than once.

Conflict 3: Speed versus caution. Always appoint someone to lead the Web initiative, but build cross-functional teams to support the effort. Whenever possible, try to "buy" rather than "build." The only way to effectively transition to the light speed of Internet time is to quickly build to standards and use outside talent whenever possible. Develop and maintain an implementation schedule to track your efforts. Too often, Internet development projects take on a life of their own and expand well beyond the original time allocated.

Conflict 4: Web world versus the Big Picture. Do not be fooled by how easy it looks. The Web can be a black hole for many companies that fail to plan and organize.

Since we are still in the early days of global Webtrade, companies need to maintain a balanced perspective between the Web and standard business practices. By effectively devising strategies to fit these new technologies into the overall business puzzle, companies can expect to enjoy an almost instantaneous mean time to payback, provided they do not misread the desire or ability of their customers to assimilate the new technologies.

External Plan of Action

At the same time, companies also need to develop an external global Webtrade strategy. There is a need to develop trained staff who can respond to the technical and operational issues raised by doing business over the Web. They will also need to adjust to the emerging data-centric model of the Web.

In its earliest incarnation, the Web originally presented itself as an info-centric medium, where information was published and not modified until a human revised or removed it. In this model, a user's visit to a site did not affect any of the information that could be found at that particular site. The new Web, however, is emerging as a dynamically changing global database, driven by "hooks" into underlying transaction processing systems.

These new Web sites are being referred to as *datawebs*, where users are constantly interacting with data to create newly updated information. Unlike a static

Web site, which does not change each time a user interacts with it, a dataweb is a dynamic Web environment in which users call up specific information from large databases to access current information. In many cases, users also input new information into the databases, which are then enhanced and updated by each new visit by the user. In some cases, datawebs can even generate specific user "profiles" each time a specific user arrives, so as to provide selective views of datasets to one user that another may not care to see.

Datawebs are, in effect, three-tier solutions. Tier one is the browser, which is used to request and receive data. The middle tier is the Web server, which stores the dataweb's logic and applications. Tier three is where the data is stored. At a dataweb, users can now receive live data instead of snapshots of data that have been periodically updated. Companies such as Federal Express and UPS provide real-time Internet-based cargo tracking systems using datawebs.

This is not to say that all companies must operate datawebs to participate in global Webtrade. But companies should know what is happening on the cutting edge of the Web because their customers will have rising expectations about each Web experience they have. While it is admittedly impossible to keep up with the rapid pace of change in business technologies, change is an inevitable constant when one steps onto the moving platform of Internet technologies.

At the same time, never before has there been so much opportunity for innovative companies to rise above the crowd. The world economy has never been more receptive to entrepreneurial activity. Companies have unprecedented opportunities to position themselves as key players in shaping the future of global business. Success will come to those companies that are able to bring together resources that create value for their customers. This will be a major step for most companies that are currently tied to traditional business hierarchies of control.

The new strategic paradigm demands that control be abandoned in favor of leadership because companies that do not innovate will soon see the dark side of current business evolution—they will have no choice but to make history or be history. To survive into the next millennium, companies must realize that the future is now.

UNDERSTANDING GLOBAL TRADE USING THE INTERNET

2

Before building an international Web site and opening your business to limitless opportunities in the global market, it is critical that both you and your employees make yourselves aware of the complexities involved in selling products overseas. If you're planning to export only by responding to unsolicited offers you receive through your Web site, there is probably little reason for you to worry. However, if you see exporting as a great growth and profit opportunity for your company (and you definitely should), then you must learn the costs and risks of exporting and develop an exporting strategy.

The ingredients of success in exporting are *information, preparation,* and *commitment.* Failure in foreign markets usually can be attributed to weakness in one of these three ingredients. Commitment is something that you'll need to establish yourself and is outside the scope of this chapter (although the fact that you are reading this book is a good sign!). The Internet is an excellent tool to assist you with the other two areas. You can find various resources on the Web that give you the kind of information you need, tell you where you can find that information, and how to interpret it to help you prepare to do business in foreign markets. This chapter covers some of the most critical questions you should be asking and tells you where to get the best answers.

What Do I Need to Know about Online Research?

While the Internet offers practically an unlimited potential for research, it also comes with dangers and pitfalls. When conducting research online, you need to be particularly careful to avoid potentially damaging situations, most of which involve the quality and reliability of the information you find. Of primary importance are issues such as the following:

- The timeliness of the information
- The reliability of its source
- Its continuous availability
- Whether it is worth subscribing to fee-based services

Timeliness of Information

Unlike printed material, many Web documents and data don't let you know how recent the information is. This can become a huge problem, particularly if the information is time-sensitive, such as laws, regulations, tax rates, or market information. Considering the fast pace of the current business environment, you can't risk basing decisions on outdated information. Therefore, before starting to read a document or process any data, you should make it a practice to verify its timeliness. Try to find some indication of when the document was created as well as the time frame of the analysis. Some documents will include this information in the title, or just below the title, and others may include it at the very bottom of the page. If there are any data in tables, look at the last column to see the latest year for which data are provided. Skim the text to see if there are any references to specific dates. If you're unable to find a date, contact the author or owner of the document and ask for this information. If this method fails, treat that information as questionable, and do *not* use it unless you find a second source to at least partially verify the timeliness of the information.

Source of Information

Another problem with conducting research on the Web is verifying the reliability of information. Verification needs to be done on two levels: *where* the information actually comes from, and *who* is publishing the information on the Web. The latter typically becomes a challenge because boundaries between Web sites are invisible. As you click on links to skip from one page to another, you may not be aware that you're traveling from site to site. In fact, it's likely that when you find the piece of information you're looking for, you'll be at a completely different site than the one you started searching from. Why is this a problem? One of the reasons for the Internet's rapid growth is that it's so easy to put information online. Anyone with a computer and a modem can create a Web site and put up whatever content he or she want. No entity monitors or verifies the truthfulness of the information on the

Internet, and you should therefore make it a habit to verify for yourself the source of each and every piece of information you find on the Web.

The first step in verifying the source is figuring out whose site is posting the information. To do this, look at the URL and identify the site name (Figure 2.1), which will usually tell you the organization or company that owns the site. If it's a government site you can be pretty confident about the reliability of the source. For the United States, the site name will end with .gov; for other countries, the site name will end with .gov followed by the country identification code—for example, .gov.au would indicate a government site in Australia, .gov.tr, a site in Turkey, and .gov.uk, a site in the United Kingdom. The information is likely to have been created internally by an agency and to accurately represent the information originally created. However, if the site is educational (.edu), commercial (.com), or organizational (.org) or is a network service provider (.net), verifying the source gets a bit trickier. Many such sites allow their employees and third parties (customers who rent Web space from these companies) to create their own sites. Therefore, you'll have to figure out whether the information was actually provided by the organization that the site name represents or by a third party. By looking for the logo of the organization or a copyright notice on the page you should be able to figure out who the primary owner of the site is.

Once you've figured this out, the question boils down to whether or not that organization is reliable. Most educational institutions and well-known organizations, such as the United Nations, are pretty reliable. For commercial companies, it's mostly a judgment call. Some companies, such as Trade Compass, form strategic alliances with government agencies, educational institutions, and international organizations in order to provide useful information and data. On the Web sites of reliable companies, you can usually find a section dedicated to explaining who they are, why they're putting information online, and how they acquire information. Always be extremely cautious of what you find on a company's site where the information is presented as part of an effort to sell products or services.

Figure 2.1 Identifying the site.

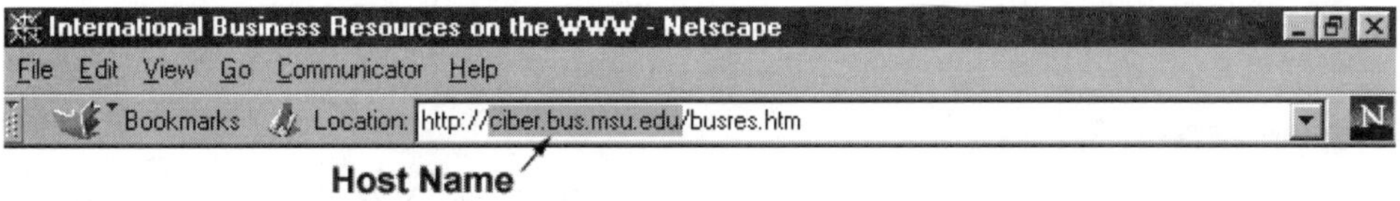

To verify the reliability of information, do one of two things: either ask the site owner to tell you how he or she acquired the information published on the site or find a second, independent source that duplicates at least a portion of the data and compare the two sources for consistency. Your plans and forecasts depend on the results of your research. You will spend your time, money, and effort based on these plans and forecasts. Therefore, it is extremely important to be fully confident about the reliability and accuracy of the information you find.

Availability of Information

The Internet is dynamic. Unlike the contents of books or magazine articles, the information you find on a Web site may change daily. A site that exists today may not exist tomorrow or may provide completely different content. Therefore, whenever you come across a page with potentially useful information, print it and file it, save a copy of it on your hard drive, or copy and paste its contents into a word processor file. This ensures that you can refer to that information when you need it in the future.

Subscription-Based Services

Another issue you may want to consider is whether to subscribe to the fee-based services that some sites offer. As you get more deeply involved in research, you'll come across sites that require an annual or monthly subscription fee to access some or all of the information on the site. Before subscribing, make sure the site offers enough value-added content to ensure you get your money's worth. Most sites will give you either a guest access or a trial period to test out the site. Use that time to go through the site and assess whether it will be beneficial to you and, more importantly, whether the information provided on the site is available elsewhere on the Internet for free. While some sites try to sell you information that you can easily get somewhere else for free, other sites such as STAT-USA (http://www.stat-usa.gov/) and Trade Compass (http://www.tradecompass.com/) provide original, value-added information and services to exporting and importing companies. Therefore, you may find it beneficial to subscribe to such services. Also note, however, that many services duplicate each other (for example, a subscription to Trade Compass also includes access to STAT-USA), so make sure that you review the offerings of each service extensively before you take out your wallet.

How Do I Start?

The first step in understanding the complexities of exporting is to have an overview of the complete process. Each of the resources mentioned in this section will take you through all aspects of exporting in a step-by-step manner. Although many sources provide similar information, each has a unique perspective to offer. The basic steps are as follows:

Assessing the business and its products. Before exporting, evaluate your business and products to assess strengths and weaknesses. Determine whether your company is export-ready. In addition, you will need to evaluate your product's export potential.

Identifying potential markets. Conduct ample research by looking into foreign market trends; country demographics; and political, social, and economic environments, laws, and regulations. This information is crucial to identifying the target markets where your product will be successful.

Develop a business plan. A solid, comprehensive, well-thought-out business plan is your recipe for success. Such a business plan should include your choice of market entry method, product positioning strategies, pricing decisions, advertising and marketing plan, forecasted budget, and other important business decisions.

Documentation and logistics. Every exporter needs to be in compliance with numerous packing, labeling, documentation, and insurance requirements. These requirements will vary according to the product you are exporting. You will have to meet both the U.S. and the foreign government's regulations and requirements.

Financing. As an exporter, you will naturally want to get paid as quickly as possible. In turn, the importers will usually prefer to delay payment at least until they have received and resold the goods. Therefore, financing and being able to offer good payment terms become critical issues in exporting. Determining your options carefully and establishing financing in advance will give you a competitive edge in the foreign market.

These steps may sound overwhelming at first, but with careful planning and preparation exporting is really quite easy. The following resources should help you get detailed information on the exporting process:

A Basic Guide to Exporting. Prepared by the Department of Commerce, this guide is a great beginner's resource. Taking a step-by-step approach to developing an exporting strategy, the guide explains the costs and risk associated with exporting. Because it's an invaluable reference, you may wish to buy a hard copy for your personal library. You can also access the full text at numerous locations on the Web. The first location is the Department of Commerce's National Trade Data Bank (NTDB), which can be accessed through STAT-USA (http://www.stat-usa.gov/). If you have not yet subscribed to this database, a free-access copy is located at I-Trade (http://www.i-trade.com/dir01/basicgui/), which is another useful site for exporters and is sponsored by Trade Point USA.

Breaking into the Trade Game: A Small Business Guide. Another useful resource is this guide provided by the Small Business Administration (SBA), which covers the entire exporting process, from developing an export strategy and doing market research to identifying buyers and financing. You can contact the SBA for a free copy or accesss the electronic version at the SBA Web site (http://www.sbaonline.sba.gov/OIT/info/Guide-To-Exporting/).

I-Trade Export Guide. This guide is prepared by Trade Point USA, a nonprofit trade information and services company established with the cooperation of the United Nations Conference on Trade and Development. Taking an approach similar to the first two guides, this resource can answer many of your questions on exporting. It can be found at http://www.i-trade.com/dir01/exprtgui/.

Other resources. You can find various other guides and resources that can provide you with a detailed overview of the export process. Ohio State University's Center for Information Technologies in Management provides an online tutorial called the Export Process Assistant–ExPA (http://citm.cob.ohio-state.edu:1111/expadocs/) that offers detailed information on the process as well as links to several relevant sites throughout the guide (Figure 2.2). Similarly, Michigan State University has developed ExporTutor (http://web.miep.org/tutor/index.html), which incorporates a ten-step road map to foreign markets, as well as Quick Consultant, a reference guide to terms and concepts that an exporter needs to know.

Virtual Universities

If you do not find these self-study guides sufficient or you would like to formalize your learning process there are several virtual courses on exporting being taught over the Internet. An advantage such courses offer in comparison to the export guides is their value-added content. One of these is "Managing Export Operations," offered by the Center for International Business Education and Research (CIBER) at Michigan State University (http://ciber.bus.msu.edu/). The course uses a modular structure to explore the field of international business manage-

Figure 2.2 The Export Process Assistant (ExPA).

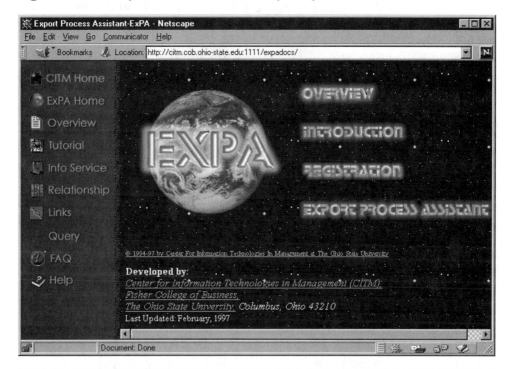

ment. In addition to providing the same information that the export guides provide, the course provides you with access to decision support systems, self-test assessments, resource databases, articles, cases, and discussion groups as well as access to other exporters, practitioners, and academicians to which you can directly ask questions and get real-time answers. Of course, another advantage is the professional certificate that you receive upon completing the course! Trade Compass also provides a similar certificate program as part of its International Business Academy program (http://iba.tradecompass.com).

How Do I Classify My Product?

Before exporting, you need to classify your product. The Harmonized Tariff System Classification (HS) is a standardized numerical method for classifying traded products. The identifying number assigned to each product is used by customs officials around the world to determine the duties, taxes, and regulations that apply to the product. The HS number (also called Schedule B) must appear on the shipper's export declaration and other documents in order for exports to leave the country. Standard International Trade Classification codes (SITC), developed by the United Nations, are also used for certain applications. It's a good idea to find your product's classification under each system in advance. Knowing which classification codes represent your product can also help you track where similar products are being shipped, what quantities are being shipped, and the revenue generated from the shipments.

There are several sources that you can refer to find these classifications. The U.S. Census Bureau has a site (http://www.census.gov/foreign-tradc/www/) that you can search using keywords. If you know your Standard Industrial Classification (SIC), you can use various translators available on the Internet to find the appropriate HS and SITC codes. One of these is provided by Professor Jon Haveman of Purdue University (http://intrepid.mgmt.purdue.edu/Jon/Data/TradeConcordances.html). His site includes the complete classification systems as well as translators for translating from each system to another. Similarly, Trade Compass HS-SITC-SIC classifier can help you with the task (http://hs-stc.tradecompass.com).

How Do I Assess My Product's Export Potential?

The best way to determine your product's export potential is to see if the same product is being exported by another business. You can find this information through census data and import/export statistics. The U.S. Census Bureau (http://www.census.gov/foreign-trade/www/) provides historical and current trade data by country as well as commodity. You can analyze this information to see whether your product has been well received throughout the world. The Government Information Sharing Project at Oregon State University (http://govinfo.kerr .orst.edu/impexp.html) provides detailed import/export statistics as well. The National Trade Data Bank (NTDB, http://www.stat-usa.gov/) also lets you search for these statistics by commodity or country.

The most powerful of such tools is provided by Trade Compass. Named World Trade Analyzer (http://www.tradecompass.com/trade_analyzer/), this site features fifteen years of trade data searchable in a variety of methods. Using this database, not only can you assess your product's export potential, but you can also research historical trade patterns, identify the largest markets for your products, and locate the fastest-growing markets for your products.

How Do I Determine Where to Export?

Since there are more than two hundred countries in the world, it is not feasible to attempt to export to every single one of them. Your time will be more effectively spent by identifying the most lucrative countries for your product. You should take the following sequential approach in your efforts to identify potential markets.

Preliminary Screening

In this first step, preliminary screening, you should attempt to narrow the number of countries you will focus on. From the universe of more than two hundred countries at the beginning, you should end up with no more than a dozen target markets at the end of this step. Although you can start to analyze countries from scratch, it really isn't necessary. The Internet provides you with many invaluable resources to simplify this task, which are described in the following paragraphs.

Market Potential Indicators for Emerging Markets. Michigan State University CIBER maintains a market potential index that ranks twenty-three emerging markets on seven dimensions that determine market potential (http://ciber.bus.msu.edu/publicat/mktptind.htm). This index, developed through years of research and experience, is continuously updated, making it one of the richest sources of information for the preliminary screening stage of the analysis (Figure 2.3).

National Trade Data Bank. The National Trade Data Bank (NTDB, http://www.stat-usa.gov/) provides various resources to help companies identify target markets. Categorized under "Market Research Reports" and updated monthly, these resources are extremely valuable, not only in preliminary screening, but also in the later stages of the market selection process. These reports are also available from Trade Compass under the site's STAT-USA Plus product (http://statusa.tradecompass.com/).

The Best Markets Report (BMR). BMR covers several industry sectors and provides information on the best markets within each industry. These markets are listed in order of total market size and include data on import opportunities in the United States as well as exports from the United States. The report also rates market receptivity to U.S. products and gives qualitative assessments of the competition and market barriers that U.S. exporters may encounter for each country.

International Market Insights (IMIs). IMIs are profiles of specific foreign market conditions or opportunities prepared by the Department of

Figure 2.3 The Market Potential Indicators for Emerging Markets.

Countries	Market Size		Market Growth Rate		Market Intensity		Market Consumption Capacity		Commercial Infrastructure		Economic Freedom		Market Receptivity		Country Risk		Overall Market Potential Index	
	Rank	Index	Rank	Index	Rank	Index	Rank	Index	Rank	Index	Rank	Index	Rank	Index	Rank	Index	Rank	Index
SINGAPORE	23	1	1	100	9	60	10	65	2	87	6	67	1	100	1	100	1	100
HONGKONG	21	2	9	66	1	100	8	72	5	82	1	100	2	68	4	78	2	90
S.KOREA	6	13	3	86	14	48	6	83	13	24	5	68	6	14	2	83	3	60
ISRAEL	20	2	8	70	6	75	1	100	6	75	8	61	4	17	9	61	4	57
CHINA	1	100	5	76	23	1	9	69	19	7	23	1	20	5	13	51	5	56
PORTUGAL	22	2	15	49	4	76	-	-	7	70	3	73	11	9	3	82	6	44
CZECH REP.	15	4	19	38	13	55	4	90	3	83	2	80	5	16	10	59	7	43
MALAYSIA	16	3	2	89	20	33	13	47	11	31	15	45	3	35	6	76	8	42
GREECE	17	3	16	48	3	91	-	-	1	100	11	60	13	8	11	57	9	41
INDIA	3	55	10	64	17	42	7	78	23	1	21	27	21	2	15	40	10	40
HUNGARY	19	2	21	29	10	60	3	98	8	69	7	63	10	10	4	78	11	36
POLAND	9	10	14	51	15	45	2	99	9	52	13	58	15	7	17	37	12	33
THAILAND	14	5	4	84	19	34	13	47	21	5	12	59	7	14	8	64	13	32
CHILE	18	3	7	74	12	58	17	21	15	20	4	72	12	9	7	69	14	31
PHILIPPINES	13	6	12	59	11	59	11	64	12	27	14	53	8	11	17	37	15	25
INDONESIA	7	12	6	76	22	25	5	85	22	3	22	24	16	7	12	52	16	23
ARGENTINA	11	7	20	34	2	96	-	-	10	35	10	60	22	2	19	30	17	19
TURKEY	10	10	11	61	8	61	-	-	16	19	17	37	17	6	21	19	18	13
RUSSIA	2	60	23	1	21	32	12	51	4	82	20	32	19	5	23	1	19	12
BRAZIL	4	31	13	56	16	43	19	1	14	23	16	42	23	1	20	30	20	10
S.AFRICA	8	12	18	41	18	40	18	13	20	6	9	61	18	6	14	50	21	5
MEXICO	5	17	22	20	7	66	15	43	18	8	19	34	9	10	16	39	22	2
VENEZUELA	12	6	17	48	5	75	16	32	17	10	18	37	14	8	22	11	23	1

Commerce's U.S. and Foreign Commercial Service, the Department of State, and multilateral development banks in overseas markets. They may focus on specific projects, industry profiles, finance and marketing trends, regulation, and import changes as well as trade show opportunitites or goverment policy updates.

Industry Sector Analyses (ISAs). ISAs are in-depth profiles of a selected industry subsector. They include an analysis of the market opportunities, end-users, competitors, market access, distribution channels, market barriers, and financing options.

Big Emerging Markets. Analyzing the interests of the United States in the world economy, the Department of Commerce has identified several markets that offer the greatest commercial opportunities for U.S. exports (Figure 2.4). As a result of this ongoing research, the International Trade Administration maintains a Web site to provide exporters with information on these markets (http://www.stat-usa.gov/itabems.html). These markets are of utmost importance since the Department of Commerce provides numerous additional services to companies exporting to these countries.

Top Targets for Trade Promotion. Another program developed by the International Trade Administration, this site lists specific market segments (country and industry) with strong sales potentials for U.S. exporters in the upcoming years. The listing is provided by country as well as by industry and is updated annually. It can be found at http://infoserv2.ita.doc.gov/Tradebase/toptar.nsf.

Detailed Analysis of Industry Market Potential

Once you have narrowed the number of potential markets to a manageable number, it is time for the second stage of the process. In this stage, you should gather detailed information on each potential market and try to determine present and

---

Figure 2.4 Big Emerging Markets.

---

future demand and sales potential. Table 2.1 provides a list of factors you should consider when selecting your target markets. Use this list to create a spreadsheet. Create a new column for each country in your list, and rank them on a scale of 1 (excellent) to 10 (poor) in terms of how they fare on each of the factors listed). In the end, you should have a pretty good idea of which markets offer the greatest potential.

Table 2.1 Foreign Market Potential Assessment

Demographic/Physical Environment:

> Population size
>
> Urban and rural distribution
>
> Climate and weather variations
>
> Shipping distance
>
> Product-significant demographics
>
> Physical distribution and communication network
>
> Natural resources

Political Environment:

> System of government
>
> Political stability and continuity
>
> Ideological orientation
>
> Government involvement in business
>
> Government involvement in communications
>
> Attitudes toward foreign business and trade
>
> National economic and developmental priorities

Economic Environment:

> Overall level of development
>
> Economic growth: GNP, industrial sector
>
> Role of foreign trade in the economy
>
> Currency: inflation rate, availability, controls, stability of exchange rate
>
> Balance of payments
>
> Per capita income and distribution
>
> Disposable income and expenditure patterns

The list in Table 2.1 may look somewhat daunting, at least initially. Once you start researching, however, you'll see that most of this information is readily available on the Internet. The following list contains some of the best places you should go to find the information you are looking for.

Table 2.1 Continued

Social/Cultural Environment:

Literacy rate, educational level

Existence of middle class

Similarities and differences in relation to home market

Language and other cultural considerations

Market Access:

Limitations on trade: tariff levels, quotas

Documentation and import regulations

Local standards, practices, and other nontariff barriers

Patents and trademarks

Preferential treaties

Legal considerations: investment, taxation, repatriation, employment, code of laws

Product Potential:

Customer needs and desires

Local production, imports, consumption

Exposure to and acceptance of product

Availability of linking products

Industry-specific key indicators of demand

Attitudes toward products of foreign origin

Competitive offerings

Local Distribution:

Availability of intermediaries

Regional and local transportation facilities

Source: "Guidelines for Export Market Research," in International Marketing Strategy *by Hans B. Thorelli and S. Tamer Cavusgil, 3d ed., 1990, Pergamon Press.*

Country Commercial Guides. These guides contain information on the business and economic situation of foreign countries and the political climate as it affects U.S. businesses. They are produced annually by U.S. embassies with the assistance of several U.S. government agencies. For each country, each guide provides information on leading trade prospects for U.S. business, the economic and political environment, marketing U.S. products and services, trade regulations and standards, the investment climate, financing, and business travel. The Country Commercial Guides can be accessed for free at the Department of State's Web site (http://www.state.gov/www/about_state/business/com_guides/index.html).

The World Factbook. Published annually in August by the Central Intelligence Agency, the *Factbook* (http://www.odci.gov/cia/publications/nsolo/wfb-all.htm) includes detailed information on each country compiled by various government agencies. The guide includes trade statistics for each country and information on the geography, demography, economy, government, and infrastructure.

Country Reports on Economic Policy and Trade Practices. These reports are intended to serve as general guides to economic conditions in specific countries. Prepared annually by the Department of State and U.S. embassies, each report provides information under nine headings: key economic indicators, general policy framework, exchange rate policies, structural policies, debt management policies, significant barriers to U.S. exports and investment, export subsidies policies, protection of U.S. intellectual property, and worker rights. These reports are also available at the Department of State's Web site (http://www.state.gov/www/issues/economic/trade_reports/index.html).

Ernst and Young's Guide to Doing Business around the World. The well-known accounting, taxation, and consulting firm prepares an information guide for each country it operates in, summarizing the business conditions of that particular country. Focusing mostly on regulations, accounting standards, and taxation issues, each guide is concise and provides a wealth of information on the country and particularly its legal structure (http://www.eyi.com/cgi-bin/foliocgi.exe/dbi.nfo?).

Other resources. Although the preceding four guides (in addition to the guides discussed in the previous section) should provide you with enough information, you should be aware that much more information on the business climate of each country is also available on the Internet. If you wish to find additional information, a great starting point is the "International Business Resources on the WWW" index (http://ciber.bus.msu.edu/busres.htm).

What Forms Do I Need to Fill Out?

A vast amount of documentation can be required for an export transaction. The documentation required varies from order to order and country to country. In addition, such documentation needs to be very precise. Even slight discrepancies can prevent the order from being exported. It is critical, therefore, that you fully understand the documentation process. If you have not had prior experience in exporting, it is advisable that you consult a trade specialist or freight forwarder for your documentation.

The documents typically required in an export transaction can be found in most of the export guides listed in the beginning of this chapter. Most of these guides give a brief explanation of the purpose each document serves. In addition, TradePort (http://www.tradeport.org/ts/t_expert/details/ship/docs.html) provides an extensive description of each document required as well as sample forms and instructions on how to fill each one out.

Most goods being exported do not require an export license. Under certain circumstances, however, an export license may be necessary. These typically apply to commodities in high-tech and defense industries, as well as dual-use items. You should contact the Bureau of Export Administration (http://www.bxa.doc.gov/) to determine whether you need to acquire an export license.

How Can I Obtain Financial Assistance?

A multitude of sources is available to help a business finance its export operations and transactions. Be aware, however, that export financing is different from other types of financing. Your situation and your buyer's situation determine the types of financing you need. A good place to get detailed information on the types of financing as well as a selection of sources is TradePort's guide to obtaining financing (http://www.tradeport.org/ts/financing/).

For a comprehensive list of trade financing sources, you should visit the International Trade Administration's "Financing Information" page (Figure 2.5). The ITA pages include information on various government agency programs, nonprofit associations, and commercial banks that provide financing. It also includes a directory of alternative financing services to fill the unconventional needs of U.S. exporters when traditional services fail to meet those needs (http://www.ita.doc.gov/how_to_export/fininfo.html).

Figure 2.5 ITA's Financing Information page.

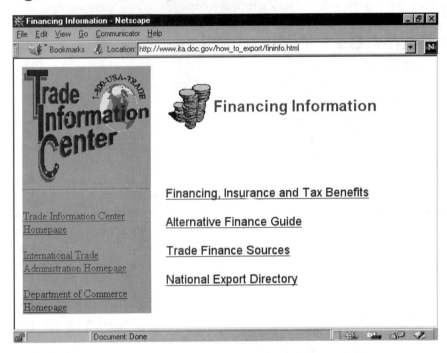

Where Can I Get Legal Information?

The most extensive and comprehensive site on international trade law is the International Trade Law Project (http://itl.irv.uit.no/trade_law/). This site has an extensive collection of international trade law materials, including most of the treaties, conventions, model laws, and rules on international trade. The site also features an extremely large trade law reference library.

A second location to visit is Ernst and Young's World Tax site (http://www.eyi .com/itax/). In addition to the *Doing Business* guide mentioned previously in this chapter, this site also includes a wealth of information on taxation issues. Particularly worth mentioning is the Worldwide Corporate Tax Guide, which contains a summary of the corporate tax systems in more than 130 countries.

Another useful resource for export-related legal information is the Export Legal Assistance Network (ELAN), which is a cooperative program sponsored by the Federal Bar Association, the Department of Commerce, and the Small Business Administration. The network provides free initial legal consultation to companies making their first entry into the export market (http://www.miep.org/elan/).

Where Else Can I Go for Assistance?

A variety of nonprofit organizations and government agencies provide free or inexpensive assistance to exporters. The obvious ones are the U.S. Small Business Administration's Office of International Trade (http://www.sbaonline.sba.gov/OIT/) and the U.S. Department of Commerce International Trade Administration (http://www.ita.doc.gov/). We already referred to both agencies' Web sites earlier in this chapter. In addition, the following three organizations are worth mentioning:

Service Corps of Retired Executives (SCORE). A resource partner with the SBA, the SCORE program is dedicated to assisting small businesses. Members of the SCORE program, many of whom have years of practical experience in international trade, provide one-on-one counseling and training seminars. SCORE also assists small firms in evaluating their export potential as well as in strengthening their domestic operations by identifying financial, managerial, or technical problems (http://www.score.org/).

The Commercial Service. A part of the U.S. Department of Commerce, the Commercial Service is committed to assisting U.S. firms in realizing their export potential by providing expert counseling and advice, information on markets abroad, international contacts, and advocacy services. The Commercial Service is located in Export Assistance Centers throughout the United States. You can find a directory of Export Assistance Centers on the Commercial Service's Web page (http://www.ita.doc.gov/uscs/).

Small Business Exporters Association (SBEA). The SBEA provides a variety of services to exporters who choose to join the association. Education, certification, networking, export financing assistance, and advocacy campaigns are only some of the services that SBEA provides (http://www.sbea.org/sbea/).

Being well prepared often spells the difference between success and failure for an export venture. The resources discussed in this chapter will certainly assist you in considering the various facets of exporting. Using these resources, you should create a business plan that covers market choice and entry, distribution, pricing, and financial strategy. Once a business plan is set, you are ready to operationalize it by building your own Web site and utilizing the other opportunities the Internet provides to start exporting your goods online.

SELLING ONLINE TO THE WORLD

A Case Study

3

The Internet is becoming the high ground of global commerce. As Nicholas Negroponte pointed out in his book *Being Digital* (Knopf, 1995), the shift from atoms to bits is releasing us from the limitations of geographical proximity. In 1994, people said of the Internet, "It's too hard to use." In 1995, they said, "It's just a fad." In 1996, they said, "It has potential." In 1997, they said, "It can help us make money."

According to a study presented at the Internet 98 Conference in October 1997, new users are logging onto the Internet at a rate of seventy-one thousand per day, and even though electronic commerce (e-commerce) is in its infancy, there are already close to a million commercial transactions a day occurring on the Internet, and an estimated $10 billion in goods and services were purchased via the World Wide Web in 1997. The Web is physically growing. The number of URLs grew from seventy-two million at the end of 1996 to more than two hundred million by the fall of 1997.

Estimates vary, but market research firm International Data Corp. predicts that the volume of commerce on the Internet will reach $220 billion a year by 2001. The number of businesses connected to the Internet was 4 percent in 1996; that's expected to reach 33 percent in the year 2000.

This is not merely an interesting trend. It is one that portends life-and-death consequences for many citizens of the business world. Nowhere does electronic communication loom more importantly than in the arena of global business. Globalization is an inescapable fact. It is business that knits the world together, more so than politics or culture. It is business on a global scale that drives growth. It is therefore natural that the first generation of e-commerce should be born from the cradle of business-to-business electronic communication.

Only a few years ago, most technology observers believed that the first commercial application of the Internet would relate to business-to-consumer marketing. For a variety of reasons, that application has not taken off as quickly as expected. It now appears that business-to-business applications will carry e-commerce into its first full bloom.

The same firm that predicts Internet commerce will reach $220 billion by 2001 says that 80 percent of that amount will come from business-to-business commerce. AMP Incorporated, the world's leading connector and interconnections systems company, is already an innovator in using the Internet to provide information on its vast array of products to customers all over the globe. A Fortune 300 company founded in 1941 and based in Harrisburg, Pennsylvania, AMP makes close to half a million products—primarily electrical and electronic connection devices. More than 130,000 of AMP's products are available commercially. The balance consists of items that are in the process of being discontinued or are special, proprietary products designed and built for specific customers such as Mercedes, Hewlett-Packard, and General Motors. AMP has eighty-eight thousand customers in forty-seven countries, and its sales in 1997 were $5.7 billion.

The New Market Channel

In the past, AMP used four channels to reach its markets: direct contacts via the field sales organization, telephone sales, relationships with suppliers and subcontractors who build AMP products into their products, and a general distribution network. Commerce on the Internet, through an online catalog called "AMP Connect," now offers a new channel to market, one that overarches but also complements all the old channels.

AMP Connect gives customers all over the world the ability to find out about nearly ninety thousand products in eight languages—all without leaving their office chairs. They can search the database by viewing pictures of AMP products, by reviewing an alphabetical listing of products or industry names for the products, or by requesting information by means of AMP part numbers.

Information available over the Internet encompasses all of the information available from AMP's paper catalogs, fax-back system, and CD-ROM system. This includes customer drawings, application specifications, product specifications, instruction sheets, and 3-D CAD models.

AMP Connect is commerce-enabled, meaning that online transactions are possible. Orders are taken from customers over the Internet, through which customers are able to make payments and monitor the status of their orders.

The Evolution of Internet Commerce at AMP

Why would a conservative company like AMP get involved with e-commerce? The reason is the tradition of serving our customers well through a variety of sales and marketing channels. E-commerce—AMP's online catalog—is simply one more channel (see Figure 3.1).

In addition, online catalogs save money by reducing expenses connected to printing and staff time. In the past, AMP delivered product information through paper catalogs, as our competitors have done and are still doing. Even now, more than four hundred paper catalogs are produced approximately every twenty-four months. These updates require a publishing budget of roughly $15 million.

Fax-Back

In late 1991 AMP established a new standard in the delivery of product information: a fax-back system called "AMPFAX." This system allowed customers to call a toll-free line and request information by part number. The information was then faxed back to the customer. The fax-back system provides customers with easy access to very current product information.

Soon after its introduction, the success of AMPFAX became well known in the electronics manufacturing industry. Because it was so effective, AMPFAX imme-

Figure 3.1 AMP's online catalog.

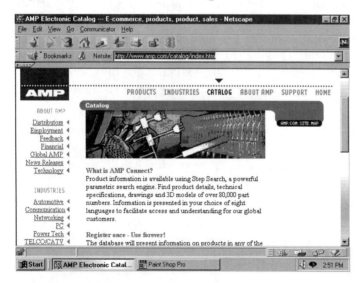

diately became very popular, receiving between three thousand and four thousand calls per month.

By 1994, AMP competitors had begun to emulate the fax-back system. But with an annual telephone bill approaching $1 million, AMP's fax-back system was not necessarily the most cost-effective way of providing product information to customers. While competitors were building fax-back systems, AMP was already moving toward an even better method for providing product support and information to customers. This next step was the use of CD-ROM technology.

CD-ROM

In 1992, AMP began using CD-ROM technology with a program called EADS, the Electronic Application Design System. The objective of this system was to offer customers a way to get engineering CAD drawings of our AMP's products. AMP supplied the engineering data on disks to customers in order to save them design and specification time. This program wound up being used by more than fourteen hundred customers.

After the introduction of EADS, Jack Usner, manager of AMP FutureView Group, came up with the idea of putting the catalog on CD-ROM. A pilot project was begun late in 1993 and completed in the early part of 1994. AMP developed a search engine and moved about five thousand part numbers for appliance industry products into an electronic CD-ROM catalog and then shared the catalog on a trial basis with a number of clients in the industry.

Customer feedback on the CD-ROM catalog was very positive. On further analysis, AMP discovered that what customers liked most was the search engine. They said the CD-ROM catalog was more usable and user-friendly than a paper catalog, but it was really the search engine (Figure 3.2) that they found so helpful. The search engine had been developed jointly by AMP and one of its contractors, Sherif Danish. The Step Search system that AMP uses today in AMP*e*Merce is its descendant.

AMP also realized that the CD-ROM medium had shortcomings much like those of a paper catalog. Once a CD-ROM catalog is mastered—the equivalent of a paper catalog being printed—it begins to age very quickly. It's a challenge to keep a CD-ROM catalog updated in the same way it's a challenge to keep a paper catalog updated.

It was at that point that AMP began to think about the possibility of using the Internet as the delivery vehicle for an electronic catalog. In 1994, AMP asked

Figure 3.2 Search engine of AMP CD-ROM catalog.

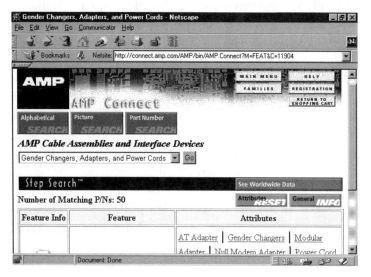

Sherif Danish to adapt the search engine used for the CD-ROM to the client/server environment of the Internet.

Pulled toward the Internet

In 1994, AMP's marketing strategy involved the challenge of finding a way to attain market growth in a period in which the market had matured. AMP's move toward the Internet also involved its perception of its customer base. AMP believes its customers are segmented into three tiers or strata.

Tier 1, the top tier, consists of a limited pool of about eighty customers who collectively account for a large number of high-volume transactions but relatively low growth and low profit margins. Tier 1 customers are companies such as IBM, Hewlett-Packard, and Motorola. These companies typically negotiate a very tough bargain; and while AMP clearly wants their high-volume business, Tier 1 is not necessarily where the growth opportunity is in the marketplace.

Likewise, AMP's approximately three hundred mid-size Tier 2 customers present limited opportunities for market growth. At the other end of the spectrum, Tier 3 consists of approximately eighty thousand customer companies that engage in relatively low-volume transactions but offer a high-growth opportunity. This is the segment where new businesses are formed and rapid growth takes place. Typically, the margins on products in this segment are better than the margins in Tier 1. So this is the area of the market where it's important to play—and play very aggressively.

If you looked at AMP's traditional channel-to-market coverage plan at the time, you would have seen a strategy in which salespeople covered Tier 1 customers by knocking on doors, calling on customers, and meeting needs on an individual basis. Distribution partners were used to address both Tier 2 and Tier 3 customers (the small companies and those in the middle, respectively).

In reality, the sales organization and distribution partners worked toward each other. Both salespeople and distributors tended to focus on the larger accounts because such accounts represented, after all, large transaction opportunities for them. Instead of distributors providing deep coverage down through Tier 3, they tended to cover the top of Tier 3, all of Tier 2, and the bottom of Tier 1.

That left a big chunk of Tier 3 unattended. AMP wasn't taking advantage of the market growth that it could have. The challenge—the opportunity, really—was to find a way to focus on the low-volume, high-growth, high-margin area called Tier 3. AMP saw the Internet as the solution.

AMP looked at the different media it had used to purvey product information in the past and how those media had met the demands of their customers. It found that its customers need a full range of product information and product specifications. They need to be able to cross-reference competitors' products to AMP's. They need price and delivery information. And they need to be able to enter orders and check on the status of those orders.

Comparing Capabilities

Paper catalogs provide product information and specifications. So does the fax-back AMPFAX system. The CD-ROM prototype catalog AMP developed also provided product information. But it is the Internet that gives AMP the capability to provide customers with *all* of the information they need and want on a current, almost up-to-the-minute basis.

Speaking more generally, the Internet is a *network* that provides the capability to meet the customers' information requirements at all stages of the buying cycle. With the big, high-volume Tier 1 customers like IBM, you can afford private networks, if necessary, to provide the requisite information; it's justified by the return. Not so with Tier 3 companies, however. Private networks with a large number of small Tier 3 companies would be cost prohibitive. But the Internet is the public data network. Because it's relatively inexpensive, it's the perfect choice for connection to Tier 3 customers.

The Internet gives AMP the ability not only to provide product information and specifications, technical and testing data, competitive cross references, price information, and delivery information, but the company could also use it to take orders and track them.

Getting Management's Blessing

AMP began by putting up on the Internet essentially the same database of five thousand products related to the appliance industry that they'd used for the CD-ROM project. They decided at this point that AMP needed input from the outside world about how well its search engine worked. It took its search engine and five-thousand-product Internet database to the second annual World Wide Web Conference in Chicago in October 1994. The feedback was tremendous and very, very positive. The technology attracted a lot of interest, as did the concept of AMP's application and utilization of the Internet. Companies like IBM, Hewlett-Packard, and Microsoft watched what AMP was doing with envy.

Back in Harrisburg, AMP realized that it needed to patent the process used by the search engine. They've since done that, and the search engine is now available as Step Search from a company called Saqqara Systems. Saqqara Systems was formed by Sherif Danish, AMP's consultant, and is based in Sunnyvale, California. AMP has invested its intellectual property rights in the company and is a stockholder.

AMP distilled what it wanted to do into a vision statement to be presented to its management team at the end of 1994. The vision statement was as follows: "That AMP can realize its tactical and strategic goals in significant part as a result of the competitive advantage realized by the implementation of leading-edge electronic commerce initiatives."

The vision was built upon what AMP had already achieved. They wanted to establish an electronic catalog and then link the catalog to the specification information available on AMPFAX. They also wanted to be able to put together customized catalogs that would allow for application-specific or industry-specific views of the product database. They wanted to provide cross references both from competitors' products to theirs and also from their customers' part numbers to AMP's part numbers. They also saw the catalog as holding strong potential for communicating marketing information from their sales and marketing organizations to customers. Finally, they wanted to be able to share price and availability information on products and actually take orders and track them.

The presentation to top AMP executives was scheduled, but fate was somewhat unkind. That morning, newspaper headlines declared that General Electric's computer system had been penetrated by hackers. You can imagine the questions about Internet security that greeted the presentation.

AMP senior management expressed some concerns. One was concern about the customers' willingness to accept and use the Internet. The other concern was security. Could AMP secure a Web site and also secure their legacy system so that the company would be safe from hackers?

As is sometimes the case, you want to find peers and other organizations that are thinking in line with you. AMP had the good fortune to have the opportunity to join an organization called CommerceNet, a not-for-profit consortium of companies who view the Internet as a potential source for doing business, want to understand its challenges, and want to put in place programs and guidance regarding how to confront some of those challenges.

Members of this organization range from American Express and Apple Computer to Wells Fargo and Xerox. You might describe CommerceNet as a kind of chamber of commerce for the Internet. Partial funding for CommerceNet initially came from the federal government. The government allocated several million dollars and the then-forty-plus member companies provided matching funds during the organization's first three years. CommerceNet now has about five hundred members worldwide.

AMP rightly thought that the people and companies involved in CommerceNet had some of the same concerns they did. AMP worked with them to understand the challenges related to security on the Internet. Much of the work that has been done in the area of Secure Socket Layer technology was a direct outgrowth of this organization's guidance.

In late 1997, CommerceNet was chosen to serve as the facilitator on a project funded by the U.S. Commerce Department's Advanced Technology Program. The project is designed to investigate and develop an open component-based architecture for Internet commerce. The Advanced Technology Program began in 1990 at the National Institute of Standards and Technology. Its mission is to invest in promising but high-risk technologies that may lead to economic growth.

Finding Out If Customers Are Ready

The next step for AMP was to look at its own customer base to determine its readiness to accept and use the Internet as a delivery vehicle.

Beginning in early 1995, AMP reviewed the status of four hundred customers who were in the million-dollar-plus category. They found that 46 percent of them already had begun to use the Internet and had registered domains. That indicated that they were at least using the Internet for email or sending files by FTP (file transfer protocol).

AMP then went to each of those registered sites to find out in more detail in what other ways the Internet was being used. It found that 25 percent already had home pages. This was a good indication that there were many other large corporations out there interested in using the Internet, at least as a medium for marketing and corporate information.

The four hundred customers AMP reviewed accounted for about 61 percent of its revenue at the time. It had to be concerned, however, about the other 39 percent because that's where the low-volume, high-profit, high-growth opportunities existed—with the Tier 3 companies discussed earlier.

When AMP analyzed the marketplace, it quickly realized that despite the fact that a lot of its revenue comes from rather large companies, a sizable mass also comes from its very small customers (less than a few hundred thousand dollars). So AMP needed to understand what its small customers' use of the Internet might be.

AMP realized that if it was going to be successful, it had to serve both ends of the spectrum with the Internet. Clearly, it couldn't go out and sample all eighty-eight thousand AMP customers to see how many had registered Web sites. Instead, they did a random sampling of three hundred smaller customers and found that 30 percent had registered Internet domains, a finding that was again very supportive of what they wanted to do. In fact, the expectation at the time was that AMP would have been lucky to find something in the range of 5 to 10 percent. Thirty percent seemed so incredible that they did a second sampling of another three hundred smaller customers. This time the result was 32 percent with Internet sites!

A year later, at the beginning of 1996, use of the Internet had expanded appreciably with those same four hundred big customers. Seventy-three percent now had registered Internet domains, and nearly 66 percent had home pages. It was apparent that people saw a tremendous opportunity to communicate their companies' stories to the public in this manner. Of the six hundred smaller customers (the two groups of three hundred), close to 60 percent had Internet registrations at the start of 1996, and more than 50 percent had Internet home pages. Quite a startling progression of growth was apparent from the beginning of 1995 to the beginning of 1996.

The growth in the use of the Internet by AMP's customers was enough to convince its senior management that they were looking at tremendous potential in terms of meeting the needs of customers.

Doing It for Real

As sometimes happens, vision becomes mission. AMP's mission was to have the electronic catalog in place and available to customers globally by the end of 1995. The goal was to put up a catalog that would include components that account for more than 80 percent of AMP's revenue. That meant including approximately thirty thousand parts just to make sure that each of the appropriate product families were rounded out.

Senior management wanted AMP's project to meet the needs of its global customers, the implication being that they had to use multiple languages. And the regional executives and the country managers wanted to make sure that when a customer first viewed products for delivery into a specific country they viewed the standard stocking parts for that country. That would give AMP a better chance to serve the customers' needs without having to pull products from around the globe.

It was management's desire, as well, that AMP be self-sufficient. The thinking was that if, in fact, the Internet was going to be a significant competitive advantage, and if, in fact, it was going to become an important channel to market, then AMP should possess its own in-house expertise. It turned out to be a prescient position for management to take.

The year 1995 was spent developing software, building the database, and conducting pilot tests. AMP conducted one very extensive pilot effort that involved a dozen companies and two distributors from various places on the globe. Those dozen companies and two distributors were represented by fifty-four individuals in the pilot; those fifty-four people gave AMP input that allowed it to refine and improve its system interface and also to add additional functional features that it thought would be valuable.

One of the strong advantages of the Internet and Internet technology is the fact that it is relatively easy to adapt. AMP was able to communicate, on a weekly basis, with pilot participants to get their input. Usually about a week later they would be able to implement changes based on participants' requests and then get additional feedback.

May to October of 1995 was a period of rapid change and development in the way the interface looked and in the facilities AMP provided to the customer. One thing that happened in that period was that AMP developed the search engine in the Windows NT platform and in parallel on a Unix platform, so that they effectively had two search engines.

Turning On the Lights

In December 1995, AMP did load testing to determine that its systems and software could handle the demand presented by queries to the catalog. They introduced the AMP catalog to each of the pilot companies. They did it across the pilot company's entire engineering base one day at a time. AMP was able to watch the load build on the system and determine if it had any bottlenecks or any problems that needed adjustment. The results were very positive, such that by the time AMP closed for the holidays, it had significant confidence that the public release of the system would proceed as scheduled.

The public release took place on January 11, 1996, at the following address: http://connect.amp.com. The catalog debuted with thirty-two thousand product part numbers available in five languages.

Of immediate interest to catalog users was that the search engine operated in a nonhierarchical archival fashion. This means that the user searches by clicking in input, guiding the search engine to deliver back the right product or information for the right product based on the customer's needs and the order of priority of those needs. It is a superior and very dynamic search approach as compared to the more traditional top-down, or drill-down, method.

Another revolutionary element of the AMP online catalog was the introduction of dynamically created pages. Prior to this, the industry had used static HTML pages to convey information. However, AMP began building HTML pages in a dynamic fashion. (The best analogy for understanding static versus dynamic HTML pages is to compare yesterday's manual typewriter to today's word processor. With the manual unit, changing a document means starting all over. With a word processor, changes are made effortlessly and permanently throughout the system.) Based on the clicks from the user, the system takes the search parameter, goes to the database, and pulls up the appropriate information. The contents of the HTML page come from the Oracle 7 database. In effect, the users get a customized page to look at based on the information they have entered (Figures 3.3A and 3.3B). The information entered is a description of what the user needs, in a particular priority sequence.

Because of the multiple language capability and the fact that AMP purveys only the standard stocking parts for a particular country, they are able to deliver a customized presentation to the individual user. As part of the registration process, the user selects his or her language preference and the country the product will be delivered to. Using that information along with additional feature preferences selected by the user, AMP can create a customized response. For example, users may want to see the catalog in German but have the part shipped to Spain; AMP presents the contents in the German language and lists the standard stocking parts for Spain.

Figure 3.3A Information for customized search.

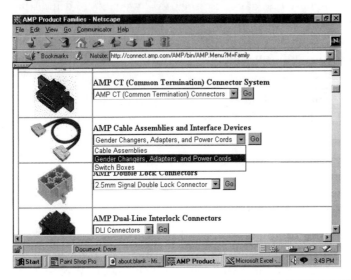

In addition to customizing the catalog by language and country of delivery, AMP enables its customers to navigate through the catalog by specifying product requirements. AMP then uses the specifications to respond with the right product. This flexibility is very different from standard catalog technology and is what captured the attention of the WWW show in Chicago in October 1994.

As mentioned, the catalog went public in January 1996 with thirty-two thousand part numbers on the system, exceeding AMP's original expectations. The catalog offered five languages (English, French, Italian, Spanish, and German), a part number search, a picture search, an alphabetic search, and the new Step Search technology.

Release 2, shown in Figure 3.4, was announced in June 1996. It featured sixty-four thousand part numbers and the addition of the Japanese, Chinese, and Korean languages. This release was the first use of a Unicode-based database from Oracle of Redwood Shores, California, to support multiple languages. The design of the Web pages came from NetImage of Camp Hill, Pennsylvania.

By the fall of 1997, AMP Connect had more than ninety thousand part numbers online and was receiving 115,000 hits a day. The Internet project, under Global Electronic Commerce director Jim Kessler, was launched with four full-time employees and a team of temporary data-entry employees. They worked on database design and the use of Oracle 7 database technology with Sherif Danish and his team of consultants on Step Search applications, together with the company's own Systems Services organization.

Figure 3.3B Customized search result.

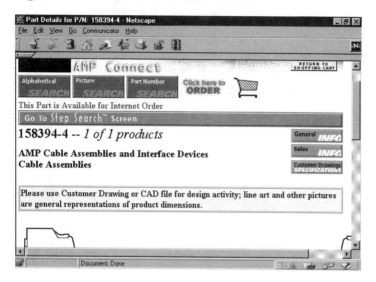

Figure 3.4 AMP Connect, Release 2.

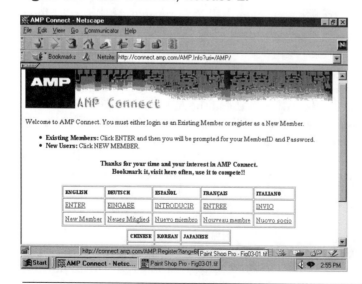

Some Lessons Learned

AMP realized the potential marketing power of the Internet in 1994 and aggressively pursued the project with its senior management. There were naysayers who didn't believe the project would work. They criticized Internet performance and security. Often the criticism was founded on a lack of understanding of the Internet.

The Internet in its most rudimentary sense is nothing more than the use of the existing telephony system to communicate messages. The Internet uses the same long-line carriers as the telephone. Data and telephony messages and both private networks and the public Internet all use the same physical plant. The messages are packetized, coded, and passed from one system to another on copper or fiber-optic lines. One message is voice; the next is composed of data. It may be private data at one moment and Internet data the next. Any combination of voice or data messages travels down the same pipe. The infrastructure to support the expanding reliance on the Internet is, in fact, in place. There are no fewer than a dozen Internet providers today, a number more than adequate to meet the demand.

AMP located its site very cautiously. Performance was going to be a key element in the acceptance of its offering. They understood that a major site like theirs had to be co-located near the backbone of the Internet so customers would be able to access the catalog easily.

In January 1996, as AMP prepared to go public with its online catalog, it sent packages of information to all its salespeople. These packages included introductory disks that allowed customers to load a browser on their system and use the browser and the Internet free for one month. That provided AMP's sales force with an opportunity to introduce AMP Connect and show customers how easy it was to use.

Although customers could have used any browser to access AMP Connect, the Internet was too new to expect everyone to have a browser and an Internet connection. AMP therefore teamed up with IBM and the Advantis organization to produce the introductory diskette and provide free Internet time so customers could become familiar with using the Internet. In addition, AMP sent along a fifteen-minute videotape about the Internet, a PowerPoint presentation, and URL cards with the address of the catalog. All communications from AMP, including advertising, press, and magazine material, carried the URL address so people outside AMP would know how to reach AMP Connect.

AMP also asked its users to register, despite having been advised that customers wouldn't take the time to do so. In fact, customers began to register. As of this writing, AMP has over 160,000 registered users from 138 countries around the world. That's eighty more countries than it has offices in! Clearly, AMP has reached new markets.

AMP Connect receives approximately 170,000 hits a day. This figure represents roughly fifteen thousand users exploring the catalog every day. Of further importance is how many of those are first-time users and how many are repeat users. The more repeat users, the more the catalog has become a tool for customers to find product information. Repeat use of the AMP catalog—which is adding new users at the rate of ten thousand per month—has grown at a compound rate of somewhere between 10 and 15 percent monthly, which the company considers a very significant growth rate.

AMP can track who is in the catalog and what they are doing. From the registration, they can learn a customer's position and occupation, what country he or she is from, and what company he or she represents. AMP has learned that 68 percent of its users are engineers, the primary target audience for the online catalog. Fifteen percent are purchasing oriented. The remainder fall into a variety of categories, covering all types of industries and not excluding any of the major industries served by AMP.

More than 450 new users sign up and register in the catalog every day. This is a predictable number: every weekday, 450 new users sign up; on Saturday, between 50 and 70; and on Sunday between 80 and 100. These numbers have been consistent, except for the Christmas holiday week of 1996.

AMP receives feedback directly from customers through a feedback area on the catalog.

The impact of AMP Connect has been significant. It won British Telecom's Internet Award in 1996, and AMP was named the top award winner in CommerceNet's Very Innovative Practice (VIP) competition in 1996.

Looking over the Horizon

AMP is not stopping with AMP Connect. AMP has added the Platinum Program, a specific marketing program that allows AMP's select customers to personalize their interactions with the online catalog. The program offers "interest view" access—or access to product groupings based on customized interest—as well as secure administration, secure delivery, and customer cross reference. Another enhancement is called Expert Mode, which was put in place late in 1997. Typically, there are several hundred products in a product family. There may be as many as twelve or fourteen feature groups, and after that five to ten options in each feature group. Suddenly, you have a range that produces a huge set of possible combinations. The goal is to provide guidance to the customer, so he or she ultimately gets one of the products offered. You never want the customer to enter a string of data and ultimately be told, "We don't have a product like that."

Expert Mode uses Java scripting technology to provide gentle guidance by limiting options that either are no longer available or don't lead to an existing product. Users can enter, in a single query, two or three sets of criteria. If the clicks the user enters do not lead to a match, the system peels off the last click and then uses the previous clicks. This continues until the user has a hit. The system then presents that hit as the response to the user. The user can go forward and further refine his or her requirements.

AMP is also putting in place industry and application interfaces. Users can indicate what industry they work in and get a view of the catalog specific to that industry. For instance, if the user works in the appliance industry, he or she can view all the connectors built for, sold in, and typically used by the appliance industry. Likewise, the user can view the catalog from the perspective of applications for different kinds of connectors, such as wire-to-wire or board-to-board connectors. Another feature AMP believes has tremendous demonstrated value is supporting the electronic catalog with a database that is updated every day. The catalog is always current as of the close of business the day before. That makes the online catalog a source of current information in a way a paper catalog could never be.

The Publishing Interface

AMP can now use the same database that supports AMP Connect online for its own printed catalogs, using software it has acquired from Database Publishing, Inc. of Boston. Database Publishing worked with AMP from the middle of 1996 through the early part of 1997 to build a proof-of-concept system that allows them to extract information from the database and use it to produce a custom-printed paper catalog. The custom paper catalog can be organized by a specific group of products, a grouping of product numbers, or by industry. The publishing software provides printer-ready output in either QuarkXPress or PostScript files. These files only need to be reviewed for formatting; as long as the database is accurate and up to date so, too, is the output.

This system cuts the production time of a paper catalog down to a few weeks, from what had been up to nine months. While the amount of revenue generated over the Internet is an important measure of success, the costs that are avoided, such as those related to the printing and publishing of paper catalogs, are just as important. AMP will save an estimated 40 percent of its catalog publication costs by producing printed paper catalogs from the database used for the online catalog. If, like AMP, you are spending $7 million to $10 million to publish catalogs, the savings is indeed significant. This process also considerably reduces costs for AMP by eliminating the time required for engineers and product managers to spend updating, refining, and redlining the old catalog and then running the changes through several rounds of proofing.

It's not likely that the printing of paper catalogs will be entirely eliminated in the near future. The way paper catalogs are printed will be changed and refined. Over time, CD-ROM technology and fax-back technology will atrophy. As more and more people become aware of what is available on the Internet, and become comfortable with using it, there probably will be a steady decline in the use of other, older technologies, which in turn should result in cost savings.

New Kinds of Corporate Assets

A parametrically searchable product description database and an image assets database are at the heart of global electronic publishing and create the ease that enables the system to locate the product or products within the vast catalog. In the past, the only repositories for this data tended to be in printed, paper catalogs. Mary Ann Swartley and her team created the parametric database for AMP. It's a huge physical challenge to find all the information, enter it into the database, and make sure it is correct. It is also a costly project. More than half of the total developmental budget for AMP Connect was spent reverse-engineering paper catalogs into a parametrically searchable database.

Where do you get the images? This is another challenge, a very big challenge. Most corporations do not have a single repository of digital images. This is a new kind of asset that corporations will need to create in the future. Image storage has traditionally been disorganized. Figures were stored as hard copy or as computer graphics files. Corporations did not have a set of standards so images could be utilized by the entire company. Today, the need for a repository of preapproved images of the product or products is immediate.

One concern is image resolution: Does the image meet the resolution requirements of the Internet, currently at 72 DPI (dots per inch)? Does it meet the higher resolution requirement (600 DPI) for printing?

To meet this challenge, AMP uses Image Assets, a product from New Mexico Software Company in Albuquerque, New Mexico. Image Assets is based on a Flash Pix technology patented by Kodak that allows you to maintain one image in your digital database and extract it at whatever resolution level is necessary to meet your needs. The image can be enlarged, sections may be cropped, or the colors may be changed.

A related benefit to maintaining large, parametrically searchable databases is savings. When you use a database in multiple languages, you suddenly reduce the expense of localizing catalogs by language. Without this database, AMP had to have the catalog translated each time it published a paper catalog, resulting in a high per-word cost. With this database, AMP translates each word only once and saves it in the database. Aside from updates related to product deletions and additions, an occasional text review for language misuse (improper idioms) is all that is required. Once the translations are in the database, they may be used to publish new catalogs. The database does not have to be retranslated. It only has to be maintained and updated.

Developments in electronic publishing such as those discussed here have benefits related to consistent message, consistent quality, customized message, reduced cost of publishing, and reduced cost of translation. These benefits typically are not understood when companies plan for an electronic offering over the Internet. They are very anxious to see the revenues generated from new sales. AMP believes that there will be considerable revenue generated from new sales over the Internet. For example, because customers are finding it relatively easy to use the Internet for product data, fewer may make calls by voice telephone to find and obtain the information they want. That may mean a drop in the call volume to customer service. If that happens, you can save money by reducing the size of your customer service staff. Fax-back can be used less by using Internet technology. AMP spends approximately $800,000 a year for outbound faxing; this cost will shrink as more customers utilize the Internet instead.

The Paradigm Has Changed

The paradigm for product information has changed. It used to be that manufacturers, end-users, retailers, distributors, and original equipment manufacturers (OEMs) were all part of a value-added hierarchy of channel-to-market partners. Now, the end-user, the retailer, the distributor, and the OEM are on an equal plane. The best place for all of them to find product information is AMP Connect, the electronic catalog on the Internet.

This paradigm change will cause distribution to adjust its business model. In fact, this is already happening for AMP. One of its distributors has taken a very aggressive posture toward changing the value paradigm it brings to distributing products. This distributor is helping smaller manufacturers, those that don't have the resources to utilize the Internet as AMP has. It shows the companies how to get on the Internet and use it to introduce new products and create forums on the quality of products. The distribution paradigm will continue to change in the future.

Some major organizations have already successfully taken advantage of the Internet. Amazon.com, the online bookseller, is one example. In one quarter of 1997, its net sales were $27.9 million. Boeing Aircraft, another example, takes part orders over the Internet from all over the world. Dell Computer Corporation is said to be selling computer equipment from its Web site at a pace of $730 million a year. Cisco Systems is projected to be selling $1 billion to $2 billion a year on the Web. Those companies and others in technology-related businesses, such as Gateway Computers, are taking orders, communicating product information, and helping their customers by means of the Internet. In fact, AMP*e*Merce, an offshoot of the AMP catalog effort that provides e-commerce consulting services to companies, has helped Hershey Foods create an Internet ordering system for chocolate novelty items sold in its Chocolate World store.

Are there any limitations on the kinds of products that can be marketed over the Internet? Probably not, with the possible exception of perfumes, because the sense of smell cannot be conveyed or replicated (at least not yet). Even the ability to market tactile-sensitive products over the Internet will improve as new technologies and bandwidth improves. Three-dimensional walk-throughs of automobiles or homes probably will become possible. The technology of virtual reality will allow you to place yourself in a virtual room and turn and see the different aspects of a room or the inside of a vehicle. You'll see the light and shadows change and get a sense of space.

Will the complete transaction, in such instances, be concluded over the Internet? The answer is probably no, for the time being. You're probably still going to want to go and actually sit in the automobile. But the sales process itself may radically change. For instance, once you've physically sat in the automobile of your choice, you may go back to the Internet to negotiate the final deal. Already you can get detailed vehicle model information and comparisons online, along with a commitment for financing.

Getting Started

For those interested in e-commerce, the first key is to have a clear idea of where you want to go with your Internet initiative. What do you want to accomplish?

Establish a specific mission and a set of measurable objectives that you can use to gauge your success. Carefully evaluate what you want your site to do for you. What business problems are you addressing? Then use your communications skills. Think about your Web site as if you were a magazine editor evaluating an ad. Think carefully about content. Are you reaching the right audience? How do you get your audience to return?

Put a high priority on front-end planning and keep your expectations realistic regarding what can be accomplished. Do a test version of your Web site and use the information gained to hone your site more precisely. A word of caution: The moment you ask for customer input, be prepared to operate a twenty-four-hour facility and to respond within hours. This can become a black hole into which you throw unlimited resources. Make sure beforehand that you can really handle whatever it is you're planning to offer.

If you do that, and if the work that you do is properly designed and laid out, you should meet your expectations.

Finding a New Business

In the latter part of January 1996, AMP Connect personnel started getting calls from companies outside of AMP who wanted to collaborate with them in the design and conception of e-commerce initiatives for their businesses. By April 1996, it became apparent that this was a business opportunity for AMP. AMP formed AMP*e*Merce Internet Solutions with the idea of sharing with the outside world the expertise they had developed while building and launching AMP Connect. AMP*e*-Merce—a group of thirty-two full-time employees supplemented with a number of contract agencies—provides Web site planning, site design and development, catalog analysis and conversion to parametric databases, Web site commerce enabling, Web site hosting, translation services, and support and systems integration.

There are many consultants who sell cataloging and search technologies and any number of elements on the component level. What AMP*e*Merce has is the know-how and the demonstrated capability to take all the components, all the existing tools, and integrate them into solutions that meet customers' needs and Web site missions.

AMP*e*Merce is currently exploring how people use Web sites in order to better understand how to customize e-commerce services. By building a portfolio of customer interests and preferences, as would be done by the traditional salesperson, AMP*e*Merce consultants can advise on how to capture the attention of a given customer set. For example, if AMP knows what products, applications, or industries a customer has been interested in, it can provide follow-up via announcements and new information and other material that is in line with the customer's interests— every time he or she returns to the Web site.

Imagine an engineer who frequently visits a Web site. He touches upon a certain area or product that has to do with a new application and suddenly there are new developments in that area. AMPeMerce links to articles on those new developments. They aren't involved in publishing the information, but they are aware of it and help guide the engineer to it. In that way, AMP can guide all the users of its electronic catalog to anything that will be pertinent to them. Such a site becomes value-added.

Given the overall size and scope of AMP, AMP*e*Merce is probably not going to be much more than a tip at the end of the tail from a revenue point of view. But whether it is using its expertise for itself or for another company for a fee, AMP is pleased to have the opportunity to participate in the pioneering of e-commerce. It knows what's going on out there and is committed to helping set the standards for a fully integrated solution in e-commerce initiatives.

The Importance and Impact of E-Commerce

AMP Connect and AMP*e*Merce serve as models for e-commerce applications. More than ever time is money. E-commerce allows a business to gain control over both. AMP believes the evidence is overwhelmingly positive that Internet commerce will evolve and grow rapidly.

Internet commerce shortens the buying cycle. With commonly available Internet access, customers can quickly access the online product database free of charge. Using a parametrically searchable database, customers can locate their desired product within their required parameters without having to waste time paging through irrelevant data.

Internet commerce reduces the cost of sales. By making information directly available to customers, sales and marketing costs connected to low-volume buyers can be dramatically reduced. Online publishing reduces and/or eliminates the need to maintain product information in a variety of media, such as paper or CD-ROM, so printing, shipping, and distribution costs can be greatly reduced. Adding a database publishing capability to the electronic database allows the user to publish catalogs on an as-needed basis. In the future, the capability to print custom information directly from the database is a likely scenario.

Internet commerce guarantees timeliness of product information.
With a few key strokes, an entire database is corrected, ensuring customers and employees alike of the most timely and factual product information. Depending on one source of easily reproducible information is
far less cumbersome than correcting and printing hundreds of publications or CD-ROMs.

Internet commerce facilitates round-the-clock transactions. Customers in all parts of the world can use the database at their convenience
without having to wait.

Internet commerce adds another channel to market. At AMP, traditional channels to market, such as the sales force, distributors, and in-
house customer service representatives, are complemented by the
electronic catalog. It provides yet another avenue through which customers can do business with the company. This development promises to
be the most momentous of all. It will bring a shift in the very foundations
of traditional business practice. Clearly, e-commerce is fully capable of
supplanting conventional channels while also saving money. In fact, a
Price-Waterhouse study recently said that doing business over the Internet, if done efficiently and effectively, can cut the cost of your distribution channel by 25 to 35 percent.

AMP has seen electronic or Internet commerce evolve through several phases.
The most basic level, of course, is the publishing of static HTML pages. These provide simple online information. This basic offering serves as a bridge from paper
to electronic catalogs. But it is limited by its inability to help the user search for
customized information. On an HTML page, information is accessible, but searching for it remains difficult.

The next level is database publishing. At this level, users are able to conduct
a search for information within the context of a set of requirements. By using a
parametric search engine, the user selects from sets of product characteristics and
searches the database for the appropriate match. Technology on this level meets
several challenges:

- It offers a maintained, timely database of product information.

- It provides language translations that support true global marketing.

- It creates dynamic, customized information to customers.

The third level is that of customer self-service. Here customized information is provided to specific users. This level provides search-assisted catalogs and service diagnostics that customers can download from the company. Information on product pricing and availability is integrated with the company's legacy systems.

The fourth and most complex level enables customers to complete a full transaction, from gathering information to purchasing, fulfillment, billing, and payment in a single environment. Concerns about security of transactions on the Internet have now been addressed by Secure Electronic Transactions technology. IBM, for example, has developed crypto-lopes, secure electronic envelopes. You can specify who can view them and who can open them.

No Turning Back

Internet or electronic commerce is plainly in its infancy. Today's high-tech solutions, over which we exclaim in amazement, will become the buggy whips of tomorrow. We will not know until after the fact which technologies will indeed turn out to be the dominant ones.

But despite such uncertainty, there is no turning back from the Internet, from electronic communication, from e-commerce. As global competition and technological innovation continue to drive the decision-making of business, we come to the inescapable and nearly universal recognition that we live in an electronic world. The paradigm has already shifted. The transition to e-commerce, like the transition to the twenty-first century, is well underway.

THINK LOCALLY, ACT GLOBALLY

As the first true global marketing medium, the World Wide Web provides an immediate and cost-effective means of communicating with your customers worldwide. By localizing your Web site, you deliver your Web content to targeted customers throughout the world with the same clarity and cultural sensitivity as in your printed localized materials. The essence of localization is communication. As with any form of corporate communication, Web site localization is more than just the transmission of information. It evokes trust, it commits the audience, and it gets the buy-in. The difference is that it has to achieve this in multiple languages.

Web site localization, therefore, must be more than just an afterthought. Localizing a Web site implies a host of technical challenges beyond the issues normally faced with other multilingual communications. Effective localization requires as much thought and planning as any other communication strategy. It is a careful balancing act of culture, people, and technology.

Keeping these elements in proper balance is also crucial to developing a multilingual site that works for everyone. We'll look at some of these critical elements in this chapter, along with several solutions chosen by various corporations to meet the challenge of globalizing their Web sites.

Before You Localize

Web site localization is not something to venture into haphazardly. It is an investment in your company's communications strategy. As with any investment, it requires careful and thorough consideration. A decision to localize cannot be made until there is complete understanding of the risks, challenges, and rewards involved.

An educated decision will mean the difference between simply a translated Web site and an effective vehicle of communication for reaching your target market.

Therefore, a company must consider effective multilingual communication from the very beginning. The language element can add technical, typesetting, and logistical challenges that you must accommodate from the outset. Without proper planning, the introduction of complications during the process will mean costly and untimely delays in getting your communication tool to market. The Internet is, in essence, a time-sensitive conduit of information. Because it is easily updated, users will assume that information will be up to date. Viewers' expectations dictate the need for haste in launching Web sites and revisions. Your own strategy, most likely, will necessitate a more efficient approach. This requires forethought.

Understanding Your Audience

Effective communication begins with understanding your target audience. What your audience likes or dislikes, is indifferent toward, or is emotionally drawn to can affect the tone and style of your copy. Now add another element: over five billion people who speak another language! With such overwhelming numbers and the appalling lack of Web content available to those who speak any of hundreds of languages, those few who make the decision to localize will be greeted enthusiastically. Demand and need are there, and opportunities abound for suppliers to take full advantage of them. There are two components of your audience to consider: language and culture.

Linguistic Differences

Let us assume your audience speaks French, Spanish, or Chinese. Knowing this, are you now ready to begin translation? No. Country-to-country linguistic differences will determine the target language for your specific audience.

Chinese illustrates the need to understand the linguistic differences and the sensitive political issues present in any culture or country. The word Chinese, in fact, is not even the appropriate name of the language. In the People's Republic of China (PRC), to be literate one needs to know at least four thousand characters out of a possible tens of thousands! To read English, it suffices to be familiar with twenty-six letters and various punctuation marks.

In addition, the PRC has over two hundred spoken dialects, which linguists have grouped into ten manageable categories. This can be a major hurdle for communication. While Mandarin is the official language in the PRC, it is spoken mainly in the north. In the southern provinces of Guang Dong and Hong Kong, the Cantonese dialect is spoken. With the gaps in China's spoken language, the written language became a strong unifying element. However, with the sheer number of characters to learn, the threat of widespread illiteracy, and thus political disunity, loomed.

In 1956, the Chinese government adopted a strategy to maintain language unity. It introduced 515 simplified characters; another 2,236 were added in 1964. This shortened and stylized form became official in the PRC in 1957 and was commonly known as Simplified Chinese script. The long form, or Traditional Chinese script, is still used in Hong Kong, Taiwan, and in Chinese populations off the mainland.

Traditional Chinese has become the script for the literary elite; most classic literature is written in long form. It is also a powerful symbol of political independence from the PRC. Thus, in the years following Hong Kong's handover to China in June 1997, it will be interesting to see how the evolution of its name to Xiang Gang (Mandarin language, not Cantonese dialect) will influence its political and economic development.

It is wise to be aware of the undercurrents that dictate language use and therefore your customer's perception of your message or product. Thus, to determine who your audience will be, the question to ask is: Will it be Mandarin in Taiwan, mainland China, or San Francisco? The constituency of your audiences will decide the nature of your copy.

Similarly with Spanish, will your target audience be from Spain, Mexico, Argentina, or Los Angeles? Each country or region has expressed the Spanish language in a unique way. Vocabulary words that appear to be cognates and benign in one country can be misleading or even completely offensive in another. Furthermore, one word may have very different meanings depending on the region. In Mexico, for example, the word *coche* means car. In Guatemala *coche* means pig. If you want to sell a car in a Spanish-speaking country, it helps to know who your specific target audience is, or those customers looking for a pig will be sorely disappointed.

A good example of a Web site sensitive to linguistic differences is the one constructed by The San Francisco Partnership, a cooperative project between the City of San Francisco and local corporations. In March 1997, the Partnership launched a marketing campaign designed to attract new business to the city. An integral part of this campaign was a seven-language Web site (see Figure 4.1).

This terrific Web site (http://www.spf.org) is a valuable tool for the Partnership in that the Web is the main source of information for those who provide consulta-

Figure 4.1 The San Francisco Partnership promotes global business with sensitivity to linguistic differences on its multilingual site at www.sfp.org.

tion to businesses looking to relocate or expand. One of the Partnership's hot prospects is Asia, and it has particular interests in Hong Kong, the PRC, and Taiwan. Based on these target markets, the Partnership chose to localize its Web site into both Simplified and Traditional Chinese characters to reach these diverse audiences. With San Francisco's international flavor attracting tourists from all over the world, the Partnership's ability to communicate successfully in other cultures creates an environment conducive to global commerce.

Cultural Differences

Another significant component of your audience to consider before you make any localization decision are cultural differences. Political, economic, and religious environments will dictate the content of your copy. Although beliefs in these areas may serve as warning signals to let you know what ideas to exclude, they can also provide valuable insight into what other ideas to include to communicate your message more effectively. For instance, in Latin America, religion plays a strong role in family life, and its power can be harnessed in your message.

Other cultural issues to remember include customary payment methods, the information required for ordering in specific countries, and customer service expectations. You might need to offer alternative means of payment for cultures that do not use credit or state the dimensions of household items for countries in which living space is a constraint and influences purchase decisions or provide more customer service in places where it is expected and frequently used. Even seasons will affect your product positioning. In Southern Hemisphere markets, holidays and vacations will conjure different images than in Northern Hemisphere markets. There is no white Christmas in Australia!

The formal or informal style of communication in the target country will also affect the way your copy is written. This is a factor for the Internet but less so for corporate intranet sites. Global corporations have unique subcultures within each country that allow them to use their own copy style and tone with limited consideration for cultural issues.

Typesetting Issues

Once you have decided which languages are most appropriate for your site and what your content will be—whether it should be uniform across all languages or unique for each target language—your next challenge is layout design. The three main areas of concern for Web site localization will be text length, text appearance, and technology. These issues can be discussed within two distinct language groups, those with Roman-based characters and those with non-Roman-based characters.

Roman-Based Characters

Translating into languages that use Roman-based alphabets will expand the size of your text up to 30 percent. When designing your page layout, leave ample white space to accommodate this text expansion. This is particularly pertinent for text-embedded graphics. Text might expand beyond the frame of the graphic, which will require that the graphic be redesigned. Other strategies for accommodating text expansion include increasing line length, reducing font size, and adjusting leading or kerning.

Grammatical and structural rules will also determine how text appears. For instance, differing hyphenation rules may leave rags, or uneven right edges in a paragraph, which might not create the same look and feel as the original English. Translated words tend to be longer than English words, and hyphenation is often difficult, awkward, or prohibited for certain word constructions. In Figure 4.2, Broderbund Banner Blue's German Web page contains words that are longer than the original English counterpart. This is a good example of how different line length and rags can be from one language to another.

Figure 4.2 Broderbund Banner Blue branches out with a page dedicated to its German-speaking audience at www.familytreemaker.com. Note the long word lengths and how hyphenation rules can create extreme rags on the right edge.

The appearance of the text is more than an aesthetic feature in localization: it serves a functional purpose. Rules about bolding, underlining, capitalizing, and the like are more strict in some languages than others since they affect the readability of the text and the placement of accent marks.

Non-Roman-Based Characters

Non-Roman-based alphabets create more challenges for the localization process. For scripts such as Chinese, Korean, and Japanese text length may decrease. This means heads and subheads will be shorter. However, the grammatical and structural rules of these languages are very strict. Chinese, Korean, and Japanese scripts are generally justified. This requires that kerning be varied between characters to achieve the effect of justified margins. Justification aids readability and satisfies readers' visual expectations. These languages traditionally read vertically, but contemporary standards allow for horizontal left-to-right typesetting. Other languages, like Arabic, read from right to left. As Figure 4.3 shows, taken from Direct Language Communications' (DLC) site, the Arabic text is visually unique.

Figure 4.3 DLC's site at www.dlc.com communicates with a global audience and tackles technical challenges, like those presented by Arabic.

For character-based languages (such as Traditional/Simplified Chinese, Korean, and Japanese) the size of the characters must be larger than English letters. Scaling fonts below nine points is not recommended because the intricate characters may plug up—the space between the strokes will fill in, rendering the characters illegible. These character-based languages are also illegible in reversed-out format, that is, white text against a black background. The intricate details tend to be lost.

In addition to the typographical issues there is a technological challenge. All non-Roman-based scripts require localized applications and/or operating systems as well as specialized fonts. This issue is best addressed by further dividing the non-Roman-based group into two subgroups: single-byte and double-byte languages.

Standard operating systems can process only the typical 256-character set of most Roman-based scripts—these 256 characters include accent marks and punctuation marks. In the binary system, this processing requires only a single byte of information to encode the characters. Languages that are not Roman-based and yet still single-byte include Thai, Laotian, Tagalog, Hmong, Cambodian, Greek, Russian, Arabic, and Hebrew (see Figure 4.4). Some single-byte languages do require their own localized operating systems, such as Arabic and Hebrew.

Figure 4.4 Cisco's fourteen-language site, at www.cisco.com, includes double- and single-byte languages, like this Russian page (Russian is single-byte and non-Roman-based), all of which require localized systems and esoteric font sets in order to view the page properly.

Chinese, Korean, and Japanese scripts have over ten thousand characters in their alphabets. To process this vast amount of information, operating systems, applications, and output devices need to be able to process information at an exponential rate. This requires two bytes of information to encode the characters. Such devices are commonly referred to as double-byte-enabled. In Figure 4.5, Millipore Corporation, a biomedical instrumentation company, opted to keep double-byte viewing for its site. Millipore's target market for this site is Japan, which means appropriate systems will be available for viewing the site in the Japanese language.

The decision to use double-byte viewing makes especially good sense for a company like Millipore, which does 70 percent of its business with clients from outside the United States. After careful consideration and some market research, Millipore developed a six-language Web site to communicate with its clients. Of the six languages Millipore chose—French, German, Italian, Japanese, Portuguese, and Spanish—Japanese proved to be the most technically challenging. Millipore had to acquire a double-byte-enabled operating system in order to mount the Japanese language pages on its server. Millipore declined the option to create graphics files

Figure 4.5 Millipore Corporation's Japanese Web page at www.millipore.com can be viewed only with a double-byte-enabled system and Japanese fonts.

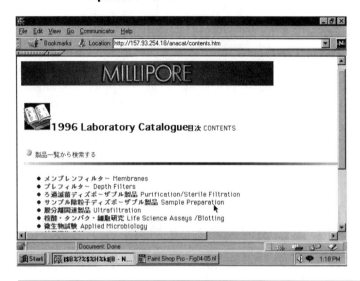

of the Japanese-language pages, which would have eliminated the need for any unique operating systems.

But this latter option to create graphics files for its Japanese pages would have defeated Millipore's purpose. "The site is a dynamic catalog of Millipore products," according to Philip Onigman, the company's marketing director. "In choosing to create the various language pages in HTML [HyperText Markup Language], Millipore is able to maintain the dynamic flow and keep the Web site as a true interactive medium." Since the localized site went online in April 1997, it has received positive feedback from its global clientele and will be adding eight more languages.

The Millipore project also reveals an unfortunate but still evolving dilemma. Outside the United States, Internet access is still limited and slow. It can be frustrating to surf the Web when the waves are coming in at only 14.4 kbps, a snail's pace for those in the United States accustomed to the basic 33.6 kbps. Millipore thus keeps its graphical element to a minimum to reduce viewers' download time. Access is improving, but in the meantime Millipore offers clients a "Wireless Web" CD-ROM. The CD-ROM collapses the corporation's entire Web site onto a fast, removable medium with complete HTML interface capabilities. It furthers Millipore's aim to provide an efficient interactive environment for its clients.

Believe it or not, in many cases the choice of fonts is highly critical to the legibility of localized languages on multilingual Web sites. The esoteric font sets of each language are not generally compatible with other font sets. Likewise, localized applications are not compatible with each other.

Although the localized software and systems market is small and about six months to a year behind English versions in development, it is rapidly catching up and will ultimately eliminate compatibility issues. In the meantime, keep in mind that simple functions, such as wrapping text, can take longer in localized text because of the absence of upgraded software. Also, technology support is not widely available. Once again, it is a matter of market demand and supply. The emergence of true globalizing efforts on the Internet will bring the supply market in line with trends.

Although the challenges of localization may seem overwhelming, knowledge of the critical issues can prepare you for anything. And, as companies like Millipore and others have already discovered, knowledge of the target audience and flexibility will help you develop appropriate solutions for your market. For the rest, you can depend on the professionals in the field.

Selecting an Agency

Professional Web localization agencies have the experience needed for localization and are dedicated to this specialized and demanding task. What specific criteria should you look for when selecting a qualified agency to manage your Web site localization investment? The appropriate agency for you should address your needs in three areas: project management, qualified language resources, and technological capabilities.

Project Management

Project management involves more than just coordinating the rudimentary elements of a project and producing a final output. What you should seek is a Client Management Network: an agency who can provide a responsive support network for all your requests and a partner who understands your requirements and knows how you like to work. These attributes are absolutely critical when you consider the dynamic environment of the Web and the demand for current information.

Web sites are constantly being revised. Your responsibility of continually updating the content of your Web site is taxing enough without the added stress of managing your agency. You should be able to rely on a team that is familiar with your technology, your industry, your protocols, and your vocabulary. The pace of change does not afford you the time to search for a new agency every time information on the Web needs to be updated. The long and steep learning curve associated with bringing on a new agency should be avoided. Thus, your initial selection process should be thorough.

Team Management

Ideally, the agency you choose will provide you with one team to coordinate your project. This team might include project managers, project coordinators, assistants, technology support personnel, and language resources. This team will be highly knowledgeable about your multilingual requests. Should one team player be unavailable, others could answer your questions. The importance of maintaining the same language team will be discussed further in the following section on project coordination. This network of support coordinates all details of your Web site localization project, from acquiring the correct HTML file to coordinating your in-country reviewers to delivering the HTML-translated files.

Project Coordination

Scheduling is critical in project coordination, especially when dealing with time-sensitive information that is to be released in all language versions simultaneously. The translation process is multiphased—involving editing, proofreading, and reviewing in addition to the translation itself. In most cases, it is important to have your own in-country affiliates review the translations to ensure the copy is consistent with any other in-country material. Be aware of any political motivations in-country affiliates may have that could influence their judgment of the translated text. Also be alert to cultural environments in which deadlines are viewed differently than in the United States. The human element is a critical component to consider when scheduling your project.

An example of the scheduling issues involved in going global was Cisco Systems' experience interviewing team members for its operations as a leading global provider of internetworking solutions for corporate intranets and the Internet. The team agreed they wanted a fourteen-language introduction to their Web site, which walks users through the steps for navigating the Cisco site (see Figure 4.6).

Cisco's site is a dynamic site from which clients can place product orders—30 percent of Cisco's orders are placed through the Web site. The site allows Cisco's diverse worldwide clientele to access various in-country Cisco servers in fourteen languages from anywhere in the world. Only the first two levels, primarily menu

Figure 4.6 Cisco Connection Online at www.cisco.com helps viewers navigate through fourteen languages, like this page in Finnish.

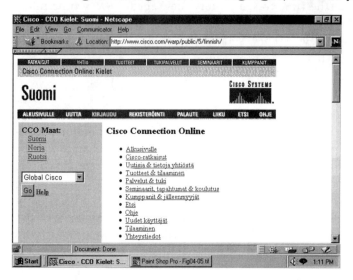

pages, were translated to help orient the viewer to the vast undergrowth of dynamic Web pages. This decision was appropriate since the nature of their industry and clients meant that most viewers are fluent enough in English to read the nontranslated pages that follow the translated instruction pages.

According to Lembit Marder, Cisco's Web globalization manager, the fourteen-language project proved to be a scheduling challenge. Direct Language Communications (DLC) worked extensively with Marder to develop an efficient timeline. However, the Cisco in-country reviewers required more time to review all the translations. Their understanding of the urgency and timeliness of their feedback was different from that of the head office in San Jose, California. Fortunately, DLC came to Cisco with experience in Web site localization and was able to compensate for the delays, thus meeting the deadline for the final HTML-translated files. Marder advises that other key challenges to consider are revision management and simple protocols, such as having the same file-naming conventions between your company and the agency.

Communication

Communication among the members of the team becomes vital during project planning. Although it is obviously important to let everyone involved in the project know the schedule in advance, it is doubly important to allow input from all concerned during the schedule development. In-country affiliates should always be consulted to assure them that they play an integral role in the process and to ensure that scheduled deadlines are realistic.

Qualified Language Resources

The nucleus of the multilingual communications industry are language specialists. Having appropriate language resources for your project ensures a high-return investment. When you are considering an agency to manage your localization projects, you should understand its procedures for screening and qualifying language resources. Language specialists are educated and trained specifically in translation. Uncle Joe down the street who took high school French is not a language specialist. Any translator who has not had higher education in his or her language of expertise or has been away from his or her native country for a significant period of time is not a qualified language specialist. Language specialists have a singularity of purpose. This ensures that they pay attention to details that might otherwise be overlooked by, for instance, someone in your accounting department who happens to speak Spanish and is translating your annual report.

Qualifying Process

A qualified language specialist is tested and evaluated by the Web localization agency. These evaluations confirm the specialist's claimed expertise in languages, skills, and subject areas. Language specialists are native speakers of their language of expertise, which ensures that translations sound fluid and natural. A specialist's skill sets include the ability to translate different document types such as technical documents or high-end marketing copy as well as such strengths as translating or editing. Subject areas include specific industry knowledge (such as computers, medical instrumentation, advertising, etc.). If your product is networking technology for the financial industry in Japan, your language team should consist of specialists who are proficient in networking vocabulary, who understand financial industry needs, and who are from Japan. Likewise, your language team for your promotions should have marketing and advertising skills, just as your team for product use information should have extensive technical writing experience.

In addition, the agency should be part of the translation industry. An agency's involvement with its language resources is indicative of its stability and consistency in providing you with the appropriate language specialists for all your future projects. While these requirements may seem inconsequential, you can demand, and expect to receive, them from a qualified agency.

Technological Capabilities

Another criterion for selecting a qualified Web localization agency is the quality of its technological capabilities. As mentioned earlier, the technical requirements for multilingual typesetting are extensive. An agency's ability to deliver properly formatted material on time will depend on its in-house technical capabilities. There are a few questions you can ask to ascertain the agency's technical capabilities:

- Does it have double-byte-enabled capabilities?

- Does it have localized operating systems and localized applications?

- Does it have a broad selection of esoteric font sets?

- Most importantly, does the agency have a team structure that can support all these vital components?

- Does the agency have personnel versed in the necessary technology, including technical support and multilingual staff? A computer graphics artist working with a layout application in a language he or she understands can be much more efficient than one who is not familiar with the language. A multilingual staff will also be more sensitive to linguistic details.

If these capabilities do not reside in house, the agency must outsource the services, which usually adds variables like cost and delays to the equation.

These criteria for selecting an agency are only guidelines for your decision-making process. Your own business methods and strategies will dictate the specific requirements for your localization projects. The vital components will fall into place, and you will be able to build a client-management team appropriate for you.

The Process

After you select an agency partner for your localization project, the next step is understanding the entire process. The process can be divided into two main phases: translation management and testing.

Translation Management

This multiple-step process is designed to provide the most efficiently and accurately translated material for your project. It is a procedure that has proved successful for many agencies experienced in Web site localization.

HTML Extraction

The first step of the translation management process involves the HTML-coded text. HTML is the set of codes or tags that distinguish text from commands in the programming language of the Web page. HTML assigns various attributes to the text, such as font information, line breaks, accent marks, and the like. HTML also defines the hyperlinks that direct viewers to remote or local Web pages. These codes can be difficult to maneuver for those not familiar with the codes.

For example, the following is the original HTML document pulled from Broderbund Banner Blue's Family Tree Maker site:

```
<P>
<IMG SRC="wftdot.jpg" ALT="*" ALIGN="TOP"><FONT SIZE=4> <A
HREF="#goals">The Goals of the World Family Tree Project</A></FONT>
<P>
<IMG SRC="wftdot.jpg" ALT="*" ALIGN="TOP"><FONT SIZE=4> <A
HREF="#submit">How to Contribute to the World Family
Tree</A></FONT>
<P>
```

Language specialists may not be familiar with HTML code because they are primarily concerned with the text. To ensure the integrity of the HTML codes and to facilitate the translation process, the text must be separated or extracted from the HTML. However, the HTML codes must somehow remain intact and linked to the text to which they apply. In effect, the HTML codes must be made invisible. The ideal procedure extracts the text and codes each line with a number that represents each set of HTML codes related to that line.

This is the same Broderbund document with the text extracted and tagged:

```
[5][The Goals of the World Family Tree Project]
[6][How to Contribute to the World Family Tree]
```

Translators would touch only the text between the brackets.

With only the pure text visible and the HTML codes properly linked, the document is manageable, and the HTML is secure from accidental interference.

Glossary Development

The next step will be to determine the words and phrases specific to your industry, product, or company that are used frequently throughout your material. This will become your glossary. Identifying these words in advance and developing a corresponding list of translated terminology will help you maintain consistency. Problematic terms and phrases can be pinpointed, translated, and preapproved prior to the localization process, saving translation time during localization. You should also decide which trademark names and acronyms should remain untranslated. Once the glossary is compiled, you can transfer it to your offline material and leverage terminology from publication to publication, thereby maintaining consistency from one project to the next.

Glossaries also serve as references during the proofreading and review stages. The glossary is ideal for large multilingual projects that may have many language teams because it gives all teams a common frame of reference. Thus, you can maintain the integrity of your communications across all languages.

The Translation Process

The third step in translation management is developing language teams. A language team consists of a translator, an editor, and a proofreader. The members of the language team should always be native speakers of the target language with knowledge and experience in your specific industry or product. The translator localizes the text to the target language and target audience. After the translator has finished, the editor compares the translation with the original source-language text to ensure accuracy, completeness, and consistency. The proofreader reviews the translation, without the source text, checking for integrity, grammar, punctuation, and spelling and, most importantly, ensuring that the translation reads as if it were originally written in the target language. Each team member refers to the glossary to ensure consistency of terminology.

This process leverages the skill sets of the three language specialists and provides for multiphase quality control. The translation/editing/proofreading process occurs in the extracted text. Knowing that so many hands will touch the text, it is easy to understand why the HTML-extraction process is so critical.

In-Country Review

Once a translation proof is ready, it proceeds to in-country affiliates for review. Your in-country affiliates are well situated to understand your market in that country and what wording is most appropriate to and consistent with your existing in-country material. Free of the burden of the translation process, they have more time to provide valuable insight into nuances of the economy, your consumers, and the political environment. In-country reviewers and language teams will work hand in hand to manage your global image.

Text Reinsertion

After all rounds of proofreadingare completed, the final translated text will be reinserted into the HTML codes. The numbering assigned to the text lines during the extraction process will serve as a guide. During reinsertion, accent marks will be assigned to HTML codes. This procedure ensures that accent marks will be viewed properly on all platforms. The HTML codes will reconcile any font-compatibility issues in Roman-based character sets. Keep in mind that double-byte languages will still require that viewers have localized operating systems. With the HTML codes in place, the file is ready to be mounted to your Internet server but is not yet ready for the public domain.

Format Review

At this stage, the format of the Web site should be reviewed. The integrity of the translations will be reviewed to ensure that word and line breaks are correct and that accent marks appear correctly. This phase is also a test for functionality. Graphics may need to be replotted to accommodate any text expansion or compression that occurred during translation. Additionally, hyperlinks associated with words might need to be reengineered. For instance, the following phrase from a Web page contained a hyperlink: the red car. The word *car* was originally engineered to link to a page with pictures of other cars. When translated into French, it became "la voiture rouge." The link was transferred to the word *rouge* (red) because the phrase was inverted in the translation and *rouge* took the place of *car*. The link should be reengineered to apply to the subject word *voiture* to reflect the hyperlink on the original page so that viewers can correctly expect to be transported to a page of cars and not red things.

Usability Testing

The next step in the translation management process is usability testing. The main focus is on hyperlinks, both remote and local. Remote links connect viewers to Web sites outside of your corporate domain. For instance, you might have a page listing some of your clients. Clicking on one will transport viewers to that client's Web site. Local links will take viewers from one page to another inside your domain. Say, for instance, that you have a list of products. If these products are linked internally, then clicking on one will take viewers to product description and ordering information.

In a multilingual Web site, you should consider whether you want to transport your viewer to another language page. If a viewer is on a Japanese page, will you want to have all linked pages be in Japanese? If, as in the Cisco Systems Web site (see Figure 4.6), translated pages are meant only for orientation purposes, linked pages can remain in English. What makes sense for the link and for your strategy is your decision.

An example of a unique Web site localization strategy is that undertaken by Aldon Computing, a developer of computing tools for programmers. Aldon developed a multilingual Web site—in French, German, Portuguese, and Spanish—to communicate with its global customers in Europe and South America. "This clientele represents 40 percent of all software orders downloaded from our Web site,"

Figure 4.7 Aldon Computing at www.aldon.com chose to develop language pages in parallel with the English page but not as mirror copies.

according to Matt Scholl, Aldon's marketing director. He continues, "Our audience consists of information systems directors who are ahead of the curve when it comes to the Internet. Aldon wanted to be able to provide this savvy clientele with a level of customer service they deserve."

However, Aldon's translated pages are not exact counterparts of the English pages. Each localized section—numbering twenty-plus pages per language—is a customized version of the English sections, scaled down and with unique features. Figure 4.7 compares the English and French home pages.

Global Investment

The choices made by the corporations cited in this chapter clearly reflect the power and potential of the Internet. These companies have made strategic decisions appropriate for their needs and their audiences. Coupled with general market trends that are driving demand for localized content—such as telecommunications deregulation, which makes Internet service affordable to more markets; rising computer purchases, which indicate a more savvy market; and improvements in secure online sales, which bring viewers to the Web—these companies' Web investments will reap large rewards for them in the coming years.

Customizing your communication is an involved process. It requires that you invest time to understand who your audience is and to find a Web localization agency qualified to manage language resources, processes, and technology. With these components in place, you will have an effective communication vehicle that will not only further your partnerships with existing clients but also help you reach new markets with new potential. The localization strategy you choose will help to continue a trend that is putting the "World" into the World Wide Web.

LEGAL FACTORS

5

Our economy is currently undergoing a fundamental shift in its foundation. Prior to the 1800s, the world's economy was primarily agricultural in nature. Then in the nineteenth century came the Industrial Age, and the economy shifted to one based on manufacturing. Today, we are once again experiencing a cultural shift and are now entering the Information Age.

The Internet and online services have created new ways of using and distributing information. They have also placed a host of new entities, including Internet access providers and Internet service providers and every corporation with an interoffice network, into the role of disseminating vast amounts of third-party content.

Changes in technology, consumer behavior, and commerce are occurring at an unprecedented rate. We have new forms of communication such as email, group online conferencing, and electronic bulletin board posting areas. We now have electronic commerce, banking, and online shopping. The World Wide Web has revolutionized information services by enabling consumers to find information on every conceivable topic posted by hundreds of thousands of diverse parties. Additionally, consumers can communicate globally via email over the Internet by the touch of a button.

These new media markets may offer marketing gold mines for the business community. However, current legal land mines threaten to deprive businesses and consumers of their full potential. Since the development of technology has outpaced the law, many issues have not been legally clarified. In this chapter, we will attempt to sensitize you to various legal issues that can arise in connection with business use of the Internet.

Copyright Law in Cyberspace

Of all of the areas of the law that must be reexamined in light of the rise of cyberspace, copyright poses the greatest challenge because it is a strict liability statute. Thus, providers of Internet services, commercial online services, and corporate network services—all known as service providers—have become concerned over their potential liability for copyright infringement because they have transmitted communications initiated by others. Content owners, on the other hand, are worried that the value of their content may be diluted by powerful communications technologies that permit the instant and global distribution of their works.

By way of background, a copyright can exist in any original work of authorship that is fixed in a tangible form. Under copyright laws, a copyright owner possesses several different exclusive rights with respect to this copyrighted work. These rights encompass the exclusive right to control the reproduction of the work and the exclusive right to control the preparation of derivative works from the original work, such as screenplays from a book, new versions of software, an audio reading of a book, and many other types of derivative works. The copyright owner's rights also include the exclusive right to control the distribution of copies of the work, the right to publicly perform the work, and the right to publicly display the work.

The Look and Feel

With the advent of the Internet, there are many issues that arise under the copyright laws. For example, one issue is who will be the owner of the copyrights for the look and feel of an Internet or Web site? Typically, the creator of a Web site is known as a Webmaster. One issue that arises is whether the Webmaster as opposed to the owner or sponsor of the Web site owns the copyright to the look and feel of the Web site. The look and feel consists of the graphics, the layout, any audiovisual works, and the overall flow of the Web site.

Under U.S. law, as well as many other countries', if the owner or sponsor of the Web site does not have a written agreement with the Webmaster who creates the Web site, the copyright laws will deem that the creator or author, in other words, the Webmaster, will own the copyright to the look and feel of the Web site. This is an unacceptable result for many owners or sponsors of Web sites who compensate Webmasters to create these Web sites for them. It is therefore incumbent upon the owner or sponsor of a Web site to obtain a written agreement with the Webmaster wherein the Webmaster assigns all of the copyrights to the owner or sponsor of the Web site in exchange for the compensation.

Content

Another issue that arises with respect to Web sites is who is the owner of the copyright for the material or content included on the site? The owner or sponsor of the Web site must ensure that it either owns all of the copyrights to all of the works that are posted on the Web site or that it has an appropriate license to use all of the works on the Web site in their designated manner.

In the mad scramble to post content on the Internet, many companies are searching through their archives for additional content to include on their Web sites. However, these companies may have potential liability in their use of these materials. For example, many newspapers have old articles or stories in their archives. The original license granted from the author of those works may only apply to distribution of the work in newspaper or paper format or may be silent regarding the medium for publication of the work. The author of the work may not have contemplated distribution in new media, such as the Internet.

Many disputes have arisen between authors and sponsors of Web sites relating to whether or not the original license allows the Web site sponsor to use the work in this new medium. In a decision in August of 1997, the U.S. District Court for the Southern District of New York handed publishers a victory on a related issue. The court ruled that under Section 201(c) of the Copyright Act the right to revise a contribution included in a collective work permits electronic publication in databases and CD-ROMs of works that were originally in print publications without the need for the consent of or additional payments to the author for these electronic versions. The decision is limited to CD-ROM and Nexis database technology, but it is not difficult to analogize it to distribution of a collective work via the Internet.

It remains advisable for the owner or sponsor of a Web site, however, to avoid disputes and to try to obtain the necessary license rights from an author before publishing a copyrighted work on a Web site. The license could explicitly state that the sponsor of the Web site has the right to use the material in an electronic media such as the Internet. In Scotland, for example, a Web site owner must have a grant from an author of the cable programming rights. In order to be safe, a license should grant the Web site owner the right to use, distribute, reproduce, display, and perform the copyrighted works in connection with the Internet medium.

Moreover, Web site sponsors should secure rights for the future use of the licensed material in any electronic or other future media in order to cover new technologies that may arise in the future. A very broad all-encompassing grant could include the right to reuse, resell, syndicate, or create derivative works from the original work and may also encompass all media and platforms on which the content will be distributed.

Third-Party Content

Once the Web site owners ensure that they have all rights to the Web site and the content they want to display on the Web site, what happens when Web site sponsors find that unauthorized copyrighted material they did not place on the site is uploaded onto the site by a third party? Is the Web site owner liable for copyright infringement for material that is uploaded onto the site by someone else? The answer is yes: Under the current U.S. law, the Web site owner is held liable for copyright infringement that occurs when unauthorized copyrighted material is uploaded onto its site or its bulletin board by a third party.

In a 1993 case involving Playboy Enterprises, a subscriber to the defendant's Internet bulletin board service uploaded digital copies of photographs for which Playboy owned the copyrights onto the service. The defendant was held directly liable for unauthorized distribution and display of Playboy's copyrighted photos even though he had no knowledge that his subscriber had uploaded the photos onto the bulletin board. The court held that an innocent infringer is still liable under the current copyright laws.

Liability of ISPs

Another issue arises when an Internet access or service provider is merely providing the physical facilities through which communications occur on the Internet. Can the Internet access provider also be held liable for the infringing acts of its subscribers?

Under the current U.S. law, in the majority of jurisdictions, Internet access or service providers can be held liable for copyright infringement committed by their subscribers. Because it is a strict liability law, the copyright law does not require any knowledge or intentional infringement.

A 1995 California case, however, reflects the position of a minority of jurisdictions. The court considered whether the operator of a bulletin board service and Netcom, the large Internet access provider, should be held liable for copyright infringement committed by a subscriber to the bulletin board service. The court found that Netcom was not liable for *direct infringement* because it did not maintain an archive of files for users and was therefore merely a conduit for communications. However, Netcom had received a letter from the copyright owner complaining of the infringement, and this raised the question of whether Netcom knew of the subscriber's direct infringement, therefore creating the issue of Netcom's potential contributory infringement. Therefore, even from the point of view of the minority of jurisdictions, an Internet access or service provider may be held liable for contributory copyright infringement where it has knowledge of the infringement.

Legislation was introduced in Congress in July 1997 that would exempt online service providers from direct or vicarious copyright infringement liability based solely on the transmission of infringing materials by third parties in certain situations. The proposed exemption would not apply, however, if the service provider has notice of the infringing material. However, the legislation is currently stalled because of disagreements between content providers and service providers over the measures.

Hyperlinks

An additional issue that has arisen is whether a party that provides a link to a Web site containing infringing material can be held liable for the copyright infringement on the linked site. In a 1996 United Kingdom case, the owner of the site linked to the second infringing site was held liable for the infringement on the second site.

A second hyperlinking case, this in the United States, has been cast under an unfair competition theory. In April 1997, Ticketmaster Corp. sued Microsoft over Microsoft's use of unauthorized hyperlinks that connect Web users directly from Microsoft's Seattle Sidewalks Web site to the ticket sales portions of Ticketmaster's Web site, bypassing the Ticketmaster home page and its associated advertising. Ticketmaster's complaint alleges unfair and deceptive trade practices and the dilution of its trademark.

In its answer, Microsoft responded by arguing that any business, such as Ticketmaster, that participates in the Internet and the World Wide Web invites other participants to use the business's Internet addresses and URLs to contact it. Microsoft made a counterclaim for a declaratory judgment that it lawfully used hypertext links. Microsoft argues that if businesses, such as Ticketmaster, can prevent hyperlinks, the free workings of the Internet will be chilled. The case is still pending.

Framing

In addition to the use of hyperlinks, it is also possible to set up a Web site on the Internet so that the viewer will click on a hyperlink and a second Web site displayed within a frame will pop up on the first Web site. This framing technique can be used in ways that the courts could construe as copyright or trademark infringement or unfair competition.

One recent example of the framing issue involved the TotalNews Web site. This site used framing technology in such a way that the content of various newspaper sites (along with their logos) was displayed within a frame on the TotalNews site. The advertisements seen on the bottom of the screen, however, were those of the TotalNews site. In February 1997, the Washington Post and several other newspapers filed suit against TotalNews claiming misappropriation, trademark dilution and infringement, false advertising, unfair trade practices, copyright infringement, and tortious interference with their advertising contracts. The case settled in June with an agreement in which TotalNews would be allowed to continue to link to the newspapers' sites but may not do so in such a way that the content of the newspapers' sites appears in a frame within the TotalNews site display.

Caching

Another issue under copyright law has arisen in the area of caching. Caching is the process of storing data in a storage medium. On the Internet, caching occurs at multiple levels. First, many people who browse the Internet cache locally by storing recently visited Web pages in their computer's memory. For example, a person running Netscape Navigator who selects the Back button will, in many cases, retrieve a page from the computer's RAM (random access memory) instead of a fresh copy downloaded from the actual Web site. Caching also occurs at the server level and is known as proxy caching. Online services such as CompuServe and America Online, for example, store the most frequently requested Web pages on their own computers. Then, when a user requests a page that has been cached, the online service delivers a copy from its own computers' memory not from the Web site in question. Caching is helpful because it speeds user access to Web pages and reduces the demand on the limited infrastructure of the Internet.

Technically, caching can be considered to be copyright infringement. Caching implicates a number of the exclusive rights of copyright holders, including the reproduction right, because it makes an extra copy in RAM or possibly on a hard drive. And, in the case of proxy caching, it implicates the distribution right, the public display right, and possibly the public performance right. However, caching may be conduct considered to be a fair use, thereby providing a defense to a copyright infringement action. Under the Copyright Act, the use of a copyrighted work can be considered fair if it is used for the purposes of criticism, comment, news reporting, teaching, or research. The argument in favor of a finding of fair use would be that the caching process makes the Internet operate more efficiently, and it's also a noncommercial use of the work. And some have argued that caching is permitted because Web site owners have granted an *implied license* to make a copy of their site by making their content available over the Internet. In other words, it can be argued that the copyright owner who posts a copyrighted work without any express prohibitions on its use or technological blocks to prevent that use has granted viewers an implied license to use the posted copyrighted material. However, one flaw in this theory is that there is no other area under existing copyright law where a copyright holder's failure to use technology to reduce infringement creates an implied license to infringe. Indeed, placing the burden on copyright holders is inconsistent with the general legislative trend toward increasing protections for copyright holders.

The World Intellectual Property Organization

Because of the issues discussed in the previous sections as well as other issues arising from the new technology and because of the failure of the current copyright laws to address the new technology, the World Intellectual Property Organization (WIPO) met in December 1996 in Geneva to propose amendments to the Berne Convention on copyright laws. The Berne Convention is an international treaty, to which the United States, as well as most of the other industrialized nations in the world, is a signatory. Under this convention authors are entitled to enjoy the same protection for their works in other foreign member countries as those countries accord their own authors. At the end of a contentious three-week conference, the delegates ratified two treaties that supplement the Berne Convention. The first treaty, the WIPO Copyright Treaty, amends the Berne Convention and addresses protections for literary and artistic works, which the treaty defines as including computer software. The second treaty, the WIPO Performances and Phonograms Treaty, is a new international agreement addressing protections for sound recordings. These treaties represent important steps toward global uniformity of copyright laws because previously there were no global agreements concerning protection for computer software or recordings. However, the WIPO delegates did not specifically address the question of liability for copyright infringements on the Internet. They did, however, make significant decisions concerning the extension of the exclusive rights of copyright owners that directly affect liability.

The WIPO Copyright Treaty specifically defines a protected literary and artistic work to include computer software. The delegates proposed to extend the reproduction right to include direct and indirect reproductions of literary and artistic works whether permanent or temporary, in any manner or form. In other words, whenever an Internet computer server makes an automatic temporary copy through caching, the user would be at risk of infringing copyrights, unless distribution of the work was authorized by the copyright owner. In light of the concerns raised over this proposed extension, the delegates declined to define the reproduction right in a way that would give copyright holders the exclusive right to authorize these automatic technological processes. The delegates also narrowed the reproduction right, which was proposed in the Performances and Phonograms Treaty to exclude coverage of temporary copies. The result was that there was no change in the Berne Convention's existing reproduction right. The WIPO Conference did create a new reproduction right for performers and producers of phonograms that tracks the language of the Berne Convention.

Additionally, Article 8 of the WIPO Copyright Treaty provides that owners of literary and artistic works shall have the exclusive right to authorize "any communication to the public of their works, including the making available to the public of their works, by wire or wireless means, in such a way that members of the public may access these works from a place and at a time individually chosen by them." The Performance and Phonograms Treaty contains similar language. These provisions extend exclusive rights over communicating content or making content available to the public to cover new ways of disseminating content in the digital environment, including interactive and on-demand access. An example would be posting infringing material to a Web site. Therefore, the treaties are consistent with the developing U.S. case law.

The language of the treaties is somewhat unclear, however, in that they employ the terms *communication to the public* or *making available to the public* and do not seem to apply to the mere provision of server space, communication connections, or facilities for transmission. The delegates appear to have been focused on the infringer who posts or sends the infringing content and not on the service providers who carry or transmit the communications. However, because the language is unclear and has yet to be tested, uncertainties over its scope remain. Bills have been introduced in Congress seeking to implement the WIPO treaties' provisions.

The challenge for the Internet for the near future is that until new technologies such as encryption and other copyright management technologies are available and are widely deployed, the courts and the policymakers must balance the interests of content owners in deterring and recovering for copyright infringements in cyberspace with the interest of the public in protecting the ability of service providers to carry an enormous volume of third-party communications quickly and inexpensively.

Trademark Law in Cyberspace

The Internet represents one of the greatest technological achievements of the twentieth century. It has helped to bring together people from the four corners of the Earth, opened doors that would have taken three times longer to open before it was established, and turned the business community into a truly global marketplace.

Trademark owners throughout the world, however, are struggling with the emerging issues presented by electronic communication and electronic advertising that is accessible throughout the world, specifically as these issues affect protection for trademarks and domain names. Since trademark protection is territorial in nature and the Internet is global in nature, owners of trademarks are finding it increasingly difficult to protect those rights while attempting to take advantage of the new technology.

By way of providing technological background, every computer connected to the Internet is assigned a numeric address that other computers on the Internet use to communicate with it. Because these numeric addresses are difficult for people to remember, Internet authorities assign them alphanumeric addresses or domain names. Examples of domain names include mcdonalds.com, whitehouse.gov, and the like. From the standpoint of consumers of goods and services and users of the Internet, an Internet domain name identifies the company, institution, or organization to which the Internet site is attached. Because people increasingly use domain names to locate Web advertising sites in the worldwide marketplace, companies doing business online want domain names that are easy to remember and that relate to their products, services, trade names, and trademarks. Owners of very famous trademarks, such as Coca-Cola, will want to register their trademarks as domain names. Many consumers will first choose the principal trademark of a company when attempting to locate the company's Web site. Depending on how domain name registry systems are ultimately designed throughout the world, the Internet therefore represents an opportunity to either destroy or to enhance the existing trademark system.

Domain Names

Under the present system for assigning domain names in the United States, the National Science Foundation (NSF), the Internet Society, and the Internet Assigned Numbers Authority (IANA) established the Internet Network Information Center, known as InterNIC, to provide domain name registry services in the United States. InterNIC contracted with Network Solutions (known as NSI) to register names for domains using certain generic top-level domains or TLDs of .com, .org, .gov, .edu, and .net for entities that are commercial, organizational, governmental, educational, and represent network infrastructure, respectively.

Unrelated to NSI, in many other countries worldwide various independent agencies or individuals assign domain names using certain two-letter country code TLDs such as .ca for Canada, .uk for the United Kingdom, and .fr for France. However, the top-level domains of .com, .org, .net, and .edu have become popular choices for TLDs for users worldwide and have become alternatives to the two-letter country code TLDs. These generic TLDs have become so popular that by the end of 1996 the number of .com domain names exceeded six hundred thousand. The domain names, including the .com suffix, now form the overwhelming majority of the names on the Internet, and the longer a person or company waits to apply to NSI for a .com domain name, the greater the chance that the choice will not be available.

NSI's policy is to assign domain names to people who request them on a first-come, first-served basis for a certain fee. Only one user can register the .com address that matches its name. As you might guess, this policy has caused problems. Two or more companies may have the same name but may be selling goods or services in unrelated industries. For example, I can think of a company known as Apple Records and a company known as Apple Computers. If both of them wanted to register the domain name apple.com, NSI would only grant that domain name to one or the other.

Moreover, certain "cybersquatters" have been known to apply to NSI for domain names that correlate to certain famous trademarks in order to exchange the domain name for a ransom from the trademark owner. Trademark owners who do obtain their desired domain name may find that there are other domain names that are only slightly different from the trademark owner's mark and, therefore, cause confusion among Internet users.

As disputes between owners of domain names and trademarks have arisen, the domain name registries have found themselves under pressure to take sides in the controversies. NSI was forced to formulate a dispute resolution policy. Its position is that its only purpose is to register domain names, not to perform trademark searches or arbitrate trademark rights. NSI contends that it is not equipped or funded sufficiently to perform these searches and that it is not responsible for any trademark infringement that takes place involving the domain names it registers.

The most recent version of NSI's dispute resolution policy was issued in September of 1996. Under that policy, an owner of a U.S. federal or foreign registered trademark may challenge another person's domain name registration by sending notice to the domain name holder and NSI that the domain name is identical to the trademark owner's registered mark and, thus, violates the trademark owner's legal rights. Of course, there have been numerous criticisms of NSI's policy. One criticism is that it does not require the trademark owner to allege actual trademark infringement; it only requires that an allegation of a violation of legal rights be made. The trademark laws may allow the two marks to peacefully coexist.

Therefore, technically, the trademark owner would not have to have evidence of a likelihood of confusion but could rely on other theories of violations such as general unfair competitive acts. The cornerstone of proof that must be met in order to find trademark infringement is that there is a likelihood of consumer confusion between two uses of the same or similar mark.

In order to determine whether a likelihood of confusion exists, a number of factors must be considered, including the degree of similarity between the two marks at issue; the degree of similarity between the parties' goods or services; the degree of similarity between the channels of trade for and/or prospective purchasers of the parties' goods or services; the degree of similarity between the advertising media utilized by the parties; the second user's intent in adopting the mark; and any evidence of actual confusion by consumers. Where two parties use the same mark but for completely different goods or services, there may be no likelihood of consumer confusion and, thus, no trademark infringement (e.g., "Apple Records" and "Apple Computers"). Another criticism of the NSI dispute policy is that the only challenges that can be lodged are for domain names that are identical to registered marks. Domain names that are merely similar to registered marks are not contestable under the NSI policy.

Once a trademark owner has lodged a protest, the domain name holder must then come forward with a trademark registration of its own within thirty days or NSI will place its domain name on hold. This registration of the domain name holder must predate the complaint lodged by the trademark owner. NSI does not get involved in arbitrating who is entitled to rights to the domain name; it only places a disputed domain name on hold. The disputed domain name will remain on hold until NSI is presented with a court order declaring which party can use the name. Therefore, the parties to the dispute are required to initiate a legal action in order to determine who is entitled to use the domain name.

Resolving Domain Name Disputes

Most domain name registries around the world do not have their own dispute resolution policies but typically follow a policy issued by the IANA. Under the IANA policy, the registration authority will have no role in a dispute between domain name registrants other than to provide contact information to the parties to allow them to fight among themselves. The IANA policy also provides that a domain name has no trademark status. However, under the IANA policy, a domain name applicant has a duty to ensure that he or she is not violating another's trademark rights.

Some countries' registries do maintain their own dispute resolution policies. For example, under the Irish and Bulgarian registries' policies, an applicant for a domain name must select a domain name that corresponds with the applicant's name, an abbreviation for the applicant's name, or the applicant's trademark. If the applicant's requested domain name is already in use, the applicant must select another name. Where the proposed name is, in the opinion of the Irish or Bulgarian authorities, likely to lead to confusion with another's trademark or trade name, the registry requires the applicant to select another name.

One of the most publicized early disputes was between the McDonald's Corporation and one of the first cybersquatters in 1996. This individual registered a number of famous trademarks as Internet domain names, including the name mcdonalds.com. Eventually, McDonald's agreed to donate a certain amount of money to fund a local school's purchase of computer equipment in exchange for the individual's agreement to transfer the rights to the domain name to McDonald's.

In another famous 1996 case, Roadrunner Computer Systems (RCS) sued NSI to have NSI enjoined from placing its domain name roadrunner.com on hold because of a trademark challenge from Warner Brothers, which owned the rights to the Roadrunner cartoon character. Warner Brothers obtained a federal trademark registration for Roadrunner in 1995 and challenged RCS's use of the domain name roadrunner.com. RCS had been offering computer services on the Internet under this domain name since 1994. To prevent NSI from putting its domain name on hold, RCS obtained a trademark registration for Roadrunner from the country of Tunisia. At the time of this action, NSI's policy was unclear whether a domain name registrant had to have a U.S. federal registration when responding to a challenge to its use of a domain name or whether a registration from any country was sufficient. RCS took advantage of this loophole. The country of Tunisia does not conduct an examination, and, therefore, an applicant can receive a registration quite quickly. Although RCS used its Tunisian registration to successfully respond to Warner Brothers' challenge, the case was subsequently dismissed after a settlement agreement between the parties was reached.

In another 1996 case, Hasbro, the toy manufacturer, claimed that an Internet site that had the domain name of candyland.com and was a sexually explicit site, diluted the value of Hasbro's trademark "CANDYLAND" for a children's game by tarnishing the goodwill and reputation it had established in connection with that game. Hasbro also alleged that children searching the Internet might mistakenly come across the candyland.com site and think it was related to the Hasbro game. The court agreed with Hasbro under its trademark dilution theory and required the Internet site operator to adopt a different name.

Outside of the United States, there have been several reported decisions in domain name disputes. For example, in Germany, one court held that the private registration of the domain name heidelberg.de infringed on the City of Heidelberg's rights to its own name. In another case, the United Kingdom ordered a cybersquatter to hand over the domain name harrods.com to the famous Harrod's London department store. The court held that registering this domain name constituted infringement of Harrod's registered trademark.

Needless to say, because of the large number of disputes that have arisen and the inconsistent rules among domain name registries, many commentators feel that there should be a uniform worldwide approach to resolving domain name disputes. Therefore, many organizations are attempting to promulgate new models for dispute resolution between trademark owners and domain name holders.

For example, the International Ad Hoc Committee (IAHC) was recently formed under the auspices of the IANA to discuss some alternatives. The IAHC announced a proposal in February 1997 that calls for the creation of new categories of generic TLDs, which would segregate the .com category into the different types of goods or services provided for different industries. For example, some of the new TLDs proposed are .firm, .store, and .arts. Additionally, the IAHC recommends the formation of a trademark domain name space wherein trademark owners will register their trademarks as domain names. The IAHC also recommends the creation of new domain name registrars and the harmonization of policies worldwide. The IAHC further recommends that all applications for domain names be published for public review and that disputes between domain name holders and trademark owners be heard by an international arbitration panel of intellectual property experts. It recommends that the World Intellectual Property Organization (WIPO) administer these arbitration panels. The arbitrations would be conducted online whenever possible.

One criticism of this proposal is that the addition of a greater number of generic TLDs could result in a significantly increased policing burden for trademark owners, who would have to search through the many more generic TLDs for potential infringers. However, one advantage of this proposal may be the online challenge mechanism, which could result in the resolution of disputes much more quickly and in a less costly manner than litigation in court.

Of course, it remains unclear whether any of the new proposals will be implemented and, if they are, when the implementation will take place. Something will have to be done in the near future, however, as NSI's contract for serving as domain name registrar expires in 1998, and the NSF has indicated that it will not be renewed.

Corporate Internet Access and Security Policies

Permitting employees to use the Internet via corporate computer networks may expose companies to liability for infringing various intellectual property rights, disseminating unlawful information, defamation, and other unlawful practices. For example, employees who download and display pornography in the workplace may expose their employer to liability for sexual harassment by creating a "hostile work environment."

Other potential liability scenarios could be the following: (1) an employee loses his temper in an online debate and posts a message from his company-provided account to a bulletin board service falsely claiming that the person he is upset with has a prison record; or (2) an employee uses her work account to download copyrighted software to a company-owned computer. Plaintiffs' lawyers would not hesitate to include the employer in the lawsuit for copyright infringement.

The risk for employers is real. Fully half of all Internet users gain access to the Internet with accounts supplied by their employers. Already, some companies have received undesired publicity from the online antics of their employees. A recent Nielsen survey revealed that numerous employees use their work accounts to make visits to online editions of sexually explicit magazines. A large company recently fired more than a dozen employees who had made thousands of visits to sexually explicit Web sites using their company accounts.

Under general *respondent superior* legal principles, an employer may be held liable for the acts committed by an employee when the employer knows or has reason to know that it has the ability to control the conduct of the employee and understands or should understand the necessity for exercising such control. The few courts that have considered the issue have concluded that an employer has a right to monitor its employees' use of email and Internet accounts.

Although it is clear that a company cannot control each and every risk associated with its connection to the Internet, a company providing Internet access to its employees should follow certain procedures when establishing access and should institute a policy for the proper employee use of the Internet. Adopting and enforcing an Internet use policy should reduce legal risks and security risks to employers in two general ways: (1) if employees know the risks, they will be less likely to engage in conduct that exposes their employer to liability, and (2) if an employee engages in conduct that violates the policy, the employer will be in a better position to argue that it should not be held responsible for the employee's conduct.

Issues That a Corporate Internet Policy Should Address

Your corporation's Internet use policy and related procedures should be designed as an extension of your general corporate policies and should adhere to corporate goals and procedures. However, your policy should be flexible. Policies should be reviewed periodically by users and system administrators and updated so they comply with legal requirements and user needs.

Limited Access

At a minimum, an Internet policy should require that each user of the internal network enter an appropriate user identification or login code and password in order to obtain access to the internal network.

Moreover, to prevent outside users from entering into the internal network, system administrators should technically limit inbound access to the internal network, configure the network so that certain machines and services may only be accessed by key personnel, maintain and review user activity logs to detect unauthorized activity, keep computers containing the most sensitive information separate from the network and the Internet, and alert users not to post or transfer sensitive or confidential information online. (For example, large financial transactions should not be performed on the Internet until security and encryption is improved.)

Viruses

Another security threat is posed by computer viruses that may enter your corporate computer system through a connection to the Internet. Typically, viruses are disruptive or data-erasing programs inserted into unauthorized entrances or "trap doors" in a computer system. The viruses can then replicate themselves and invade other systems. Viruses can infect programs by altering them and can also cause widespread damage to computer systems. Viruses have also found their way into commercial application software. To guard against viruses on computer networks, system administrators should institute mandatory virus checks of any software downloaded from the Internet as well as any disks containing software to be used on the internal network.

Email

Before installing and using Internet email service, businesses should adopt a clear and concise email policy that should cover several key issues.

First, employee use of the Internet to transmit email or to browse the Web should be restricted to business uses only to limit potential liability for unlawful communications and to ensure that email is used productively. Companies should provide notice that viewing, downloading, copying, sending, and processing information is limited to business uses only. Employees should be prohibited from accessing sexually explicit material. Further, employees should be aware that misuse of email or the Internet can be the basis for discipline or dismissal.

Second, companies should develop policies governing third-party access to employee email and information concerning the employee's access to the Internet. The right of companies to view email messages sent and received by employees may raise legal issues involving the employee's privacy rights.

If corporate management chooses to monitor or intercept email messages, the Internet use policy should do the following:

- Provide notice to employees that email messages will be reviewed by appropriate personnel and disclosed to third parties as deemed necessary

- Include a statement that all employees waive any right to privacy in email messages and consent to such monitoring and disclosure

- Explain that employees should treat email messages like shared paper files, with an expectation that anything in them will be available for review by authorized representatives of the corporation

- Reserve the company's right to disclose email messages to law enforcement officials or other third parties without notice to any of the parties to the messages

The Decision to Retain or Delete Email

The casual, often careless way many people create email messages and their surprisingly frequent and prolonged preservation of them make such messages a fertile ground for the discovery of evidence if your company is ever involved in litigation.

Among a company's email data are probably many pages of comments that would never appear in more traditional forms of written communication. Many people treat email and voice mail messages as transitory and ephemeral, not realizing that they often create a permanent record. Users treat email as casually as whispering a confidence to a friend or at least as carelessly as an unplanned oral communication. People say things in an email communication that they would never commit to in a letter or memorandum.

Electronic messages, however, differ from oral communications in several ways. Electronic message systems permit recipients to easily forward messages to others on the system or to archive them. Recipients can easily print out email messages or have voice mail messages transcribed or copied onto tapes, thus creating discoverable documents of which the sender is often unaware. In a number of recent lawsuits, audio tapes of threatening or harassing voice mail messages have been introduced into evidence, and archives of email messages have been fertile sources for discovering relevant evidence.

In the case of email, even if the sender and all recipients have deleted the message, it may still exist in some electronic storage medium. The system may have copied it to a backup storage medium before it was deleted. Until another file actually overwrites the deleted file, the original file still exists in the backup storage medium and is easily retrieved. And even programs that erase data from hard disks don't always work completely. One solution to this problem is a software tool called an electronic shredder, which destroys the data in a deleted file even before it is overwritten, so it is not recoverable.

It is advisable to educate employees about the permanence of emails. And one way to reduce liability exposure for a corporate employer is to develop and enforce a records retention policy covering the retention, organization, and destruction of email and archival email. An email retention policy should do the following:

- Educate employees that email messages are often permanently recorded, so email should be created and distributed with the same care as letters or memoranda.

- Email retention/deletion policies should provide for deletion in the shortest period of time consistent with business needs. Users should be instructed to delete emails as soon as they are read. Company information services managers should be instructed to delete archives periodically. Emails with permanent value can be preserved in a separate file for a longer period of time. Additionally, email messages that include attorney-client privileged communications should be segregated so as to avoid an unintentional waiver of the privilege.

- Email messages that are retained should be organized with uniform, descriptive titles. This will avoid the cost and burden of reviewing all retained emails for their relevance to a discovery request.

- Once litigation has commenced, the company should consult with an attorney regarding what it may legally and ethically destroy.

- A well-established email retention/deletion policy can provide a line of defense in the course of litigation. Good faith destruction of business records pursuant to routine policies can avoid unfavorable evidentiary inferences. (In contrast, the destruction of business records where no records retention policy is in place can lead to sanctions against the company for destruction of evidence.)

Employee's Unauthorized Statements Concerning the Company's Products or Services

One of the most overlooked areas of potential online liability for an employer is its employees' participation in online discussion groups relating to the company and its products or services. In these online groups, customers can post questions, comments, and complaints about the performance and reliability of a company's products or services. A company's employees may participate in these discussions and perhaps offer a temporary fix for a customer's problem (perhaps one not yet tested or approved by the company) or they may disclose information about the company's new products or services (weeks before the marketing department had planned a new product announcement, for example) or they may discuss problems with the company's products or services. All these statements could expose the company to defective product claims, breach-of-warranty claims, and the like by constituting admissions by the company that there are or have been problems with the company's products or services. With respect to new products, the online statements could also be disclosing the company's confidential trade secrets.

The company's Internet use policy should therefore prohibit employees from making any online statement about the company, its position on any issue, its business, or its products or services unless the statement has been approved by managers who review and approve other corporate communications. And any newsgroup that concerns the company or its business should be monitored and managed by an official online relations manager rather than on an ad hoc basis by unauthorized employees.

Offensive and Obscene Communications

Your corporate Internet use policy should conform with your other policies related to corporate communications since employee communications over the Internet may be interpreted as statements by the company. Users should be aware that information placed on servers connected to the Internet becomes available to all Internet users. Corporate policies should include "netiquette" provisions, which inform employees about proper conduct online. Companies should advise employees to refrain from sending offensive, provocative, abusive, or objectionable messages. And because sexual harassment laws prohibit an employer from letting its employees create a hostile work environment, the company should prohibit employees from accessing or downloading sexually explicit material from the Internet. Even ubiquitous jokes containing sexual innuendo, which many people view as harmless, could create a liability problem for a company when they are forwarded from person to person on the company's network.

Trade Secrets and Unsolicited Ideas

It is essential for the protection of trade secret information that a corporation take all reasonable steps to protect the secrecy of such information. This is important not only with respect to the particular information involved but also with respect to any showing the corporation may need to make in the future regarding its general trade secret protection policy. At a minimum, the corporate Internet use policy should include the following points:

- Confidential electronic communications should be clearly labeled as confidential.

- Sensitive information should only be sent to those with a need to know.

- Unauthorized messages concerning the company, its business, or its competitors should be prohibited.

- The transmission of unencrypted confidential information or trade secrets should be prohibited.

- Sensitive email should be removed from the recipient's monitor rather than left on the screen for any passerby to read.

Corporations may also face liability for using unsolicited ideas submitted by email. For example, many companies operate Web sites on which they provide a variety of information about products and services as well as enabling visitors to access their site and send email to the company. In some cases, people from outside the company may submit ideas for new products and services via email. For companies that do not accept unsolicited ideas, this has raised the concern that if they independently develop products or services that are similar to an idea submitted via email, they may be vulnerable to claims for compensation from the person who submitted the idea.

As a practical matter, the best way to handle unsolicited ideas submitted by email may be similar to the way many companies (which choose not to encourage unsolicited ideas) handle such ideas when submitted by letter. Generally, a company should have a written policy with respect to unsolicited ideas. The policy should provide that employees receiving email from outside the company that contains unsolicited ideas for new products or services should, as soon as they recognize that an email contains such an idea, stop reading it, forward it to an individual responsible for responding to those ideas, and delete the original email.

The person to whom the email was forwarded, an individual segregated from the "idea generation" groups in the company, should be instructed to delete the email after responding to the original sender, saying in the response, among other things, that the email is being deleted from the recipient company's records and that the company does not use unsolicited ideas.

Persons submitting unsolicited ideas should be notified that the company does not accept unsolicited ideas for products or services and should be instructed not to send any email or in any other way communicate ideas for new products and services in the future. It may be wise for the notification to include a clause stating, "By continuing to access this Web site, and by submitting email to us, you agree that you shall have no recourse against our company for any alleged or actual infringement or misappropriation of any proprietary rights in your communication to us."

Online Copyright Infringement

Corporations should ensure that employees do not violate intellectual property laws when sending information over the Internet. A corporate Internet use policy should require that users not copy protected works illegally. If an employee downloads a copy of a hot new software program and installs it on his or her computer or on the company's network, the company could be liable for copyright infringement, especially if it is aware of this type of activity and has taken no steps to prevent it. Also, an employee may find a great utility program on the Internet that is distributed as shareware but forget to pay the license fee after the free trial period has expired. If that program is on a company computer, the company faces exposure for copyright infringement. To avoid this problem, an Internet use policy should prohibit the downloading of any software from the Internet without the company's authorization. This will also help guard against viruses that may be included in software distributed over the Internet.

Elements to Include in a Corporate Internet Use Policy

- Prohibit (or greatly limit) personal use of Internet accounts
- Protect the employer's right to monitor employee's email and his or her use of company Internet accounts
- Prohibit any messages or other communications discussing the employer or its competitors

- Prohibit access to sexually oriented material
- Prohibit the transmission of unencrypted confidential information and trade secrets
- Prohibit employees from downloading software unless it its directly related to their jobs and the company has paid all appropriate license fees
- Have an effective educational program for employees concerning the risks associated with online activities
- Address how long email messages should be maintained or how often deleted

The Internet is creating new challenges on every front, including within the courtroom and across the bargaining table. Although no guarantees exist for making a company's computer network completely bulletproof, becoming aware of the main legal factors and following some of the practical guidelines outlined in this chapter can help to significantly reduce your Internet security and liability risks.

TECHNICAL AND SECURITY ISSUES: GLOBALIZING YOUR WEB SITE

6

According to legend, an MIT student once hooked up the toaster in the shared kitchen on his dormitory floor and patched it into an Internet chat room. The toaster was used as a kind of Boolean fortune-teller, responding positively when it was making toast and negatively when it wasn't in use. By limiting its responses to short, generic-sounding phrases, the toaster—under its pseudonym "Sunbeam"—was able to convince several people that it was in fact an important participant in the discussions. This gave rise to the well-known saying, "On the Internet no one knows if you're a toaster."

This is an alarming proposition if you intend to buy or sell products on a global scale through this new medium. How do customers know they are purchasing products from a real business and not giving their money over to an electronic bandit in a TCP/IP version of three-card monte? How does a business identify that the customer at the browser end is a real person, with real money, and not a criminal with a stolen credit card conducting a virtual holdup? Can you be sure that when you flashed your credit card across multiple interconnected networks that only the intended recipient saw it? This chapter discusses the importance of global security on the Internet and the emerging technologies that can help to ensure which transactions between buyers and sellers are secure, reliable, and discrete.

These issues of identification, privacy, and overall security are compounded when one engages in commerce on the Internet on a global basis. Currently, U.S. export law limits the distribution of many American-made computer security products. This creates a disadvantage for international customers, who may have to sacrifice security to benefit from the efficiencies of Internet commerce. It also creates a disadvantage for international businesses, limiting their ability to compete in the Internet marketplace by restricting their ability to provide secure e-commerce to their customers.

What are these tools? How do they work? Can privacy and security exist on an open network where traffic passes through unknown computers? Any person interested in doing business through the Internet should understand how security on the Internet is achieved and how it is broken. One must come to understand when a secure transaction is occurring and what specific dangers are in place. While the virtual world, like the real world, can never provide 100 percent total security, it is important that all users of the Internet understand the degree of risk to which they are exposing themselves.

This chapter examines security on the Internet from three perspectives: data, individuals, and systems. What makes data secure? How can individuals protect themselves? And how can businesses ensure that their systems are safe?

What Is Security?

Security is more than just protecting data against hackers, crackers, data thieves, and other unsavory characters. Security is about protecting oneself and one's business from a catastrophic loss of data, so as to preserve the internal and external services on which the data is based. If a program crashes—through a virus, outside attack, user error, or equipment failure—and data is lost, there has been a breach of security. Just as businesses in the past were protected against theft, fire, and flood, they must now take additional measures to ensure their virtual security as well.

Data Security

For centuries, data has been protected by cryptography. Cryptography, the science of encoding information for private transmission between multiple parties, has been used by governments, lovers, and others who wish to keep their written affairs secret, even when these writings might be seen by another. Cryptography allows two parties to have a private conversation in plain view by using a secret code or other system that translates information into a seemingly meaningless jumble of letters and back again. Data that is encrypted between multiple parties can only be read by the parties involved and is unintelligible to third parties that may see the information as it is transmitted.

Private Key Cryptography

There are two widely used methods of encrypting data on the Internet. The first is a system known as *private key cryptography*. Private key cryptography works by allowing each party to know the same secret code, or key, for encrypting and decrypting information. This key, like a physical key, can be used to lock and unlock access to information. The most widely used form of private key cryptography is known as the Data Encryption Standard (DES) and is used by financial institutions and others to transmit information. Private key cryptography only works as long as both parties keep the key confidential. Any compromise of the key's security makes the system vulnerable. Private key cryptography has been the basis of most encryption systems throughout history, from the simple secret decoder rings to the infamous enigma machines built by the Germans in World War II.

Public Key Cryptography

A newer form of cryptography is known as *public key cryptography*. In a public key system one key is used to encode information, which can only be unlocked by a second key. The first key is publicly distributed to anyone who wants to send encrypted information. The person receiving the information keeps the second key secret. By exchanging public keys, two parties can communicate. Because the public key can be freely published, these two parties do not have to hide this exchange of keys and are able to set up secure communications in plain view. This provides a distinct advantage over a private key system, in which the single key must be secretly transmitted between communicants.

Public key cryptography results from a mathematical theory that states that certain mathematical operations are more difficult than others. For example, it is very easy for a computer to multiply two large numbers together, but it is much harder to determine the factors for a large number. Consider the following problem: $13 \times 29 = y$. Solving this problem is quite simple, but what about $x \times y = 377$, where x or y is not equal to 1. To solve this problem one must try multiple values for x and y until an answer is reached. This operation takes considerably longer than simple multiplication. When working with computers one must simply increase the size of the numbers to make the problem harder for the computer to solve.

This one-way difficulty is exploited in public key cryptography to create what are in practice one-way mathematical functions, in which it is very easy to encode data but very difficult to decode data unless the factors are known. Essentially, the factors become a private key, known only to the individual who needs to decode the information, and the product of the factors is a public key, used to encode the information and send it to the recipient. Because this public key can only be used to encrypt data, it can be made freely available to any person wanting to send confidential information to a specific person. There is no need to keep a secret between all parties wishing to share information because they can simply each provide their public keys, which will be used to transmit the information back and forth.

Through public key cryptography it is possible for anyone to instantly exchange keys and have a private conversation. Public key cryptography is so powerful that policymakers in the United States have spent several years fighting over how powerful software companies should be allowed to make crypto-systems for export, as it is feared that terrorists, drug dealers, and other criminals will use such systems to hide their dealings and communications.

A Geopolitical Aside

Cryptography has long been the tool of choice for governments to communicate with spies and hide secret documents. As the Internet spreads, security concerns will drive the private sector to adopt crypto-systems to protect company communications and secrets. The new wave of public key cryptography is surprisingly easy for a programmer to implement. There are currently programs on the Internet that provide public encryption and decryption in as little as six lines of code.

Because of the strengths and simplicity of these crypto-systems, the U.S. government has undertaken an enormous effort to limit their spread. The current strategy focuses on limiting the development of commercial encryption software. There are several ways the government is seeking to limit these programs.

Public Key Regulations

The first way the government is using to limit the spread of commercial encryption software is by placing a limit on the size of the key that can be used in software. Public key systems are vulnerable to attack by brute force factoring. The smaller the size of the public key, the easier it is to break. Current U.S. policy allows the unrestricted export of products containing a 40-bit or smaller key. These codes can be broken quickly by a typical Pentium class PC. This level of security is enough to keep out the casual snoop, but anyone who is serious about intercepting and decoding corporate email, credit card numbers, or other privileged communications probably will not be stopped. After several years of lobbying, the software industry has gotten the Bureau of Export Administration's regulations relaxed slightly. It is now possible to export software with much stronger 128-bit—and higher—keys provided the software developer submits and gets approval for a key escrow plan.

Key Escrow: The Solution?

Key escrow is the simple idea that one's private key should not be completely private. In a true private key, the key used to decode information is stored in a protected location, where only the owner of the private key can access it. This provides the data with a maximum level of protection from intrusion by hostile entities because, provided the private key is secured, no other person can decode the information.

But is this a good model for protecting information? Many experts disagree. Modern forms of cryptography are now so powerful that it is possible for a Pentium machine to encode a document so that even a fleet of supercomputers working for one hundred years could not decrypt the information. If information is stored in an encrypted form and then the private decoding key is lost or intentionally destroyed, the information is unrecoverable.

Under a key escrow system the software developer establishes a secure facility to hold copies of private keys for future recovery. This allows an enterprise to recover a private key should the need arise. The U.S. government has mandated key escrow systems for strong encryption products because key escrow provides a mechanism whereby the government can get a copy of someone's private key and then listen in on private communications, just as they would in a telephone wiretap.

The downside to key escrow systems is that the key can be recovered by a party other than the owner of the private key. This would occur at a breaking point in the security system, which will be outside of the control of the owner of the private key. Should a hacker gain access to the secure facility where private keys are stored, then a company's complete database of confidential information could be compromised.

Some countries, particularly members of the European Union, have expressed concerns that the U.S. key escrow system will make their companies vulnerable to spying by the U.S. government on behalf of American companies. While most countries agree that they do not want criminals to use cryptography to hide their dealings, they also want to protect their companies from industrial espionage.

Crypto Overseas

U.S. restrictions on the export of software containing strong cryptography have limited the number of products available in the marketplace. The Internet has created a situation in which for reasons of data privacy high demand exists for these products. The scarcity of strong crypto-software has led many companies to look for ways around the U.S. restrictions by seeking to purchase products produced overseas.

The underlying algorithms for public key cryptography have been published in internationally distributed technical journals for over twenty years. Creating software based on these publications is a trivial matter well within the reach of any capable programmer. This fact opened a market for overseas encryption software from such companies as UK Web (http://stronghold.ukweb.com), makers of a range of Secure Socket Layer (SSL) products, and Elvis + Co., a Russian firm manufacturing strong encryption products for Sun Microsystems computers. Using overseas cryptography allows foreign companies to get access to products that are compatible with and comparable to products now available in the United States. Users of overseas cryptography products, however, may encounter different problems. The original authors of a particular encryption algorithm may have a patent claim to that algorithm. Users of products containing unlicensed patented algorithms may be exposing themselves to legal problems. Furthermore, overseas products, while not subject to U.S. export controls, may be subject to the export controls of the originating country. For example, encryption software created in the United Kingdom cannot be sent to Argentina and other restricted countries, nor used in the manufacture of certain munitions.

Trusted Third Parties

As mentioned, public key cryptography allows any two individuals on the Internet to have a private conversation in plain view by simply exchanging public keys. However, in any conversation it is important to know that you are dealing with an authentic individual and not a "toaster." Because private keys are exchanged through the same insecure network, it is possible that someone could pretend to be someone else and receive confidential communications intended for that person. This problem of identity and the verification of an individual's public key is solved by a trusted third party. A trusted third party is typically a company such as GTE or VeriSign Inc. who provides certification of an individual's key. The trusted third party provides a mechanism whereby anyone seeking a private conversation with another individual can go and verify that the public key they received is that individual's public key.

There are currently no regulations for trusted third parties beyond enforcement of the contract created between the third party, such as VeriSign, and the key holder. From an Internet software standpoint it is possible for anyone to set him- or herself up as a trusted third party and request that users reconfigure their browsers to recognize their status. While this allows corporate intranets to be set up with a central server within the corporation acting as the trusted party, it also allows unscrupulous persons to establish an apparent level of legitimacy in the eyes of unsuspecting consumers. Netscape and Microsoft's Internet Explorer both ship with a number of trusted third parties preinstalled. The preinstalled parties have undergone an application process in order to be included inside these browsers.

Security Technology

The Internet is a very public place. Information traveling between a Web browser and a Web server passes through many other computers, some of which may be intercepting and reading information before it is passed along. Everything one does on the Internet is in some way visible to others, and information that is passed back and forth between the browser and the server cannot be relied upon to be private. Web servers, which offer transactional features, such as ordering products, managing financial information, and other interactivity, require a mechanism for creating privacy. Transactions that are not private are subject to interference from third parties. Hostile individuals may try to intercept transactions and capture important information such as a credit card number or financial statement. Encryption solves this problem by transforming data into a seemingly random jumble of letters before sending it through the Internet and then restoring its original meaning upon receipt. There are several commonly available technologies for protecting your privacy online.

Secure Sockets Layer (SSL)

The *Secure Sockets Layer (SSL)* protocol is a frequently used public key encryption system for transmitting secure information through the Internet. SSL is used today in Web browsers such as Microsoft Internet Explorer and the Netscape Navigator for secure connections to Web sites.

When an SSL communication occurs between the browser and a Web server, the browser will indicate it by showing a solid blue key (Netscape) or a closed padlock (Internet Explorer). Both browsers will also show a message through a dialog box upon entering or exiting a secure Web connection.

SSL is a secure protocol for data transmission between Web browsers and servers; it does not guarantee that the data that has been transmitted is accurate or that the data will not be retransmitted in some insecure fashion on the other end. Currently, Web browsers are licensed for United States-only use with 128-bit keys, while internationally they are limited to 40-bit keys. Forty-bit keys are not thought to be secure because the encryption can be broken using ordinary desktop computers. Microsoft, Netscape, O'Reilly and Associates, and others now offer Web server products for sale in the United States with 128-bit key security. There is only one internationally available 128-bit SSL Web server, Stronghold by UK Web, which is made in the United Kingdom, thereby avoiding U.S. export restrictions.

Secure Electronic Transactions (SET)

A proposed compliment to SSL is the *Secure Electronic Transaction (SET)*. SET allows a merchant, bank, and consumer to communicate in a secure fashion and exchange payment information. The advantage of the SET system is that the merchant can receive payment without collecting private information such as a credit card number. In SET, the bank is sent a message that the consumer would like to make a purchase. If the consumer has credit or funds available for the transaction, the bank sends the merchant an electronic payment. This system works more like an electronic check, where a single merchant is given a specific authorization for a single amount of funds. This is seen to be more secure than collecting credit card numbers, which can be stolen or reused without the knowledge or permission of the consumer.

Cookies

Web *cookies* are a simple means of storing information for a particular Web user. A cookie is a small piece of digital information transmitted by a Web browser every time it makes a connection to a Web server. This distinct piece of information can be used to transparently identify a person on a return visit or to store information, such as a list of items a user wants to purchase in a kind of virtual shopping basket. Cookies are vital to the smooth functioning of Web sites from an application programmer's perspective because they are a reliable way of allocating specific resources on the Web server for an individual.

While SET and SSL are encryption systems for protecting information, cookies are a function of the HTTP protocol used to create statefulness in the otherwise stateless world of an HTTP transaction. They provide a means of tracking a user's preferences and usage of a Web site. Many regard this tracking as a violation of the anonymity of Web usage, while others feel it is necessary to creating a really useful site. For example, a cookie could store your book genre preferences when you visit the John Wiley and Sons, Inc. Web page, and then on your return visit you would automatically be shown a selection from that genre. This is a pretty nice feature for some, but for others it is all a little too Orwellian in that this information may have been gathered without your knowledge or consent.

The emergence of electronic transactions between buyers and sellers has paved the way for the quantification and analysis of these transactions to increase sales and target specific consumers for marketing. While many merchants welcome this increased knowledge of their customers, many consumers are concerned that electronic transactions will mean an increased invasion of their individual privacy.

Just how much of a right one has to control what happens to personal information collected electronically by merchants and others is an increasingly important political issue. In some countries such as Germany there are already privacy laws that prevent the sale or retransmission of such information without the consent of the individual from whom the information was collected. This could have implications for any business seeking to conduct global commerce through the Internet.

One rallying point for privacy advocates has been to attack the use of cookies on the World Wide Web. Most browsers now allow a user to turn off cookies and browse in complete anonymity, though they must give up the advantages of cookies in doing so.

Individual Security

Privacy is the bridge between data security and individual security. The Internet allows individuals access to almost any kind of information, from sports scores to credit reports. While much of this information is given away, some of it is highly confidential, such as credit information, stock portfolios, and one's email. How does an individual identify him- or herself on the Internet and assure that he or she alone has access to this type of information?

Passwords and Secure Identification

Many places on the Internet require the user to select a *password* as a way to identify him- or herself on return visits. Passwords act as a convenient way to store information with a merchant for later use or as a way to limit access to a resource. In its most basic form, a password is simply a word, or often a random combination of numbers and letters, that is used to protect information. Anyone who knows the word can enter the system; all others cannot pass. Many of us are familiar with passwords. When opening a checking account one is sometimes asked to give the maiden name of one's mother. ATM cards are routinely protected by PINs or personal identification numbers, another form of password. Passwords are one of the most common systems for protecting information from outsiders.

When creating a password it is important to choose a good one. A good password will not easily be guessed by a person attempting to break into your account (i.e., a computer hacker). One should avoid using words, dates, or names as the basis of a password, as these can be easily guessed. Most computer hackers now have access to a number of programs that guess millions of possible passwords in a very short time period. The harder your password is for a computer program to "guess," the more likely your information will be secure.

To create a good password, start with a favorite phrase such as "only thirty shopping days until Christmas"; then combine the first letters of each word ("otsduc"). This will create a nonsensical jumble of letters. To make the password even harder to break, substitute numbers for letters such as zero for "o," and add a nonalphanumeric character from the keyboard such as "@," "?," or "!," creating the password "0tsduc!" This password would be very hard for either humans or computers to guess. Memorizing the password is simple: just remember the original phrase.

The Flaws of Password Security Systems

Password systems are fundamentally flawed for three reasons. First and foremost, there will always be people who choose bad passwords. In many cases, a hacker can gain access to a system by playing the odds that an individual has chosen a bad password. A hacker will often attempt to get a list of valid user names for a system and then proceed to try each account for easy passwords. Once in the system, the hacker uses the expanded access to attack the system from the inside.

A second vulnerability of password systems lies in the fact that a user is required to remember the password. This leads users to write passwords down on a piece of paper, which is then mistakenly thrown out and then picked up by a hacker who "dumpster-dives" into the corporate trash. Additionally, when users forget their passwords, they can usually call up the help desk or technical support and have their password reset. This can cause problems, from corrupt system administrators who will unlock an account for a price to clever attempts at impersonation by hackers to convince the support person that they are a specific user who has forgotten his or her password.

The third flaw in password systems is that, by themselves, they provide no means of protection beyond their secrecy. Anyone—even an unauthorized individual—who can reach a password prompt is only a few letters away from confidential information. Unlike a signature or some other physically unique attribute, using a correct password to access a Web site does not always ensure that the user is authorized to gain access.

These flaws have led security consultants and companies to consider alternative means of protecting confidential information and identifying remote users. Still, passwords are convenient and familiar to a large segment of computer users. This makes password protection systems a compelling way to serve large numbers of customers while providing at least some protection for the merchant.

Future Solutions

Passwords have become the ubiquitous first line of security for protecting information on the Internet. Programmers assume that any computer accessing the Internet has a keyboard. Therefore, every person using the Internet will be able to enter a password. As discussed in the previous section, passwords are intrinsically insecure because they rely on a few characters of information that can be easily entered by any individual. A person's knowledge of a password does not guarantee that person's legitimacy, or even provide a high degree of assurance. This has led to the development of new technologies to better protect critical information such as financial records and online transactions.

Digital Signatures and IDs

Digital signature technology is an important part of electronic commerce. A *digital signature* combines public key cryptography and digital checksums to ensure that the contents of a document have not been altered and to assure the identity of the signer. Each person's signature results from his or her unique private key, which is used to encode a specific checksum of the document. Anyone with a copy of the signer's public key can decode the encoded checksum attached to the document and then compare that with an independent checksum of the document's contents. If the contents of the document are altered in any way, the checksums will not match. The only way to encode the checksum correctly is with the private key, which is a large prime factor protected on the signer's computer. In most commercial documents such as contracts or official correspondence, it is important to have a physical signature on the document. This becomes a problem when the document is transmitted digitally, and there is no paper for pen to touch. How does one create a signature in an electronic document where each byte can be erased or edited at any time?

The answer lies in the same public key systems we discussed earlier in this chapter. It is possible for a user to encrypt information with his or her private key and then allow anyone to decrypt it with his or her freely available public key. This creates a document that anyone can read but can only be altered by the holder of the private key. As long as the private key remains confidential, the document can be considered digitally signed.

Digital signature systems are now available as a part of the most popular Web browsers. Third-party companies, such as VeriSign, provide digital signatures to consumers and a service whereby one can go and retrieve a valid public key for another individual. VeriSign and others act as "trusted third parties," ensuring that the digital signature for ABC Corp. is in reality the actual signature for that organization or individual.

With digital signatures and trusted third parties, secure and private communication can be achieved as long as the private keys remain confidential to each user. If the private key is compromised, however, the system breaks down. Digital signatures are now available as a part of the latest email packages from Netscape and Microsoft. Included with these packages are registration instructions for registering your private and public keys with a trusted third party.

Smart Cards

One proposed solution to the password problem is the use of *smart cards*. Smart cards are a kind of cross between a credit card, a wallet, and a driver's license. A smart card looks like a credit card, but it contains a small microchip that can store and process information. Like a credit card, the smart card can be used to make purchases at stores and over the phone. Smart cards contain an information storage capacity like that of a floppy disk. This information can include everything from a personal calendar to vital medical information.

This ability to store information may one day allow users to hold what some are calling "digital cash." Smart card technology works by equipping computers with smart card readers. Once inserted into the reader, the smart card can be used like a key to unlock restricted information, as an instrument of commerce to send credit and billing information, or perhaps as a means of storing personalized information for a specific user, such as a stock portfolio.

The main problem with smart cards is that they can be stolen or lost. Once in the hands of another person, they may be used like a stolen credit card, or perhaps worse. Imagine losing a card that contains access to your brokerage account, bank account, medical history, and email. Smart card security systems are now available for use in corporate security products. It is only a matter of time before home computer systems begin to come with a so-called smart card reader for use in online shopping and computer security.

Biometrics

Why carry a card with you when you already have several distinct features on your body that can identify you with absolute certainty? While a thief might manage to steal your smart card, chances are he will be unable to take your palm or retina! This is the theory behind biometric-based identification systems. *Biometric* identification relies on the measurement of a body part with a scanning device for use in identification. The best-known form of biometric identification are fingerprints, which police have been collecting at crime scenes and comparing against fingerprints of known criminals for decades.

Biometric identification systems provide a secure alternative to password-based authentication. Traditionally, the cost and speed of these systems have made them impractical security systems. Recently, however, the prices of the requisite hardware, such as digital cameras and scanners, have fallen to ranges that make these systems more widely affordable and practical. Smart card and body biometric systems both require additional hardware and software to work. For this reason, they may never be as universal as passwords and digital IDs, which can be implemented on any computer system.

Workstation Security

The advent of personal computing has created a whole industry built around protecting personal or workstation computers from attack by third parties. Personal computers are designed to run their own programs in contrast to dumb terminals, which simply provide input and display functions for mainframes or minicomputers running in another location. Not every program that a personal computer runs is a friendly program. Hostile programs, called computer viruses, run secretly on the user's machine and usually attempt to destroy data or render the computer nonfunctional. Like real-world viruses, computer viruses have a built-in ability to replicate and spread themselves to other "hosts."

Avoiding Computer Viruses

Computer viruses get to workstations from an outside source. Before the Internet, this generally meant that a user brought a diskette into the office that had been infected on another machine. By preventing or limiting the use of outside disks, most companies were able to avoid infection. This computer quarantine was effective until the rise of the Internet, which offered a new path through which computer viruses could spread.

Computer viruses travel the Internet by infecting a file, which is then downloaded and run. Fortunately for the end-user there are only a few kinds of files that are easily infected. The first is any kind of executable program file. Executable program files contain programs that are run on the local computer system. The second type is any word processing document. Word processors contain mini programs called macros. Since it is possible to write a macro that contains a program, computer viruses can be easily spread by macros.

Stopping Computer Viruses

There are several anti-virus programs available today. Symantec (http://www .symantec.com/) and Network Associates (http://www.mcafee.com) make the leading programs for Microsoft Windows. These programs screen downloaded files and floppy disks automatically for computer viruses. Since new computer viruses are created every day, it is important to keep up with the new releases of anti-virus software. A workstation with an old anti-virus program is as vulnerable as a workstation without an anti-virus program at all. Computer viruses have become increasingly difficult to avoid as computers have become more interconnected. Older rules of protection against computer viruses, such as "Don't install any software on your computer which did not come directly from a shrink-wrapped box" and "Avoid sharing floppy disks between computers," have become moot as programs are routinely downloaded, emailed, and installed on computers across the Internet. Much as one avoids illness in the real world, however, some precautions can reduce the frequency of attack. Some basic rules of protection are as follows:

- Never download an executable file or word processing document from an unknown source. While it is probably safe to download a program from www.microsoft.com, downloading one from www.hackerswarez.com is probably not wise.

- Avoid email attachments that contain executable content or word processing documents.

Obviously, these rules cannot always be followed, and so even with the best precautions one should still expect occasional outbreaks from computer viruses—which is why a screening program is absolutely necessary.

System Security

More and more companies are getting full-time, dedicated connections to the Internet. High-speed dedicated access to the Internet at small businesses may soon be as common as fax machines and local area networks (LANs). Connecting a business through a dedicated connection provides many advantages. Instead of installing modems and additional phone jacks at each workstation, all workstations can get access to the Internet through the same wires that carry the LAN.

The speed of an Internet connection can depend on an office's needs. Connection speeds can be anywhere from eight to two thousand times faster than a modem connection. With a dedicated Internet connection, a business can offer a Web server for its customers, provide remote network access for off-site employees, and give business partners access to information and products from suppliers.

Dedicated connections require additional security, especially when a business is using its connection to sell products through the Web or to provide remote access to files on the LAN. Thieves and hackers may attempt to exploit these services for their own purposes. System security is just as important as individual security on the Internet.

Physical Security

Virtual security begins in the physical world. No firewall, server, or router is safe from attack if it is not protected in the real world. The easiest way for a potential attacker to access or destroy confidential information is to walk up to the computer it is stored on and either physically take that computer or damage it. Servers, routers, firewalls, hubs, and other equipment necessary to the operation of your Internet connection and LAN should therefore be kept in a secure location with restricted access (i.e., a locked room). Mission-critical equipment should be protected with climate control systems (air conditioning), uninterruptible power supplies (UPSs), and off-site media backup.

Computer equipment is sensitive to heat and humidity; it is therefore important that systems be protected with some sort of climate control system. Too often, expensive servers fail because they've been kept in an overheated, unventilated equipment room. Ideally, equipment rooms should be kept in the sixty-degree Fahrenheit range, with low humidity.

Power failures and power spikes are also a problem for computer systems. Surge protectors and UPSs protect equipment and data from corruption and damage from power irregularity. UPSs provide a short-term battery operation for mission-critical equipment, while surge protectors provide protection against voltage irregularities from lightning strikes or other causes. Mission-critical hardware can be damaged by a sudden reboot caused by a power failure or surge, so it is very important to buy high-quality surge suppression and UPSs.

Finally, it is very important that procedures are in place at your organization to make regular backups and have the stored data taken off site to another secure location, such as a safety-deposit box. All too often, businesses have found themselves in trouble because a fire destroys their office, including the server holding their accounting system, and melts the tape backups sitting in the office safe. Always keep at least one copy of any vital programs and data in another location to protect against such an occurrence.

Protecting the Network

Once physical security concerns are addressed, the next step is to secure the network from external and internal attacks. There are several solutions for protecting systems, such as firewalls, proxy servers, and virtual private networking.

Firewalls

The Internet is a collection of networks. Connections between networks are made with devices called routers, which route traffic between networks. These devices are typically designed to make this connection as efficient as possible, with little concern for the traffic that travels through the connection. A *firewall* is a device that sits on one side of the router and monitors incoming and outbound connections.

A firewall provides a means for screening connections and preventing certain connections from occurring at all. Through this screening process, potentially hostile connections can be monitored or stopped. For example, a corporate email server may be protected by a firewall. Computers inside the network can be allowed access to email so it can be read and sent, but outside the network computers can only connect to *send* mail to recipients on the server because the firewall blocks attempts by outside computers to read mail.

Proxy Servers

Another security device used in connecting networks to the Internet is called a *proxy server*. The proxy server acts as a stand-in connection for computers on the local network that wish to access the Internet. For example, if an employee wants to access a Web site from his or her workstation, instead of connecting directly to the Web site, he or she is connected to a proxy server, which makes the connection to the site and then sends the information to the user. This allows employers to monitor which Web sites their employees are viewing and even prevent access to certain sites or restrict employees to a select list of acceptable Web sites.

Proxy servers also allow large organizations to cache the pages of popular sites for their employees, and thereby conserve network bandwidth. Instead of having one hundred employees accessing a Web site through the corporate Internet connection, the proxy server can make one request to the Web site and then show the Web page to all employees.

Virtual Private Networking (VPN)

There are times when companies want to use the Internet to extend the reach of their LAN to remote sites. The specific means for using the Internet for this long-distance networking is called *virtual private networking (VPN)*. Traditionally, companies have turned to high-speed leased lines to create dedicated connections between machines. This solution is expensive when compared to the cost of an Internet connection.

Under a leased-line wide area network (WAN), a company must bear the costs of building a network between computers. If a company has offices in Chicago and Washington, D.C., and then connects them through a WAN, it must pay for a leased line between those two points, much like a full-time long-distance call.

Since the Internet now provides an international high-speed network, many companies now want to use the Internet to fulfill their long-distance networking needs.

The Internet can theoretically be used to network any two computers attached to it. So, on the surface, VPN seems redundant to the idea of the Internet. On the Internet, information is broken down into packets and sent through any number of networks until it finally reaches the intended recipient. As has been mentioned earlier in this chapter, these packets can be intercepted in route. With VPN, however, each packet is encoded and digitally signed. This creates a secure communication in which all machines on the network are known to each other, creating a "virtual" network on the Internet that is as private as a LAN in an office or a non-Internet WAN.

Protecting Workstations and Servers

A second component of systems security is protecting individual computers on the network. There are two types of systems on a network: workstations and servers. Servers are used to store common files and applications, while workstations are used for traditional desktop computing needs.

As we discussed earlier in this chapter, protecting servers requires good physical security and good virtual security. Virtual security for servers varies depending upon the operating system that is running on the server. Every server operating system, such as Windows NT, Novell, or Unix, has features for managing and tracking access to the system. It is important that the server administrator have a thorough understanding of these security features.

Software Upgrades

Sometimes the security features of server software don't work correctly. Software manufacturers will release between-version updates to their products, which are known as "service packs" or "patch levels." It is important that server software be updated with the latest patch level or service pack. Manufacturers are constantly discovering bugs and flaws in the security of their software. As these bugs are discovered, manufacturers release a service pack or "hot fix," which corrects the bug. As these bug fixes are released, the previous security hole is documented to explain why users should upgrade their product. The result of this is to render users without the service pack less secure because the security problem is now more widely known. Typically, the operating system will display the current upgrade level when the system is started.

Security Resources

There are a number of sources for security information on the Internet. For the most up-to-date security information be sure to visit the software manufacturer's Web site.

CERT (http://www.cert.org/). The Central Emergency Response Team, or CERT, was created in 1987 to provide rapid response to security problems on the Internet. CERT issues warnings whenever security problems arise on the Internet, either with server daemons or operating systems. CERT security alerts are available on the Internet at http://www.cert.org/. CERT also maintains an FTP site that provides a number of tools for testing the security of servers and networks.

NCSA (http://www.ncsa.com/). The National Computer Security Association provides security evaluation, network security certification, and professional training on computer security issues. The NCSA also provides certification for computer security products such as firewalls and anti-virus software.

A Note on Security: There are many technologies available today for protecting data, systems, and individuals on the Internet, but there are limits on their global distribution. These limits can be overcome by purchasing products manufactured outside the United States or by purchasing U.S. products that comply with U.S. export law. Both of these solutions mean making certain compromises in order to gain a better degree of security.

No single piece of software can provide total security. Security is only achieved by protecting the entire process of data transmission, storage, and redistribution. Safeguards must be inserted at every step, from workstation, through the network, to the server. It is important to stress that no system is totally secure; the best that can be said is that the chances of a successful attack have been diminished with respect to an unprotected system. It is always possible for someone to successfully attack a system.

Security systems, like alarm systems, provide a degree of protection against attack. They do not, however, provide total security. Don't ever assume that your security system is so impenetrable that constant monitoring, backups, and upgrades are no longer necessary.

EXPANDING RELATIONSHIPS

Through Worldwide Internet Communities

In recent years, considerable attention has been given to the Internet and the promise it brings to significantly alter the approaches and practice of business. In fact, more than promise, we've seen innovators embrace electronic strategies to capitalize on new possibilities and secure competitive gains.

Consider for a moment that the Internet is relatively new to the commercial world. Consequently, many Internet strategies are also new. In order to determine the most valuable approach, one must give due consideration to what the Internet really is.

The Internet is a publishing mechanism. As such, it offers more economical, deeper, and easier information delivery and access than ever before. The Internet is a set of ubiquitous standards. As such, it unites people and systems for far-reaching opportunities. The Internet is a communications channel. Unlike traditional channels such as print, television, and the telephone, the Internet is a rich multimedia environment with direct transaction and interactive capabilities and no concern for space and time constraints.

Indeed, the Internet is a completely new business channel for publishing, for communications, and for transactions. Its interactive nature makes it a relationship technology that can significantly alter the traditional interactions between businesses, partners, and customers. For those companies that recognize its true potential, the Internet offers significant possibilities.

One of the most successful business models to emerge and capitalize on the Internet's capabilities is the creation and maintenance of Internet communities. Internet communities provide a powerful context for the integration of content, communication, and commerce. When done well, the community provides an intersection between the social need that compels individuals to participate in a community and the value proposition that meets a given business objective. Its win-win formula contributes to its success.

Internet communities are not occurring at random, however. Many factors have a hand in influencing the creation and success of this business model:

- Deregulation of trade and growing global competitiveness
- The need to unite disparate technologies and geographically dispersed resources
- Cheaper information access and delivery
- Consumers' demand to be more educated about buying choices and to act in accordance with their growing time constraints
- The benefits provided by and gained from serving customers on a one-to-one basis

In fact, as they have developed, virtual communities have been shattering national barriers, unlocking new markets, and creating profitable connections on a global scale. While the effect they can have on a company varies with the characteristics of its products and services and with the industries in which it competes, they are being employed all over the world to build new value for consumers, strengthen and maintain relationships, improve processes, and have a positive bottom-line impact.

What Is a Worldwide Internet Community?

Like any communications network, the Internet's true value is in the connections it affords between people. Worldwide virtual communities, therefore, leverage the capabilities of the network to establish and grow relationships. They form when people find the *need* to communicate online to exchange information and ideas and provide each other with mutual support. Whether the community is based on mutual age (such as teenagers or seniors), location (such as people living in Paris, Texas, or Paris, France), areas of interest (such as education or travel), or some combination of these, a need to interact with like-minded individuals compels people to find each other and share their interests online. Political barriers and physical disabilities are nonexistent, and issues of gender and race melt away. In the virtual world of cyberspace, everyone is on equal footing. The measure of a person is truly in his or her words and actions, as measured by the emerging rules and conventions of cyberspace.

No one would disagree that in recent years there has been a proliferation of World Wide Web sites. There has also been a growing number of companies who call these sites "communities." From publishers to flower vendors, companies have created a Web presence where visitors can obtain information about their products or services and can send electronic messages to the company. A worldwide virtual community demands more, however. More than merely broadcasting information, it encourages interactions between consumers and the company and between consumers and consumers, and it fulfills a need for information, interactivity, and, in some instances, transactions.

Commercial success with a worldwide virtual community, in fact, belongs to those who meet both a social and a business need. By creating expansive and relevant interactions, organizations create value for their audience and drive revenues in the form of advertising, subscriptions, and transactions.

Key Elements of Any Virtual Community

There are five key elements that distinguish an Internet community from other online ventures: the community's members, the community's organizer, its guiding principles, the institutional benefits it offers, and its interactivity. Each piece is a vital part of the whole (see Figure 7.1). If any one piece is missing, the community is incomplete.

Let's examine each of these elements in some detail:

Community members. For an Internet community to exist, it must have members, people who feel a sense of belonging vis–à–vis the site. Within a virtual community, membership is *always* by choice. Once a person gets involved in his or her community, he or she acquires a sense of ownership about everything that goes on, whether by submitting articles, posting to discussion groups, or participating in chats. Although membership may be transitory, the opportunity to connect with others who share similar interests and have an influence on the community through their contributions fosters a strong feeling of empowerment at the time of involve-

Figure 7.1 Key elements of an Internet community.

Successful Community

ment. Indeed, the community's members are the actual creators of the virtual community, and the ability to extract individually relevant information and, therefore, value is an important draw.

Community organizer. Every successful virtual community has an organizer who is responsible for the virtual space where the community resides. The organizer may be an individual or an organizing body that facilitates the growth and maintenance of the community. The community organizer's primary role is to make certain that the community is cultivated and well managed. When using the virtual community equation as a business strategy, a community organizer needs to represent a credible sponsoring body and be willing to adopt a long-term investment perspective. A commitment to eliciting participation and work from staff and employees on behalf of community members needs is a vital aspect of the organizer's role. Community organizers need to be up to speed on the information requirements of their audience and on any discussions that are taking place at the site. Ultimately, they must act less like a vendor and more like a champion of the community's desires.

Guiding principles. One prerequisite of creating communities (either real or virtual) is that some rules and conventions must govern the conduct of those who come together for common purposes. Like any community, Internet communities have guiding principles, a foundation of established rules and guidelines for its members. Virtual communities are true democracies, with everything good, bad, and ugly that human nature encompasses. In general, the guiding principles of most virtual communities include the following common elements:

- Members, not the technology, drive the community.
- Members must be respectful and tolerant of all points of view.
- Members must have a clear understanding of community's moral standards and expectations, both formal and informal.

While a certain foundation of regulations can be established up front by the community organizer, the best communities are self-directed and regulated by the group of people that forms together. If anyone were to violate the charter, the actions of the organizer as well as the group would keep them in line.

Institutional benefits. When a worldwide virtual community works, it fulfills many institutional needs that produce tangible benefits. A well-functioning community helps to save time, save money, improve processes, and strengthen business relationships. For example, building a corporate intranet or extranet with a strong community element can save time by uniting different systems and information centrally and by improving productivity through easy access to other employees, departments, and countries. Alternatively, an Internet community customer-care practice might be used to answer questions online, foster customer-to-customer self-service, provide proactive notification of new products, and collect a knowledgebase of feedback to improve overall quality and reliability.

The institutional benefits of strengthening business relationships can be attained through more efficient and effective interactions and by providing access to information through which community members can feel closer and more loyal to the product and company. The institutional benefits can also be realized through outreach and exposure since a vibrant worldwide virtual community spreads the word about its sponsor, resulting in increased traffic and community loyalty.

Interactivity. The core of any virtual community is its interactivity, which turns virtual space into a virtual home. The ability to connect and speak with others, to access rich content, and to publish and communicate information work together to foster greater loyalty. Grounded in strong intuitive technology that emulates all forms of conversation, these interactive elements keep the barriers to entry low and inspire members to participate for extended periods of time, returning again and again and bringing others with them into the community.

Equipping an Internet Community

For all the importance of the success factors described in the last section, it is also important to note that *technology* plays a critical role in the success of Internet communities, especially their interactivity. The type of tools employed; their robustness in managing groups, discussions, and content; and their capability to customize the presentation of information are just some requirements to consider.

Online communities were first formed through Usenet newsgroup discussions, in which people with similar interests exchanged email messages and generated the discussion content. Then the online services began offering forum discussion and chat facilities. Indeed, one of the best-known proprietary online systems, America Online, used chat software as a primary attraction.

Today, software exists to help any company leverage community features to enhance their Web presence. At the baseline, discussion group applications for near real-time interactions, chat software for spontaneous dialogue, and publishing tools to gather and share content from users who distribute it should be included. Depending on the community's focus, ad rotation technology and additional usage analysis technology should also be looked at. To build an effective worldwide virtual community, a site must have the appropriate applications installed to foster communication between site visitors. It should make capturing, sharing, and analyzing data easy for the community organizer. And the ability to moderate and manage users, groups, discussions, content, and profiles contributes to greater success for the organizer, more relevant targeting, and better overall value for the users.

Members of any virtual community interact and develop a level of comfort with the software in the same way a regular at a coffeehouse or a social club develops a level of comfort with the ambience and decor. The level of comfort any member has with the software will be reflected in their comfort with the structure of the virtual community itself. The significance of the software in facilitating the flow of the community cannot be overstated. In short, the software that is chosen is the essential backbone of a successful community.

Understanding and employing the elements of a worldwide virtual community described so far into an Internet approach can turn the competitive threat of new technology into a company's competitive advantage.

The Evolution of Virtual Communities

The development of online communities began with bulletin boards systems (BBS)—closed, dial-in systems that served as a place for discussing and debating issues of interest and importance to participants.

One of the Web's most famous and influential online communities is The Well. From its humble beginnings in 1985 as a large computer and a rack of modems in a lowly Sausalito, California, office, this haven for thinkers and high-tech tinkerers now serves as the quintessential model for online community building today. Members of The Well are loyal and active participants in their virtual homestead. Here social constructions for community behavior were monitored and maintained by the users. Over time, Well members engendered other communities, volunteer-run Internet mailing lists, and Usenet newsgroups that brought people together under the bond of common interest.

What developed naturally and informally on The Well and other BBSs around the world was replicated as a business model by commercial online services that charged for access and offered proprietary content. The first was Prodigy, followed by CompuServe and America Online (AOL). AOL, more than its counterparts, embraced the community paradigm. AOL transformed online interaction from an application used by a few into a service found in the homes of millions and made communicating in cyberspace easily accessible for the technophobe. Indeed, until AOL moved to flat-fee pricing in 1996, a large percentage of the company's income came from the access fees paid by those who spent endless hours participating in chat sessions.

By the third quarter of 1996, the technical elements that help to facilitate online communities, from discussion and chat software to templates for user-generated content, came into use and acceptance on the Web. And as the Web emerged as the principal conduit for online change and innovation, the environment for creating virtual communities naturally evolved from one of closed systems to open Internet, intranet, and extranet solutions.

Types of Communities

On the Internet, every need is reflected and magnified on a global scale. If you are a thirty-something jazz music fan living in Holland, you can connect with like-minded music lovers in every other country of the world. If you are a cancer survivor, you can search out other survivors and their families for support. At their heart, Internet communities are communities of interest. The point of common interest can be as basic as gender or age or as specific as a professional skill or place of residence.

Some examples of areas of interest that serve as the basis for thriving Internet communities include the following:

Geographically-based communities. Towns, counties, and neighborhoods around the country are getting wired and connecting local residents with each other and with businesses, community services, and local activities. From Blacksburg, Virginia's Blacksburg Electronic Village (http://www.bev.net/) to The Lawrence Cybervillage (http://www.ci .lawrence.ks.us/), which sees itself as the official Internet gateway to the community of Lawrence, Kansas, these geographically based communities are transforming their sense of physical place into cyberspace.

Age-based communities. Some sites work to build a community environment among members of a specific age group. In this approach, site users become comfortable because they are among peers. For example, Tripod (http://www.tripod.com) is directed to the college crowd and

Third Age (http://www.thirdage.com) bills itself as "The Web for the Grownup" and is directed to people over fifty years of age.

Support-based communities. Sites are popping up all over the Web to provide mutual aid and support to people facing similar life challenges. These sites can be for people with specific health needs, such as diseases, disabilities, or addictions. They range from national organizations like the American Diabetes Association (http://www.ada.org) and the American Cancer Society (http://www.cancer.org) to smaller and more grass-roots-focused operations such as the Kids with Cancer site (http://www.kidswithcancer.com), run voluntarily by a group of parents.

Activity-based communities. If you are an avid reader, a baseball fan, or have a professional interest in technology, there are sites that offer deep information, interactions with peers, and the ability to purchase goods and services to help you pursue your interest. Take, for instance, the renowned Internet book site Amazon.com. While it offers book reviews from reputable sources such as the *New York Times*, even more interesting is its focus on membership-generated content. Members can post their own reviews and in some instances receive an incentive in the form of book awards for doing so. The approach not only provides broader information but encourages participation and loyalty, which in turn drives increased sales for the organization.

The ability to find and relate with others who share similar interests makes the computer screen, not a window to look through from the outside, but an open door beckoning you in to participate in one-to-one interactions. These interactions build relationships, and it is these relationships that are the cornerstones of business success.

Including Communities in Your Business Strategy

Even with all the fuss over the Internet's potential, the online world is still developing and searching for successful business strategies. Building worldwide virtual communities is one such strategy that spells success because it brings together the social needs of users with the value propositions of businesses to form a logical business plan.

As a business strategy, creating a worldwide virtual community is based on an equation in which the social need that compels individuals to participate in an Internet community intersects with the value proposition that meets the organization's economic objectives. Rich content and a well-researched, targeted context make a site compelling, but it is the community element that makes a site a part of a person's life, worth visiting repeatedly as long as a need exists.

The Internet Community Equation

In today's ever-changing business market, competitive threats are everywhere. Here, for example, are some real-life scenarios:

- A very large regional real-estate agency began noticing Web sites that listed homes for sale by owners in its territory, complete with room-by-room tours and direct links to mortgage brokers boasting interactive loan calculators. Within three weeks, such online players had begun to dilute the need for the agency's style of real-estate service.

- A respected brokerage house had been in business for decades with a name synonymous with trust and integrity. From beyond the virtual horizon, a set of new players invaded the company's world, using the Internet in such a savvy way that their instant credentials appeared to place them on equal footing with the company's half-century tradition of service. Many customers said they no longer needed retail storefronts because Web sites can link amateur investors together, and stock trading is taking place directly over the Internet. The brokerage house's sales began plummeting, seemingly overnight.

- A major newspaper company found that its local and classified ad business was being challenged online from all directions. On one side, a software giant with the money and tenacity to pose a serious threat started positioning itself to encroach on the paper's local classified business. On the other side, a number of small start-up companies start picking away at the paper's better ad clients, diluting sales. Together, these new communications players began to threaten the paper's industry advantage.

What online businesses often lack in traditional business understanding they make up for with an acute understanding of the interactivity and relationship-building dynamics of Web-based environments. Understanding and integrating the elements of virtual communities into your own Internet solutions can help you turn competitive threats like these into competitive advantages.

Understanding the Internet community equation as a business strategy means more than calling each visitor who comes to your site a member of your community. It means more than putting up discussion forums and chat rooms. As I indicated earlier, the formula for success in building worldwide virtual communities is when the social need that compels individuals to participate intersects directly with the value proposition that meets a given business objective (see Figure 7.2).

Using the Internet community equation as a business strategy is smart, but it is not an end in itself. One of the Internet communities launched with great fanfare in 1996 was Electric Minds (http://www.minds.com), founded by virtual community guru Howard Rheingold. The site, initially funded to employ seventeen staffers, downsized after only a few months. Then it fell prey to the most fatal disease on the Net: lack of funds. With its initial venture funding drying up and sales failing to produce sufficient cash flow, Electric Minds was on its deathbed after only seven months of operation. Despite its financial shortcomings, however, the community was hailed by its members as a cultural success. What failed, according to Rheingold, was the business, not the community.

The lesson to be learned from Electric Minds is that building a community for its own sake is not a justifiable end in itself. A sounder path is to use the Internet community equation as a strategy to build your online presence, broaden your brand awareness, and improve your services to customers. These strategies must then be coupled with aggressive revenue models that have already been shown to work on the Internet: advertising, sales, subscriptions, and licensing content. In short, the blend of an individual's social needs and a company's value proposition breeds a stable and profitable business. A deficiency on either side makes the community unbalanced and puts the entire enterprise at risk.

Social Needs

The need for social interaction compels individuals to relate with others online. Most successful worldwide virtual communities fulfill the following basic social needs:

Figure 7.2 Internet community equation.

Gaining knowledge. These communities provide a means for learning much more about a specific subject, concern, or opportunity, very often directly from other people's personal experiences.

Voicing opinions. These communities provide safe and supportive environments in which to voice your opinions or beliefs.

Connecting with others who share common interests. These serve to connect people with similar interests or concerns.

Receiving support. Such communities function as a means to support the activities and goals of all its members.

Promoting capabilities. These communities allow members to brag a bit about their accomplishments and achievements within given areas of common interest.

Value Proposition

Why is building virtual communities on a global scale so important? While content may be what gets a person to visit the site in the first place, it is frequently the community element that keeps them coming back. Each time members return to the site, from anywhere in the world, they find shared human responses that make them feel welcome and involved. This, in turn, is what generates direct revenue, improves an organization's business process (from internal communication to external customer outreach), and facilitates online marketing and advertising revenues.

The value proposition translates into the expected return an institution or business can earn by investing resources to build a global online community. In most cases, the value proposition of building a worldwide virtual community translates into the following benefits:

Generation of direct revenue. At the moment, successful Internet sites generate direct revenues through advertising, subscriptions, direct transactions, and content licensing. In every case, a site can only generate revenues in direct proportion to its volume of traffic. High traffic results in more advertising revenue, more transaction dollars from merchandise sales, and more subscriptions sold, and it typically generates greater demand for content.

A functional virtual community serves as a terrific means of generating new traffic and drawing users back. And because members of the community contribute to the content of a site by posting messages on a forum or putting content directly on a Web page through a publishing tool, they are invested in the site. Likewise, members of the community remain at a site much longer than random visitors since they are encouraged to participate, contribute, and interact once they arrive.

Improved business processes. The Internet is a communications medium that businesses are also using to better communicate internally with their customers and with their suppliers. However, just because a company has a Web site or an intranet does not mean the people the company services will use them. Building a sense of community typically facilitates the internal use of the communications medium in a constructive and lively way. It also fosters company-to-customer communications for more personal, immediate, and satisfying customer service.

Increased brand awareness. The Internet's phenomenally rapid penetration into homes and offices around the globe is historically unparalleled. The global reach of a virtual community can help an organization rapidly build the value of its brands and its overall corporate identity.

The Social Imperative in Internet Communities

Worldwide virtual communities are predicated on strong social needs. When the need goes away, participation in the community is usually suspended or ended. These communities are not meant to be lasting elements of a member's life but to serve a specific need at a specific time. When that need ceases, a person may or may not move on to another equally compelling community.

Let us not forget, then, that virtual communities are very often temporary and transient. This transience is not a warning sign of instability, however. Rather, the transience of virtual communities mirrors the life-cycle process itself.

Like many communities, virtual communities tend to "niche down" to a specific interest and event. For example, a couple expecting a new baby may move from participating in a discussion forum for expecting mothers to forums for new parents to forums for infants, then toddlers, and so on. Or a person interested in buying a Saab may spend countless hours researching the entire Saab line of vehicles online, perhaps even participating in forums that discuss features and financing. But once that person has bought a Saab, the need to participate in the community may dissipate and he or she will move on.

Membership in any one virtual community is constantly changing, but the need to create and form new communities continues to exist. Community organizers must stay ahead of their users and continue to recruit new members to keep the community alive and vibrant.

Patterns of Communication Shift between Business and Customer

In today's information age, manufacturing is not omniscient and businesses do not dominate the landscape over customers. The incredible access to information offered by the Internet has shifted the patterns of communication between businesses and customers. The power of information is transforming customers from passive to active players in the business arena.

Indeed, with the Internet, customers can be as educated as they want to be about any product or service. The informed customer wants to interact and discuss products with the companies that produce them. Companies are finding that they get many of their best product ideas directly from their customers. Smart companies listen to and engage their customers in dialogue about their projects and those of their competitors. The open and continuous dialogue made possible by virtual communities provides the ultimate tool for this information exchange while boosting site traffic and providing customers and businesses with new and unique insights about each other.

Using Virtual Communities As a Strategic Tool

Because the Internet is an interactive communications medium, it can be used to achieve differing objectives that require differing standards of measure. If the Web site is primarily used to track executive sales, then the number and amount of sales generated will be the standard. If the Web site is used to generate leads, then the number of qualified leads is the standard. If the Web site is meant to inform the public and provide quality customer service, then the volume of use and user feedback is paramount. And if the Web site is a means of building awareness in a product, company, or service, then yet another benchmark dominates.

In every case, establishing a successful worldwide virtual community within your Web site will help satisfy one or more strategic purposes. For some businesses, building a Web site dominated by the community makes sense. For others, adding a community-building element, such as a discussion forum or a chat room, is all that is needed. And for others, sponsoring sections of an existing site, such as sponsoring a chat room or advertising in a discussion area within another related Web site, works best.

An Internet Community That Satisfies Business and Social Needs

Take Cox Interactive Media, for instance. A subsidiary of Cox Enterprises, Cox Interactive Media used its late entry into the online arena as a strategic advantage. Cox Interactive Media realized that its parent company was not so much in the de facto paper business as in the local content business. One of its first online endeavors was an Internet community for Atlanta (http://www.accessatlanta.com) with the objective of being the Internet access point for the entire geographic region. Their goal was to make their Atlanta site the first place someone thought of when looking on the Internet for information about Atlanta.

With competition in the local content field looming from all sides, Cox Interactive Media decided to use as its competitive advantage the relationship with the communities it had been serving for years with its newspapers, radio stations, and other media holdings. Cox Interactive Media decided to incorporate community-building elements directly into the Atlanta site, making it the local content site by and for the Atlanta community.

Cox Interactive Media recognized that the local community itself produces some of the best local content. From day one, they gave publishing tools to community groups and organizations so that they could generate and produce content for the site. From submissions to community calendars to specific neighborhood association areas, the Atlanta site is empowering its users to not only be consumers of information but also producers of content on and about its community.

The Atlanta site employs discussion boards and chat facilities to provide community members with a place to discuss specific topics of interest. Whether the issue is crime or the county fair, the forums are a moderated discussion defined and maintained by the community. Chat, on the other hand, is a more freestyle conversational element, which allows community members to interact in realtime. These interactive community communications facilities are moderated by its organizer, who acts to spark and manage the conversations and ensure that the facility is not abused.

Cox Interactive Media's online ventures are drawing on the programming and audiences of its other media holdings to extend traditional programming. Whether a radio station, a newspaper, or a Web site, each venture is serving a local community. This local focus allows direct off-line and online crossover. For example, if a radio talk show goes over the allotted time, the program can continue by moving to a chat room on the Web. If more material exists for a story than is published in the newspaper coverage, the supporting material can be placed on the Web site where the virtual real estate is endless.

For Cox Interactive Media, online broadcasting is a community affair, where content is generated and directed by the community either directly through its publishing tool or informally in the discussion areas or chat rooms.

Through this strategy, Cox has provided users with easy and gratifying access to like-minded individuals and unique content contributions. The company receives user-generated content at no real business cost that creates new relationships with their customers and drives an advertising-based business model. Users get the opportunity to easily find others who share their passion and participate in a community of like-minded individuals. Advertisers get access to a pinpointed audience. Together this forms a harmony of interests that creates value for all groups.

An Internet Community of Support

MedSupport FSF (http://www.medsupport.org) is another form of virtual community success story. MedSupport FSF is a support-service Web site for the disabled and their caregivers. It is run by Sue Marks, who is disabled herself. Marks has twenty-five years of experience as a registered nurse and has been running bulletin boards for the disabled for six years.

To many people, the thought of opening a Web site to anyone coming through the cyber-airwaves might sound like a recipe for disaster. Marks avoids potential problems by training moderators well and having clear written rules up front to ensure that no one abuses the privilege of participating. Marks's rules are simple: no flaming, no advertising, no language you wouldn't want a child to read. Marks has found that the policy is so well known by the users that "peer pressure alone would force an abuser off our site."

Marks has found bulletin boards to be wonderful sources of communication for her audience. The ability to log on twenty-four hours a day and get support from others with similar problems in a moderated area lends itself naturally to the feeling of community. As Marks explains, "Everyone feels comfortable and secure in MedSupport FSF and many letters refer to our 'family.' Just write a 'newbie' note in one of my forums and see the supportive responses you get."

MedSupport FSF uses both discussion boards and chat and sees a difference in communication style and focus between the two. Marks has found discussions to be more topic oriented. Chats, on the other hand, are used on a more informal and casual basis, with two exceptions: (1) if a person with a problem needs to talk, (2) when there is a special event in the chat room that warrants a reserved two-hour block. For example, every Wednesday MedSupport has a Stress Management class from 8 to 10 P.M. in the chat room.

Marks believes that a feeling of community can be achieved on any site as long as there is a commitment from those running the site coupled with a strong knowledgebase on the topic. "The rest," as she puts it, "will come naturally."

An Internet Community of Learners

Magazine publisher Ziff-Davis (ZD) used a worldwide Internet community strategy for yet another end. Because technology is moving at such a rapid pace, ZD discovered that its readers needed to learn more about computers than any single issue could provide. So, in October 1996, ZD launched its ZD Net University (http://www.zdu.com) to bring busy people together to learn the latest high-tech skills in a cutting-edge distance-learning environment.

ZDU began with the deployment of discussion group software because the technology fit ZD's need for an interactive and structured online setting that allowed the teachers to teach and the students to interact with one another. ZDU can now service students around the globe regardless of country or time zone or whether they are sitting at home or at work.

Here's the way ZDU classes work. The instructor writes a lesson plan with assignments. Students read the lessons and can ask questions. Anyone in the class can post and/or answer the questions. For example, a student from Alaska might post a question after reading the lesson and a student from Japan might answer that question.

Thus, the class participants learn as much from interacting with each other as from the instructor. Moreover, each student can choose his or her level of involvement. If a student is very busy and only wants to see posts from the instructor, he or she can do that. Or a student can just look at questions posted by other students. ZDU continues to adapt and refine its software to create a learning environment that is fluid and flexible for its student's needs.

ZDU is a tremendous success, and it sees its success as tied to its incorporation of community. "The whole concept of ZDU is built around community," says Katherine Prouty, product manager of ZDU. And community does not stop when the course ends. ZDU encourages its alumni to continue to be part of the ZDU community after the course is completed by providing a place for students to meet and interact. And it's working. As Prouty sees it, ZDU is flourishing because it recognizes the importance and value of "a worldwide virtual community of lifelong learners."

An Internet Community for China

In any culture, virtual communities make sense. In January 1997, ChinaByte (http://www.chinabyte.com), a joint venture of NewsCorp and *People's Daily*, was launched as the premiere Chinese-language site for technology news. The goal of the site was to place the Chinese high-tech industry on equal footing with its Western counterparts in terms of access to industry news and events. ChinaByte is a twenty-five person operation whose entire staff consists of native Chinese except the two consultants brought in by the parent companies to help launch the venture.

ChinaByte employed discussion group software for its community-building element because of that software's malleable interface—extremely important when working with other cultures and other languages. The ChinaByte forums only discuss topics of technology—there are no social, political, or personal forums. In a country whose government is extremely concerned about subversive use of the Internet, ChinaByte tries to avoid government intervention by moderating all its forums. In its first five months of existence, the forum managers only had to pull two or three messages. However, the messages were not cut because they dealt with off-topic or inappropriate content but because they contained profanity in referring to issues of technology.

The site was an immediate success on several fronts. First, from the start it was well used and quickly became the highest trafficked site in China, receiving 100,000 hits per month. Second, its business model had a strong advertising component for the generation of revenue. It already has big-name advertisers like IBM, Informix, and Intel with many other advertisers already expressing keen interest in this market, which will shortly surpass Japan in terms of PC growth.

And finally, ChinaByte has forged a strong sense of loyalty among its users. ChinaByte knows that its window of opportunity for being first to market is closing. Other sites are already copying ChinaByte's content and format. They believe that in the end its competitive advantage will be the sense of community it has developed with its users. And this is holding true: the community feature already comprises 17 to 20 percent of the site's total impressions. As Michael Dix, the executive producer of the ChinaByte launch puts it, "Community is the gel that holds it all together."

Whatever your strategic aim, an Internet community strategy demands some consideration. The Internet is a relationship technology. To create, encourage, and support connections between partners and customers helps to build relationships and business. Whether the Internet community takes the form of customer care practices, distance-learning programs, or a marketing initiative to sell products and services, there is a global opportunity within reach. Consider this: If you don't convert your customers and partners to an online community, someone else may do it for you.

THE ROLE OF INTRANETS AND EXTRANETS IN A GLOBAL MARKETPLACE

I nformation—either in the form of raw data or more refined, analyzed records—is the most important thing a company or an individual can possess in today's business world.

Information is what distinguishes one company from another. It allows a company to understand markets worldwide, spot existing trends, and respond to crises or new trends. To position itself for future growth and prosperity, a company will strive to be one (preferably two) steps ahead of its competition in gathering and analyzing information. The rise of the information economy will probably continue, and the buying and selling of information will likely grow in size to rival the trade in physical goods.

As more and more businesses recognize the role that information plays in the workplace–and begin to explore new, exciting, and more powerful methods of collection, processing, and analysis–they can expect to experience changes in the way they relate to their clients and their markets. In the past, amassing the necessary resources to support large-scale information retrieval technologies was reserved for only the largest and best-funded businesses and institutions. Now, however, the increasing affordability of intranets and extranets is beginning to level the playing field.

Intranets are self-contained, internal networks that link multiple users by means of Internet technology. A company with a powerful intranet can have in-house and off-site employees work on the same document at the same time, provide useful corporate information to all employees at once, or even arrange online "e-meetings" between several employees in different locations.

In effect, intranets put a fence around the Internet's limitless territory, establishing controlled-access sectors where users can communicate freely and interact. Built and managed by companies or organizations (called sponsors), these networks reside on the World Wide Web, making possible cross-platform communications between authorized users in real time.

Extranets are a way for corporations to open their intranets to selected external partners. Intranets, which are built on open, public Internet standards, enable organizations to quickly deploy internal applications without the need for costly and proprietary implementations. Extranets create an electronic link between a corporation and its partners by opening up new markets, lowering costs, and reducing technology churn.

A powerful extranet can let all the vendors and suppliers of a large-scale manufacturer order parts and access individual account information online, twenty-four hours a day and seven days a week. It can provide a customer service link between key employees and individual clients and accounts, thereby making it possible to have virtual product/service teams in cyberspace. When used for customer service purposes, an extranet can usually provide a significant *return on investment* (ROI) in comparison to virtually any other communications medium.

Corporate Strategy: Efficiency and Effectiveness

Companies that manage to build successful intranets and extranets enjoy a range of benefits that fall into two broad categories: efficiency and effectiveness.

In this context, efficiency means improving the process of information exchange—that is, overcoming logistical obstacles so as to gather and disseminate necessary information in a timely manner. Effectiveness means that the organization becomes better at collaborating and making decisions.

Enhanced Efficiency

Improvements in efficiency can be readily identified and are easily measured. For example, many intranet and extranet sponsors report significant savings in such expenses as overnight mail, postage, and long-distance telephone charges. Other savings derive from reduced reliance on printed documents, such as company manuals, product brochures, or customer relations materials, which can now be distributed electronically rather than printed and mailed.

Hidden in the efficiency equation are also savings in staff time. A fully functioning intranet can drastically reduce "phone tag," the swapping of multiple document drafts, and other tasks that involve the coordination of information-gathering activities. For example, intranets speed up the peer review process for technical research publications by enabling them to be distributed quickly and responses and comments to be compiled automatically. In many organizations, an intranet centralizes the news clipping function; cutting, pasting, and circulating news articles is now done electronically from a single location.

One company's sales force makes extensive use of its intranet as a customer relations medium. Its sales representatives access online product information from clients' offices as they need it instead of having to carry multiple slide decks or a lot of printed literature. For some of the company's more sophisticated products, the marketing department has established an intranet sector specifically for customers, who use passwords to access the latest in relevant research and development (R&D) and product safety information.

A multinational trade association uses its intranet to, among other things, organize its complex schedule of meetings. At any given moment, this organization is conducting technical task force meetings and business conferences in addition to its quarterly and annual plenary meetings, which usually attract hundreds of participants from around the world.

Each of these meetings has its own attendance list, agenda, briefing materials, venue management, logistical considerations, and expected output. In the past, managing printed materials to support these meetings required five full-time staffers and cost thousands of dollars per year for reproduction and distribution. All of these materials are now posted to the intranet site, which is organized to correspond to recipients' passwords.

Scheduling and notifying members of the association's meetings are also handled via the intranet; a central calendar displays all scheduled meetings with their particulars attached so members can see them all at a glance, get the details as needed, and register online.

Enhanced Effectiveness

Less tangibly–but at least as significantly—intranets and extranets can improve the overall effectiveness of the sponsoring organization. Intranets encourage the exchange of information across traditional boundaries—both organizational and geographic. Properly managed, such enhanced exchanges become the springboard for greater collaboration between previously fragmented sectors of the sponsoring organization. By promoting coordinated interaction, the creative use of an intranet can speed up an organization's evolution from a hierarchical, top-down model to a more nimble structure.

One international law firm, for example, uses its intranet to strengthen its environmental practice. The intranet permitted the firm's environmental specialists to exchange—in a secure environment—information about current cases and emerging regulatory and legal trends that affected them and to solicit their colleagues' counsel, quickly and privately. By bringing together practitioners in each of its offices, the firm was able to capitalize on its collective expertise, improving both its attorneys' knowledge and its marketing leverage.

In one specialty chemicals company, the R&D and marketing departments reside in different countries, creating barriers to customer-responsive product development. This company used its intranet to improve communications between the two disciplines through a system that includes regular update meetings online, the participation of the R&D department by way of customer surveys, and the routine exchange of departmental news. This system has enabled the company to factor customer requirements and preferences into the product development process at the earliest stages. As a result, customers gain input into product R&D—which means the company's products are better targeted and better received. At the same time, customers have better access to the company's R&D expertise through a sales force that is better informed about new technical developments.

An international public interest organization links hundreds of chapters together via an intranet that members use to keep abreast of regulatory and social trends. Many of these chapters are small, have highly localized agendas, and rely primarily on volunteer staff. They lack the resources to monitor global issues, sponsor symposia, or attend conferences. Their intranet offers these local chapters access to each other's experiences and strategies and helps them distribute information across the full range of the membership.

Both intranets and extranets offer a way to harness the raw power of the Internet and apply it to individual organizations. The real beauty of both tools is their profound flexibility. There is no single formula or universal template, meaning each organization can—and should—define, design, and use an intranet or extranet in the way that best reflects its individual culture and supports its business objectives.

Content Is Crucial

Every successful intranet or extranet provides content—information—that users value. Of course, the nature of this content varies considerably and depends on the individual user groups and their priorities. However, a few basic principles apply to content. Intranet sponsors and users alike agree that a site's information must have the following characteristics:

Relevance. This is in the eye of the user, not the sponsor. Organizations that use an intranet only to promote the party line may be disappointed in their investment.

Timeliness. "Traffic jams" on intranets or extranets discourage users, who'll quickly revert to conventional communications when their email and message boards are slow or unreliable.

Frequent updates. Many Web sites, public and private, suffer from static content, and interest in and usage of them quickly drops. Intranets offer the capacity to update information regularly.

Accessibility. The best site content in the world has little value if users can't get to it quickly and easily. The point of the intranet is to make information available, and site design should take advantage of search engines and other features that improve user access.

In considering questions of content, it's important to keep in mind that intranets and extranets are uniquely user driven and that user needs and preferences should be factored into the initial design and engineering of the site. As with any other construction project, it is almost always more efficient to engineer in at the beginning than to retrofit after the fact. Site features and functions that make content relevant, timely, and accessible—and allow for easy updating—should be incorporated into site specifications on the front end.

The very best intranets and extranets also make a special effort to add value to the content they provide. Many purchase information directly through news feeds—both conventional sources like Reuters and Associated Press and those delivered primarily through the Internet such as News Real (http://www.news-real.com), Individual, Inc. (http://www.individual.com), and PointCast (http://www.pointcast.com).

For example, an organization could pay a service bureau $500 a month to provide targeted news feeds directly into its intranet, providing on-demand access to specialized information that is available to all employees. Employees no longer need subscriptions to newspapers and magazines, saving money, time, and frustration. They won't have to worry about articles missing from magazines, share subscriptions with coworkers, or deal with highlighted, dovetailed, and tattered paper-based information sources.

There are other content technologies that ensure the success and integration of the Internet within the workplace. For example, filtering technology exists to separate the important news from the trivial, depending on the needs of individual employees or the company as a whole. Organizations can purchase only job-specific information and subsequently route that data to all managers and employees who have a need for it. Whatever avenue you adopt, information can be tailored to provide a solution that matches your needs as closely as possible.

News feeds can provide not only outside information but also important inside information. For example, national sales figures can be made instantly and continuously available to employees—whether your organization is a $500,000-a-year start-up or a $5 billion giant. With this technology, people can see up-to-the-minute sales figures for the entire company or specific regions and departments, as well as all the other internal information that has traditionally allowed big companies to make both tactical and strategic decisions on corporate structure, budgeting, marketing, and so on. Large organizations have always been able to make these decisions with varying levels of success, but now the smaller companies are also able to leverage this information and can compete more effectively in the global marketplace.

Businesses that sell information are inevitably looking to acquire or build useful global information that is also time-valued. In today's global marketplace, information is often worthless if it doesn't reach key players in a timely, efficient fashion. As more businesses sell information, they have to turn it around faster to stay competitive, placing a burden on both technology and personnel.

An excellent example of time-valued information is a global wire service like Associated Press (AP). For example, an AP correspondent in Hong Kong speaks Chinese and English. When she covers Chinese officials giving press conferences in Hong Kong, she translates it in real time into a cellular phone, while the person on the other line types it in and puts it immediately onto the wire service. She wastes time taking notes, writing them up, faxing them to the company, and so on. It is the succinctness with which businesses can maximize their productivity that will separate the winners from the losers in the information arena.

Continuing with the wire service example, you'll often find that the people who subscribe to the AP wire need to have this information ASAP. Commodity and stock traders, for example, want the news right away so as to make trades based on this information. The extra time it could take to type, translate, and fax the report could make a critical difference. In truth, time becomes the product you are selling. Primary source information is generally available to many people simultaneously. What you are selling is accuracy and time to market, and you can rely on intranet technology to keep you ahead of the competition in many instances.

Instant access to information—such as whether the Federal Reserve has raised the prime rate or the latest consumer confidence reports—levels the playing field between historically dominant companies and smaller, specialty ones. Small organizations can now buy news feeds as easily as big organizations. They no longer need in-house departments to clip or copy news, distribute briefings and updates, or produce newsletters. All this frees up internal resources—from personnel to finances—to work on issues that are more vital to the success of the company.

The Importance of Intranets and Extranets in a Global Marketplace

The rise of intranets and extranets is another sign that the Internet and the World Wide Web are becoming powerful tools for keeping companies competitive on a global scale. This is because the technology of intranets and extranets makes geography far less important than it ever was before. It's just as simple to send an email message or post an event on a calendar for someone in another country as to send it to someone in the cubicle down the hall. This makes it considerably more practical for people to report to managers in different locations, thereby negating concerns that departments be in the same physical location. A traditional floor plan is no longer relevant with intranet technology. Individuals and companies can be connected despite geographic, time zone, or political (immigration) constraints.

The Rise of "Virtual Corporations"

One business trend that intranets and extranets have helped advance is the advent of *virtual corporations*. A virtual corporation is born when several corporations, most often those with different specialties and located in different geographic areas, work together as a single entity to service the needs of particular clients or perhaps support joint research efforts.

Intranet and extranet solutions are enabling virtual corporations to work more closely with one another, be better coordinated, and compete more directly with a single corporation. Virtual corporations can be defined as companies with little or no physical infrastructure that can exist across any geographic distance.

As the international walls of business disappear and trade barriers weaken, domestic companies are shifting their focus from a national agenda to international strategies. Today, companies are looking at international clients and evaluating the products and services they can offer them. This includes everything from writing software in multiple languages to "Westernizing" other cultures with U.S. products—or perhaps even to exporting U.S. marketing savvy abroad. To create successful sales relationships on an international level, however, businesses first must begin to understand the trends that drive culture and business environments in particular countries. Intranets and extranets offer an ideal method for tracking issues worldwide because they can leverage companies' access to information.

Making Virtual Corporations Work

There are three by-products of virtual corporations that have also been enhanced by the successful use of intranets and extranets: hoteling, telecommuting, and out-sourcing.

Hoteling is the strategy by which employees who otherwise conduct their work through the intranet reserve an office, cubicle, or conference room at a company's headquarters when they need space to work or meet colleagues and clients in. For the most part, an intranet eliminates the need for storing paper files in cumbersome file cabinets in an office. Because electronic storage eliminates the need to access files stored in a physical location, it eliminates the need to conduct work near those files.

Similarly, *telecommuting* from home gives people access to all the information stored on the intranet, leveling the playing field between employees working out of the office and those working from home. Intranets will continue to open doors for employee collaboration by allowing all employees to participate fully, regardless of where in the city or world they are.

Whether because of corporate downsizing, the decentralization of government, or the increasing sway of the computer over the workplace, more businesses are turning to *outsourcing*—the hiring of short- or long-term consultants or contractors to accomplish a specific job once handled by a full-time employee. Consultants and contractors may not come cheap, but because they are not employees of the business (meaning the business is not required to give them benefits, such as health insurance and pension plans, and even certain taxes) they often translate into significant savings. Intranets will continue to play a role in outsourcing by offering consultants or contractors a one-stop resource center for background information on the company or project, and thus in turn saving the company the hours it might require an employee to spend discussing information with the consultant. An intranet lets the employee put his or her energies elsewhere, while the consultant gets him or herself up to speed through the company's intranet.

If downsizing isn't in the company's present or future plans, new employees almost certainly are, whether they replace employees who leave or are hired for new positions. In either case, the company with an intranet in place is going to save perhaps thousands of dollars in training costs. For example, if a partner in a company leaves, typically all his or her information and expertise leave too. The information is in his or her head, in his or her files, on handwritten Rolodex cards, and in computer folders, most of which makes sense to no one but the partner.

But when this kind of information is contained entirely within an intranet, the company does not lose large parts of its "institutional memory" whenever valued employees leave or are reassigned. And if such information is also valuable to the company's vendors, suppliers, or strategic partners, then an extranet can act to extend the company's institutional memory beyond its own walls.

Determining Whether You Need an Intranet/Extranet

The key determinant of the value of an intranet or extranet is your organization's information needs. As a very general rule, either of these tools will be the most useful to organizations that have the following characteristics:

- They are geographically dispersed.
- They share common business objectives.
- They have common information needs.
- They value collaboration.

As this very basic list suggests, for an intranet or extranet to be useful it must reflect a central focus—most often a common business or organizational objective that is shared by diverse individuals or groups.

It's important to keep in mind that not every organization needs an intranet or an extranet. A small company operating from a single location may exchange information more than adequately through memos, meetings, or at the water cooler. Such an organization may well use the Internet as a resource for gathering information or intelligence, but it probably doesn't need an intranet's added power and efficiency.

By contrast, a company with multiple sales offices or operating divisions in different locations, or a trade association or not-for-profit group with numerous members or chapters, may benefit significantly from having its own intranet. Organizations such as these constantly strive to balance their managers' need for information that is comprehensive and timely with the challenges stemming from multiple time zones, incompatible computer systems, and erratic local phone service.

As a result of these and other barriers, critical decisions may not benefit from the full collaboration of all the key participants or from comprehensive background information that is equally available to all decision makers. There may be gross inconsistencies between chapters or office locations in terms of their ability to disseminate information to members or staff. Similarly, widely dispersed organizations often experience needless headaches when they relay company data (such as sales figures, financial projections, and so on) to headquarters.

At their most powerful, intranets and extranets help create and further a common vision among an organization's components by empowering the individual. For many organizations, this is in itself a revolutionary concept: achieving collective clout by distributing—not centralizing—power.

Short of this grand democratic vision of intranet usage, there are a number of uses that may be less ambitious but offer significant benefits. For example, geographic dispersion alone may suggest the value of having a central archive of corporate policy materials; a regularly updated analysis of current news or other information; or a system for automatically reporting quarterly financial data, production statistics, or membership lists. Such basic uses as these help save time and aggravation by streamlining routine reporting and assuring ready access to standard information. Although a *wide area network* (WAN) can serve as just such a central depository for files and can even share email, a WAN isn't the same thing as an intranet. A WAN doesn't have anywhere near the full capabilities of an intranet, which, even in a basic design, overshadows a WAN in the ease and efficiency with which it performs a variety of functions.

An Intranet/Extranet Checklist

Intranets are user driven, and their design should reflect users' needs. Therefore, a good way to get started is to identify those needs within your organization that an intranet or extranet can help you meet. This will help you establish realistic goals, as well as a focus for exploring all options.

Structure. Understanding an organization's structure will help you determine the utility of an intranet or extranet utility in general, as well as which of their specific functions may offer the best value.

1. Does the organization have several offices in different locations?

2. Do various staff functions (such as R&D, sales, human resources, law, engineering) reside in more than one location?

3. Is the organization hierarchical? Is it distributed? Is it centralized or decentralized?

Internal communications/information exchange. Understanding how the organization routinely exchanges information will help reveal gaps and barriers that an intranet or extranet can be used to address.

1. What are the primary information sources—inside as well as outside the organization?

2. How is business information usually delivered (by email, special delivery, telephone, meetings, or some other means)?

3. How are decisions usually made?

4. How is research usually conducted and shared?

External communications. Understanding how the organization interacts with its primary constituencies will help suggest opportunities for using the intranet or extranet to better meet their needs.

1. Are there groups outside the organization (such as customers, shareholders, volunteers) with which it routinely interacts?

2. How does the organization keep them informed?

3. What information do they need, want, or expect?

4. How does the organization receive and process information from them?

Barriers. Taking a cold, hard look at the barriers to effective communication in an organization will help you identify organizational weaknesses and assign priorities to the development of an intranet or extranet.

1. What are the primary obstacles to the efficient exchange of information?

2. Are these barriers mechanical, logistical, or cultural?

3. What is the impact of these barriers?

Resources. Evaluating available resources will help you establish a realistic starting point for the design and implementation of an intranet or extranet.

1. What is the organization's current level of computer capability?

2. What resources—staff and contractor—are required to construct and manage the intranet/extranet?

3. What resources—financial, technical, and so on—are currently available?

Setting Realistic Goals

As suggested earlier, the goals of an intranet or an extranet may be modest or ambitious, specific or very broad. Whatever the goals may be, what's important is that they be defined—clearly and in advance. As with any other major initiative, the sponsoring organization should ask itself some very basic questions before developing an intranet or an extranet:

What do we want to accomplish? This is goal setting at its most basic, and it helps establish a target and a focus for developing the intranet/extranet.

Why do we want to accomplish it? In effect, this is the devil's advocate question, forcing the organization to consider the intranet/extranet in the context of its overall business strategy. (Hint: "Because the other guy is doing it" is not an acceptable answer.)

How do we expect to accomplish it? This question helps establish a framework for project planning, including leadership assignments, technical specifications, resource requirements, a timetable, and staffing patterns.

What will it cost? A true picture of costs should include estimates of both short-term outlay and expected savings over time.

How will we monitor progress? Intranets and extranets tend to evolve over time, and it is essential to build in mechanisms for determining one's progress against one's expectations.

How will we determine success? As with any other initiative, the effectiveness of intranet or extranet is ultimately determined by making a cost/benefit analysis.

At a more specific level, sponsoring organizations of intranets or extranets also need to define the following criteria:

Who are the intended users? The universe of potential users can be as broad or as narrow as the organization requires. It may be defined as "every company employee," for example, or "all department heads." The user universe can also be defined along unconventional lines, such as "the mayors of all of our plant communities" in, for example, a project to create new alliances.

How do we expect our target audience to use the intranet or extranet? Users' interaction with the intranet or extranet will vary considerably, depending on the site's functions and the users' needs. For each user group, the organization should define a specific utility and benefit to help assure that a site is designed that meets the needs and expectations of each group. For example, middle managers may find the greatest advantage in a cross-platform messaging function, while sales reps may find the most use in a central archive.

What does the audience need in order to use it? Having defined who will use the intranet/extranet and for what purposes, the next step is to assess what's already in place in terms of computer capacity, connectivity, and resident expertise. In some cases, for example, a given user group may require extensive basic training, while for others all that's needed is connectivity and a simple user manual.

Expectations for the Future

Given the ease and relative low cost involved in building a successful intranet or extranet, the growth expectations for both of these tools are significant in both domestic and international markets.

Growth

The growth of intranets and extranets is directly related to the information explosion. As information and technology become more accessible, we will begin to see them infiltrate every sector of our lives.

For example, a power company needs to be more responsive to customers but it only has so many trucks. In the past, the company would have had to buy more trucks and hire more drivers. Now, using computer chips and an intranet, the company can instead improve the management of its current fleet of service vehicles. Computer advances in general—and intranet technology specifically—have made it easier to track this data and provide them to the appropriate employees who can deal with them in an appropriate fashion.

Intranets and extranets offer a new and revolutionary way of communicating—both as a distribution channel and an information source. The most profound characteristic of these tools is that they can provide everyone in an organization with equal access to information. They can also provide a soapbox from which disgruntled, enthusiastic, or otherwise motivated people can convey thoughts, ideas, and feelings. For organizations to take complete advantage of the new lines of communication made available by intranets and extranets, they must make a conscious effort to establish an environment in which an intranet or extranet will flourish. Although this is certainly not a simple task for any company, it is a necessity that must be undertaken if an organization truly wants to maximize the possibilities of communication.

Essentially, organizations must flatten their hierarchies, which is the 1990s version of "Empower the workers." The power of intranets is that they give every employee easy access to up-to-date information. Such access dramatically increases the pool of employees who have the information on which to base intelligent decisions. By flattening their hierarchies and giving employees the authority and support they need to make decisions on their own, organizations will cut response times, streamline decision-making, and thereby realize time and cost savings.

The important thing to remember is that a corporation's front line of employees is usually positioned best to efficiently manage its resources, resolve its problems, and advance its projects. By supporting employees with intranet-based information resources that are constantly available and consistently accurate, corporations will be able to service both corporate and client needs quickly, accurately, and successfully.

Impact

No two intranets or extranets are ever the same. Each has its own unique set of problems to solve and issues to address. However, all share the following common determinants of success:

- Vision
- Specific goals
- Realistic expectations
- A disciplined approach
- User involvement
- Follow-through

Just as technological and business trends will affect the future of intranets and extranets, so both of these tools will have a major impact on these trends. The immense synergy between business and technological trends and intranets/extranets will continue to serve as a launching pad for new ideas and technological advances, all in the name of more productive businesses and workers.

Intranets and extranets will allow businesses to change their concept of how business happens. Already, companies are accomplishing more just by using a Web browser, and the scales continue to tip toward smaller, cheaper, faster technology and technological devices.

Intranets and extranets offer tremendous potential for organizations that understand their potential and apply discipline and resources to achieving it. This potential is best met by defining goals clearly in advance and creating the support of a collaborative foundation. Encouraging collaboration and involvement on the part of all users from the beginning will help to avoid the creation of an intranet or extranet that only a select few employees understand.

In the relatively near future, users may be walking around with their computers in their pockets. Whatever the size and shape of the next wave of computers, those workers who have unleashed the power of intranets and extranets will be ready to service their clients and step up to the competition, no matter where in the world they are.

GLOBAL INTERNET MARKETS SURVEY: STATISTICAL DATA

9

key issue in international trade is *market access*—how easy or difficult is it to introduce your offering in a particular market. Some countries are easily accessible. They are open to imports and relatively free of taxes, duties, quotas, currency controls, and other barriers to trade. Other countries are tough to access and limit imports through high tariffs, onerous regulations, and restrictions on foreign products and businesspeople.

Market access is also an issue on the Internet. Although hundreds of countries around the world are already online and expanding their Net presence, the quantity and quality of electronic connections vary widely by global region, by country, and even within countries.

You have undoubtedly heard the term open door-policy used when referring to trade. The same door metaphor can be used to describe the digital market access of countries around the world—that is, how easy or difficult it is to reach and conduct business in a particular market online. Some countries are wide open and highly accessible on the Net. Millions of servers provide unfettered and constant access to tens of millions of individuals and companies online. In these markets, doing business over the Internet is relatively easy and reliable. Other countries are partially open. Here, Net connections are still significant, although far fewer in number on a per capita basis compared to the wide-open countries, and the acceptance and use of the Internet by the general population has been slower. In these markets, doing business over the Internet is viable, but many companies and individuals may be still offline. Another group of countries can be described as ajar. Like a door that's ajar, only a tiny sliver of these markets may be accessed over the Net at this time. In these locales, the connections are few in number, access may be blocked, and content may be restricted. Communicating online, while possible, is difficult and unreliable. Some countries are closed. They lack even the most basic telecommunications infrastructure and have only a tiny number of sporadic Internet connections, if any, to a minuscule audience. Doing business with these countries over the Net is virtually impossible at this time.

Like any door, the position of a country's Net door and the degree of digital market access it enjoys are not static. The door may be opened wider or closed tighter depending on, among other things, changes in government policy, upgrades to telecommunications infrastructure, and the availability of online access to the general population. A country that is ajar on the Internet one month may be wide open the next, and one that is partially open one day may be closed the day after given the appropriate political decisions and technological investments, or lack thereof.

This chapter measures the digital market access of six regions and 233 countries around the world using data produced by Network Wizards, a Menlo Park, California, computer and communications firm at http://www.nw.com. Twice a year, Network Wizards counts the numbers of hosts on the Net. Hosts are servers—computer systems that have a distinct IP (Internet Protocol) address. The systems are connected to the Internet either full- or part-time using direct or dial-up connections. Each host or computer system may contain one Web site or potentially thousands of different Web sites, depending on the power and capacity of the machine. Along with counting the number of hosts, Network Wizards also gathers information on the domain of the hosts. Similar to a passport or a birth certificate, the domain indicates the nationality of the host and identifies where the host is located.

Like any survey or census, the data collected is not perfect. In some cases, the domain of the host may not match where it's actually located. A computer with a Swiss domain, for example, may really be located in the United States. Certain domains—such as .com, .edu, .int, .net, and .org,—are generic and may be located anywhere. Some hosts may be missed by the survey and not included in the total. Whatever the limitations, tracing the precise number and location of hosts is impossible at this time, and Net Wizards' data is the best available.

For global traders, understanding this data is key to selecting markets, setting priorities, and managing expectations when doing international business on the Internet. Although only a snapshot in time and undoubtedly subject to change, this intelligence is like a reconnaissance satellite photo that reveals the current positions and movements of the nations of the world on the cyber-battlefield. It can help global businesspeople map out their digital strategies and tactics when pursuing international customers and deals online.

This chapter defines the key survey terms, highlights the major global trends, reports on leading regional developments, profiles the top twenty Internet markets, and identifies ten markets to watch.

Finding Your Way around the Survey

The following explain the methodology and key definitions of the survey:

Data. The data are estimates for July 1997 based on the Network Wizards Domain Survey at http://www.nw.com/zone/WWW/top.html. In the Network Wizards survey, five domains—.com, .edu, .int, .net, and .org—are generic and not assigned a nationality. For the purposes of this survey, these domains were assigned a nationality based on Internet usage reports and market surveys by Jupiter Communications and NUA Internet Surveys. The data can be found in Appendix A "Global Internet Markets Survey: Regional and Country Rankings."

Regional Rank. The rank of the country in its global region is based on number of Internet hosts the country has. Countries are ranked highest to lowest. If a country has no Internet hosts, rank is based on population.

Regions/Countries. The names of global regions and countries. The survey covers six global regions and 233 countries.

Global Rank. The rank of the country among the 233 surveyed based on the number of hosts: 1 is highest, 233 lowest. If a country has no Internet hosts, the rank is based on population.

1997 Population. Estimated 1997 population of the global regions and countries. Sources are the U.S. Bureau of the Census and Central Intelligence Agency.

Share of Global Population. The regional and country population divided by the total world population.

Share of Regional Population. The country population divided by the total regional population.

1997 Number of Hosts. For each region and country, the number of hosts as of July 1997. "Hosts" refers to servers—computer systems that have a distinct IP (Internet Protocol) address.

Share of Global Hosts. Number of regional and country hosts divided by total world hosts.

Share of Regional Hosts. Number of country hosts divided by total regional hosts.

1995–1997 Host Growth. Average annual growth rate in the number of hosts from July 1995 to July 1997. The asterisk symbol—*—indicates that a growth rate was not calculable for that country because the number of hosts for 1995 and/or 1997 was zero.

1996–1997 Net Change in Hosts. Number of hosts in July 1997 minus the number of hosts in 1996.

Hosts Per 100,000 Population. Number of hosts divided by population multiplied by one hundred thousand.

Digital Market Access. Each country is divided into one of four categories of Internet market access based on hosts per one hundred thousand population and the general quantity or quality of its Internet infrastructure and content.

- **Wide open.** Three thousand or more hosts per one hundred thousand population and a generally high quantity and quality of Internet connections and content.

- **Partially open.** Between five hundred and three thousand hosts per one hundred thousand population and Internet connections and content that are generally moderate in quantity and quality.

- **Ajar.** Between 0.01 and 500 hosts per one hundred thousand population and Internet connections and content that are generally low in quantity and quality.

- **Closed.** No recorded Internet hosts at this time and negligible or no Internet infrastructure and content.

Other notes. The figures for Bosnia and Herzegovina include Yugoslavia. Indonesia includes East Timor. Figures for the United Kingdom are the total of Great Britain and other U.K. domains. Figures for Russia are total number of domains for the Russian Federation and the former Soviet Union.

Global Survey Highlights

The following list summarizes the key global trends online:

The Net is growing exponentially. As of July 1997, a total of 19.5 million hosts were connected to the Internet around the world. This was nearly triple the number—6.6 million—connected to the Internet two years earlier, in July 1995, and over ten times the number—1.8 million—that were online four years earlier in July 1993.

A new host is added to the Net every five seconds. Between July 1995 and July 1997, some 12.9 million new hosts were added to the Net. On average, new hosts are added at a rate of 17,670 per day, 736 per hour, 12 per minute, and 1 every five seconds.

Countries around the world are pouring online. In 1995, 103 countries had at least one Internet host. By 1997, 194 countries had at least one host, an increase of 93 percent.

The Net is highly concentrated. While many countries are online, the vast majority of hosts are clustered in relatively few nations. Of the 19.5 million hosts, 18.6 million, or 95 percent, are concentrated in twenty countries. These are the United States, Japan, Germany, the United Kingdom, Canada, Australia, the Netherlands, Finland, France, Sweden, Italy, Norway, New Zealand, South Korea, Denmark, Switzerland, Spain, Russia, South Africa, and Austria.

Wide-open markets are all over the world. While the Internet is concentrated in relatively few countries, the "wide-open" markets—the nations with the most developed cyber-infrastructure and content—are spread all over the world. In Western Europe, these include Denmark, Finland, and Sweden. In the Asia-Pacific region they are Australia and New Zealand. In North America, they are Canada and the United States.

The Net is overwhelmingly English speaking. Of the 19.5 million hosts, 12.4 million, or nearly two-thirds, are based in five English-speaking countries. These are the United States, the United Kingdom, Canada, Australia, and New Zealand.

The United States is the undisputed champion of cyberspace. The United States accounts for 9.4 million, or 48 percent, of the Internet hosts. This is over five times the number of second-place Japan, with 1.8 million hosts and 9 percent of the total.

The majority of Net hosts are now outside the United States. While the United States continues to dominate cyberspace, its share of total Net sites has fallen in recent years. In 1995, the United States accounted for 53 percent of all Internet sites. By 1997, its share had dropped to 48 percent. This reflects the growing development of the Net in other parts of the world.

Scandinavian countries are tops in number of hosts per capita.
Four of the top nine countries ranked by hosts per one hundred thousand population are Scandinavian, namely, Finland, Norway, Sweden, and Denmark. The highest was Finland with 7,455 hosts per one hundred thousand population, over twenty-two times the world average and more than double the seventh-ranked United States.

South America, Eastern Europe, the Middle East, and Africa are tiny islands in cyberspace. Combined, the regions of South America, Eastern Europe, the Middle East, and Africa account for 54 percent of the world's population but less than 4 percent of the total number of Internet hosts.

Numerous large countries have no Net access. As of July 1997, many sizable countries had no Net hosts. These include Bangladesh, Ethiopia, North Korea, Afghanistan, and Iraq, all of which have populations over twenty million. All no-host countries and areas combined total 346 million people, or about 6 percent of the world's population.

Regional Trends

While the Internet is a global phenomenon, the nature, extent, and quality of cyber infrastructure and connections varies widely around the world. Like runners in a vast electronic race, the different regions of the world—North America, Latin America, Western Europe, Eastern Europe, Middle East and Africa, and Asia Pacific—are moving online at different speeds and at their own pace.

North America

North America leads the pack and is sprinting at full speed. Key considerations include the following:

North America has the smallest population and the most hosts.
Among global regions, North America—Canada and the United States, specifically—has the smallest share of the population, 5 percent, but the largest share of Internet hosts, 53 percent.

The United States dominates. The United States dominates the North American region both in population and hosts. Compared to Canada, the United States has nine times the population and over ten times the number of hosts.

Host growth is below world average. Between 1995 and 1997, host growth in the region averaged 64 percent annually, below the global average of 72 percent per year. Canada had a slightly higher growth rate, 66 percent, compared to the U.S. rate, 64 percent.

Tops in hosts per capita. The region averages 3,464 hosts per one hundred thousand population, the highest among global regions and more than ten times the global average. The United States had 12 percent more hosts per one hundred thousand population, 3,500, compared to Canada's 3,130.

United States

The United States alone has 9.4 million hosts. These are divided into seven segments:

Commercial **hosts account for the largest share of U.S. total.** Among U.S. hosts, the largest segment is commercial or business. Of the 9.4 million U.S. hosts, 2.9 million, or one out of three, are used by companies and businesspeople for commercial purposes. Between 1995 and 1997, hosts in this category grew 61 percent, slightly below the U.S. average.

Educational **hosts are losing share.** Hosts used by educational institutions, such as universities, accounted for 31 percent of the U.S. total in 1997, down from 40 percent in 1995. Educational hosts grew at a 44 percent annual clip, below the U.S. average and second lowest among U.S. segments.

Network **hosts are gaining share.** Network hosts—infrastructure servers such as routers and gateways that link networks and direct messages on the Net—accounted for 15 percent of the U.S. total in 1997, up sharply from a 6 percent share in 1995. Network hosts grew 168 percent a year on average, over twice the U.S. average and second highest among U.S. segments.

The military **has over a half-million hosts**. Hosts used by the U.S. military accounted for 6 percent of the U.S. total in 1997, equal to its 1995 share. The segment grew 55 percent on average, slightly below the U.S. average. If the U.S. military were treated as a separate country, the segment would rank seventh in the world based on number of hosts. The American military uses about 540,000 servers, more than many countries as a whole, such as the Netherlands, Finland, France, Sweden, and Italy.

The number of *government* **hosts lags.** Hosts used by the U.S. government accounted for roughly 5 percent of the U.S. total in 1997, down from 8 percent in 1995. Government hosts grew 24 percent between 1995 and 1997, nearly one-third the U.S. average and the lowest rate among all segments.

Organization **hosts dip.** Hosts used by organizations—mostly nonprofit organizations—composed the smallest share, 3 percent, of the U.S. total in 1997, a slight drop from its 4 percent share in 1995. Organization servers increased 47 percent, below the U.S. average and third lowest among all segments.

Other hosts **are the fastest-growing segment.** The "other" segment refers to a grabbag of commercial, educational, network, and international hosts based in the United States. Data limitations do not allow them to be assigned to more specific segments. This category composed 9 percent of the U.S. total in 1997, triple its 3 percent share in 1995. Servers in this category increased 169 percent between 1995 and 1997, the highest rate among U.S. segments.

Latin America

After crawling off the Internet starting line, Latin America is gradually picking up speed. Major trends include the following:

Latin America has the fewest hosts. Latin America has 174,000 hosts, less than 1 percent of the global total and the smallest share among global regions. By comparison, the region has 8 percent of the global population, third highest among world regions.

Growth was nearly double the world average. Between 1995 and 1997, host growth in the region averaged 120 percent, above the world average and nearly double the U.S. rate. Among countries with a population over one million, Peru had the highest growth rate, 321 percent, followed by Nicaragua at 255 percent.

Hosts per capita are one-tenth the world average. The high growth rate generally reflects the infant state of the Net in Latin America. The region averages thirty-five hosts per one hundred thousand population, the second lowest among global regions and nearly one-tenth the world average. Latin countries with especially low host-per-capita rates are Puerto Rico, Cuba, and the Dominican Republic—countries with populations between four and ten million. All have less than three hosts per one hundred thousand population, 1 percent of the global average.

Nearly half of Latin countries are new to the Net. Of the forty-seven Latin countries surveyed, twenty-four, or 51 percent, are newcomers to cyberspace. These countries have ventured online and set up their first servers only within the two-year period July 1995 to July 1997.

Four countries account for 82 percent of servers. Four countries—Brazil, Mexico, Chile, and Argentina—account for 82 percent of the hosts in the region. Combined, the countries account for 62 percent of the population.

Brazil was first in host total and growth. Brazil led the region with 40 percent of the hosts and 33 percent of the population. Between 1995 and 1997, host growth in the country averaged 144 percent per year, highest among the top four countries.

Chile was tops in number of hosts per capita. Among the leading four Latin countries, Chile has the highest number of hosts per one hundred thousand population, 132, nearly triple that of Argentina, the second highest at 54. Chile also has a large share of the Net relative to its population. With less than 3 percent of the regional population, the country has 11 percent of the hosts.

Colombia lagging. Colombia has a low share of the Net relative to its share of population. With 8 percent of the regional population, the country has only 4 percent of the regional hosts. The South American nation also lags in servers per capita. Colombia has 18.5 hosts per one hundred thousand population, nearly half the Latin American average and lowest among countries in the region with twenty million or more in population.

Western Europe

Western Europe has maintained a steady but conservative pace on the cybertrack. Progress to date includes the following:

Western Europe has the second-highest share of hosts. Western Europe has 5.3 million hosts, about one-quarter the world total and the second-highest share among global regions. By comparison, the region has 7 percent of the global population, second lowest among world regions.

Growth is below world average. Between 1995 and 1997, host growth in the region averaged 70 percent, below the world average of 72 percent but above the U.S. rate of 64 percent.

Growth spurts in selected countries. While the region as a whole lagged the world average, a few countries showed strong growth rates in recent years. These included Italy, 103 percent; Denmark, 90 percent; Belgium, 91 percent; Greece, 88 percent; and Ireland, 82 percent.

Hosts per capita are four times the world average. Western Europe averaged 1,358 hosts per one hundred thousand population, four times the world average but about one-third of the United States.

Hosts per capita vary widely between the north and south. Within the region, host-per-capita rates differ widely between countries in northern and southern Europe. Host-per-capita rates in the northern Scandinavian countries—Finland, Sweden, Norway, Denmark, and Iceland—are at least double the regional average. Host-per-capita rates in the southern Mediterranean countries—France, Italy, Spain, Greece, and Portugal—are, at most, half the regional average.

Six countries account for 77 percent of the hosts. Combined, Germany, the United Kingdom, the Netherlands, Finland, France, and Sweden account for 77 percent of hosts in the region and 60 percent of the population.

Germany leads the regional pack. With 22 percent of the population, Germany has 29 percent of the servers, the largest share in the region.

Finland is tops in hosts per capita. Finland has the highest number of hosts per one hundred thousand population, 7,455, the most of any country in the world and more than five times the regional average. Finland also has a large share of the Net relative to its share of the regional population. With about five million people or 1 percent of the regional population, the country has 7 percent of the hosts.

France, Italy, and Spain are lagging. France, Italy, and Spain have a low share of the Net relative to their populations. France has 7 percent of regional hosts and 15 percent of the population. Italy has 5 percent of the hosts and 15 percent of the population. Spain has 3 percent of the hosts and 10 percent of the population. The number of hosts per one hundred thousand population in these countries is at least half the regional average and about one-fifth that of the United States.

Eastern Europe

Although slow off the starting blocks, Eastern Europe is gaining cyber momentum. Key facts include the following:

Eastern Europe is a small Net player. The region has some 323,000 hosts, less than 2 percent of the world total and the third-lowest share among global regions. By comparison, the region has 7 percent of the global population.

Growth is nearly double the world average. Between 1995 and 1997, host growth in Eastern Europe averaged 120 percent. This was above the world average of 72 percent and nearly double the U.S. rate. Countries with especially high growth rates included Kazakhstan, 916 percent; Belarus, 850 percent; Macedonia, 826 percent; and Azerbaijan, 800 percent, all of which have populations between two million and seventeen million.

Hosts per capita are one-quarter of the world average. Eastern Europe averaged seventy-nine hosts per one hundred thousand population, one-quarter of the world average although more than double the Latin American average.

Four countries account for 76 percent of hosts. Combined, four countries—Russia, the Czech Republic, Poland, and Hungary—account for 76 percent of hosts in the region and 50 percent of the population.

Russia is the host and growth leader. Russia leads the region with 37 percent of the hosts and 36 percent of the population. Compared to the other top four Eastern European countries, Russia had the highest growth rate, 227 percent, but the lowest number of hosts per one hundred thousand population, 81.

The Czech Republic, Hungary, and Slovenia are bright spots. The Czech Republic, Hungary, and Slovenia each have a high share of the Net relative to their populations. The Czech Republic has 3 percent of the regional population and 15 percent of the regional hosts. Hungary has 2 percent of the population and 10 percent of the servers. Slovenia has less than 0.5 percent of the population and 5 percent of the hosts. In all three countries, hosts per one hundred thousand population are above the world average and more than four times the regional average.

Ukraine, Romania, Kazakhstan, and Uzbekistan are underperforming. Relative to their share of regional populations, a number of former Soviet republics are lagging in their share of the Net. The Ukraine has 12 percent of the regional population and 3 percent of the hosts. Romania has 5 percent of the population and less than 2 percent of the hosts. Kazakhstan has 16.8 million people or 4 percent of the population and only 1,136 hosts or 0.4 percent of the regional total. Uzbekistan has 24 million people or 6 percent of the population and only 153 servers.

Serbia and Tajikistan not online. Two major countries in the region are not connected to the Net. Serbia, with a population of ten million, and Tajikistan, with a population of six million, had no hosts as of July 1997. Turkmenistan—a country of four million people—had only two hosts.

The Middle East and Africa

Although further behind in the cyberpack, the Middle East and Africa has rebounded from a dismal start, and is picking up the pace. A quick overview includes the following:

The Middle East and Africa has many people and few hosts. The Middle East and Africa are home to 2.3 billion people, 38 percent of the global total and the largest share among world regions. By comparison, the region has 225,000 hosts, just 1 percent of the world total.

Growth is above the world average. Between 1995 and 1997, host growth in the region averaged 87 percent, *above the world average of 72 percent*. Countries with especially high growth rates included Lebanon, 3,259 percent; Kenya, 2,038 percent; and the United Arab Emirates, 1,246 percent.

Hosts per capita is the lowest among world regions. The Middle East and Africa averaged ten hosts per one hundred thousand population, the lowest among global regions and just 3 percent of the world average.

Three countries account for 90 percent of hosts. With a combined population of 112 million, or 5 percent of the regional total, the countries of South Africa, Israel, and Turkey accounted for 90 percent of the hosts in the region.

South Africa alone has more than half the hosts. With less than 1 percent of the regional population, South Africa has some 117,000 hosts, 52 percent of the regional total.

Israel is number one in hosts per capita. Israel has 1,105 hosts per one hundred thousand population, tops among countries in the region. This is more than three times the world average and 110 times the regional average. Israel also has a high share of the Net relative to its population. The country has 0.2 percent of the regional population and 27 percent of the hosts.

Turkey is the growth leader. Among the top three countries in the region, Turkey had the highest growth rate, 187 percent, more than double the regional average.

Kuwait, Cyprus, and Bahrain are cyber-beachheads. Three other countries—Kuwait, Cyprus, and Bahrain—are also regional standouts. All are relatively small nations with populations of less than two million each, but the number of hosts per one hundred thousand population in each is at least fifteen times the regional average.

India, Egypt, and Pakistan are underperforming. Relative to their share of regional populations, a number of countries are lagging in their share of the Net. India has 967 million people or 43 percent of the regional population and 2 percent of the hosts. Pakistan has 6 percent of the regional population and 0.5 percent of the regional hosts. Egypt has 3 percent of the population and just 0.8 percent of the hosts.

Twenty-two countries are not online. A total of twenty-two countries in the region have no hosts. The countries have a combined population of 292 million, 13 percent of the regional total, and include Bangladesh, Ethiopia, Afghanistan, Iraq, and Syria. Other countries have only a handful of hosts. Nigeria has 107 million people and six hosts. Iran has 68 million and one host. Zaire has 47 million and eight hosts. Sudan has 32 million and two hosts.

Asia Pacific

Following a timid start, the Asia Pacific is tearing up the track, and poised to challenge Western Europe for number two position in the global cyber race. A brief synopsis includes the following:

The Asia-Pacific region has the third-highest share of hosts. The region has 3.3 million hosts, 17 percent of the world total, and the third-highest share among global regions. By comparison, Asia Pacific has two billion people, 34 percent of the world total.

Growth is above the world average. Between 1995 and 1997, host growth in the Asia Pacific region averaged 100 percent, third highest among global regions. Countries with particularly high growth rates included Malaysia, 511 percent; China, 400 percent; Indonesia, 258 percent; and the Philippines, 244 percent.

Hosts per capita are half the global average. The region overall has 162 hosts per one hundred thousand population, half the global average and just 5 percent that of the United States.

Four countries account for 92 percent of hosts. Combined, four countries—Japan, Australia, New Zealand, and South Korea—account for 92 percent of hosts in the region and 10 percent of the population.

Japan has more than half the hosts in region. With 6 percent of the regional population, Japan has 1.8 million hosts or 55 percent of the regional total. Japan has 1,415 hosts per capita, over eight times the regional average, but half that of the United States.

New Zealand and Australia are tops in hosts per capita. By far the highest number of hosts per one hundred thousand population in the region were in New Zealand, 5,183, and Australia, 4,585. Both countries were at least twenty-eight times the regional average and above that of the United States.

South Korea is the growth leader. Among the top four Asia-Pacific countries, South Korea had the highest growth rate, 119 percent, between 1995 and 1997.

Singapore is a hot spot. An island nation of 3.5 million people, Singapore is relatively small in population and physical size but a regional hot spot on the Internet. Singapore has 1,753 hosts per one hundred thousand population, behind only New Zealand and Australia as the most wired country in the region. Singapore also has a 172 percent host growth rate, higher than Japan's 106 percent rate and over double the U.S. pace.

Hong Kong is among the host-per-capita leaders. Hong Kong has 1,080 hosts per capita, over triple the global average, and among the top five countries in the Asia-Pacific region ranked by host per one hundred thousand population.

China, Indonesia, the Philippines, and Thailand are lagging. Relative to their share of regional populations, a number of major countries in the Asia-Pacific region lag in their share of the Net. With 1.2 billion people, China has 61 percent of the regional population but only 0.8 percent of the hosts. Indonesia has 10 percent of the regional population and 0.3 percent of the hosts. The Philippines has 4 percent of the regional population and 0.1 percent of the servers. Thailand has 3 percent of the population and 0.4 percent of the hosts. All four countries have twenty-two or fewer hosts per one hundred thousand population, around one-tenth the regional average and one-twentieth the global average.

Nine countries are not online. A total of nine Asia-Pacific countries have no hosts. The countries have a combined population of thirty million, less than 2 percent of the regional total, and include North Korea, Laos, and Fiji. Other countries have only a tiny number of servers. Vietnam has seventy-five million people and only three hosts. Myanmar has forty-seven million people and three hosts. Cambodia has eleven million people and seven hosts.

Top 20 Internet Markets

Although nearly two hundred countries are online around the world, 95 percent of the servers are located in just 20 countries. Ranked by number of hosts, these leading markets are profiled in this section. The numbers in parentheses refer to the rank of the country in that category among 233 countries in the Internet host survey: 1 is highest and 233 lowest. The "1998-2000 Outlook" provides a brief forecast of coming Internet-related developments in an area. "Best trade prospects" refers to the industries in each country that offer the best selling, partnering, and investment opportunities for U.S. and international businesspeople. These are derived from the U.S. Foreign and Commercial Service, Foreign Affairs and International Trade Canada, and Industry Canada.

Number 1: United States

1997 population. 267,954,767 (3).

Number of hosts as of July 1997. 9,379,266 (1).

1995–1997 host growth. 64 percent (84).

Hosts per 100,000 population. 3,500 (7).

Stage of Internet development. Wide open.

1998–2000 outlook. From browsers to Net telephony to Web advertising, the United States will continue to be the global epicenter of all things Internet. With great fanfare, U.S. policymakers will launch a new GATT-like round of world negotiations on electronic commerce. Similar to past trade talks, expect a flurry of fireworks between the main players—the United States, the European Union, and Japan—over content regulation, intellectual property, security, privacy, and taxation issues. America's tariff-free, industry-led vision of the Internet—outlined in the Framework for Global Economic Commerce policy statement—is at odds with the interventionist leanings of the Europeans and the Japanese.

Best trade prospects. Processed foods, biotechnology products, medical supplies, pollution control equipment, hazardous waste disposal, value-added wood products, aircraft and parts, transportation equipment, multimedia, pharmaceuticals, advertising services, education and training services, telecommunications equipment, agricultural machinery and equipment, giftware and crafts, building materials and hardware, furniture products, and machining and casting machinery.

Number 2: Japan

1997 population. 125,716,637 (8).

Number of hosts as of July 1997. 1,778,249 (2).

1995–1997 host growth. 106 percent (51).

Hosts per 100,000 population. 1,415 (18).

Stage of Internet development. Partially open.

1998–2000 outlook. Japan will establish itself as the Internet powerhouse of Asia. Over the next five years, the Japanese Ministry of Industry and Trade alone will spend $5 billion in online, multimedia, and telecommunications services. The initiative, known as the "Fiber to the Home" plan, will connect all Japanese firms, government offices, schools, and homes by the year 2010.

Best trade prospects. Computer software; electronic components; computers and peripherals; telecommunications equipment; pollution control equipment; automotive parts and accessories; household consumer goods; air conditioning and refrigeration equipment; pumps, valves and compressors; light trucks and vans; travel and tourism; medical equipment; building products; apparel; pet foods and supplies; paper and paperboard; laboratory and scientific instruments; marine products; furniture; electrical power systems; and architectural, engineering, and construction services.

Number 3: Germany

1997 population. 84,068,216 (12).

Number of hosts as of July 1997. 1,508,370 (3).

1995–1997 host growth. 65 percent (81).

Hosts per 100,000 population. 1,794 (15).

Stage of Internet development. Partially open.

1998–2000 outlook. In January 1998, the European Union liberalized telecommunications in Germany and across Europe. This will be a boon to Internet service providers (ISPs) across the continent and will trigger an online stampede by German and European firms, which, to date, have lagged in their use of the Internet.

Best trade prospects. Computer software, computer and peripheral equipment, electronic components, franchising, telecommunications, computer services, aerospace, industrial chemicals, drugs and pharmaceuticals, plastics, scientific and laboratory instruments, airport ground support equipment, information services, medical equipment, automobile parts and services, snack foods, lumber products, fats and oils, catfish, wine and beer, citrus juice, pet food and supplies.

Number 4: United Kingdom

1997 population. 58,610,182 (20).

Number of hosts as of July 1997. 1,094,019 (4).

1995–1997 host growth. 74 percent (72).

Hosts per 100,000 population. 1,867 (14).

Stage of Internet development. Partially open.

1998–2000 outlook. While constrained in the past by metered phone services that clock and charge for every minute spent online, U.K. Internet users will benefit from the pan-European telecommunications regulation and will have access to more, better, and lower-priced online services.

Best trade prospects. Aircraft and parts, computer software, medical equipment, drugs and pharmaceuticals, apparel, defense equipment, building products, contaminated land remediation, oil and gas field machinery, hotel and restaurant equipment, sporting goods and recreational equipment, franchising, forest products, turkey meat, seafood, beer, wine, tree nuts, pet foods, and tourism.

Number 5: Canada

1997 population. 29,123,194 (36).

Number of hosts as of July 1997. 911,458 (5).

1995–1997 host growth. 66 percent (80).

Hosts per 100,000 population. 3,130 (8).

Stage of Internet development. Wide open.

1998–2000 outlook. Strategis, the Government of Canada's flagship Web site at http://strategis.ic.gc.ca/engdoc/main.html, will be the gold standard for content development and information architecture on the Web in Canada. Packed with everything from trade statistics to customizable investment reports to business chat—all free—Strategis will draw an increasing amount of Canadian and international traffic and provide a shining example of how governments at all levels the world over can provide services and deliver information online.

Best business prospects. Computer software, computers and peripherals, telecommunications equipment, automotive parts and service equipment, pollution control equipment, travel and tourism services, medical equipment, electronic components, sporting goods and recreational equipment, building products, plastic materials and resins, mining industry equipment, agricultural machinery and equipment, apparel, and materials handling machinery.

Number 6: Australia

1997 population. 18,438,824 (51).

Number of hosts as of July 1997. 845,365 (6).

1995–1997 host growth. 84 percent (62).

Hosts per 100,000 population. 4,585 (5).

Stage of Internet development. Wide open.

1998–2000 outlook. Telecommunication deregulation and network upgrades will make an already booming Internet market in Australia even hotter. Excellent opportunities will emerge in providing Internet access, along with Web-based electronic data interchange and call center services.

Best trade prospects. Computers and peripherals, telecommunications services and equipment, computer software, automotive parts and accessories, security and safety equipment, laboratory and scientific equipment, medical equipment, health care services, defense equipment, construction equipment, aircraft and parts, and food processing and packaging equipment.

Number 7: The Netherlands

1997 population. 15,653,091 (56).

Number of hosts as of July 1997. 395,976 (7).

1995–1997 host growth. 61 percent (87).

Hosts per 100,000 population. 2,530 (12).

Stage of Internet development. Partially open.

1998–2000 outlook. PTT Telecom B.V., until recently the sole telecommunications infrastructure provider in the Netherlands, will face growing competition in the Internet service provider (ISP) market. ENERTEL, a telecommunications consortium, plans to invest one hundred million dollars in a nationwide telephone network. In cooperation with British Telecom, the Netherlands Railways intends to invest almost two billion dollars to construct an information network that will cover the entire country.

Best trade prospects. Computer software, telecommunications equipment, electronic data interchange services, education and training services, electronic components, environmental equipment, building products, car customizing, medical devices, laboratory and scientific equipment, security equipment, sports and leisure wear, electrical equipment, grapefruit, wine, pecans, red meat, and honey.

Number 8: Finland

1997 population. 5,109,148 (107).

Number of hosts as of July 1997. 380,880 (8).

1995–1997 host growth. 74 percent (73).

Hosts per 100,000 population. 7,455 (1).

Stage of Internet development. Wide open.

1998–2000 outlook. Finland will emerge as a key gateway to the Baltic and Russian Internet markets. With high technical standards, a liberal telecommunications market, and extensive connections in Eastern Europe, Finland will become a platform and entry point for Internet firms in the United States and around the world seeking to provide Internet products and services in the Commonwealth of Independent States.

Best trade prospects. Aircraft and parts, electronic components, franchising, computers and peripherals, telecommunications equipment, pollution control equipment, medical equipment, computer software, wine, spirits, microbrewery beer, snack foods, health snacks, nuts, corn chips, convenience foods, frozen juices, and Tex-Mex items.

Number 9: France

1997 population. 58,211,454 (21).

Number of hosts as of July 1997. 345,879 (9).

1995–1997 host growth. 62 percent (85).

Hosts per 100,000 population. 594 (30).

Stage of Internet development. Partially open.

1998–2000 outlook. The French government will aggressively promote the use of the Net for economic competitiveness and general development. Concerned over the slow acceptance of the Internet in France thus far, French prime minister Lionel Jospin recently called for a gradual phasing out of the Minitel system, a local information network, and urged France Telecom to reconsider rates for Internet use.

Best trade prospects. Computer software, industrial chemicals, electronic components, computers and peripherals, security and safety equipment, electrical power systems, lab and scientific equipment, aircraft and parts, films/videos and other recordings, medical equipment, avionics and ground support equipment, pollution control equipment, automobiles and parts, telecommunications equipment, agricultural machinery, employment services, and insurance.

Number 10: Sweden

1997 population. 8,946,193 (83).

Number of hosts as of July 1997. 335,414 (10).

1995–1997 host growth. 65 percent (83).

Hosts per 100,000 population. 3,749 (6).

Stage of Internet development. Wide open.

1998–2000 outlook. Completely deregulated, mature, and demanding, the Swedish Internet market will seek software and services related to Web site authoring, intranet and extranet consulting, security solutions, multimedia design, online shopping systems, and technical support.

Best trade prospects. Electronic components, travel and tourism, computer software, telecommunication services, computers and peripherals, drugs and pharmaceuticals, telecommunications equipment, aircraft and parts, medical equipment, pollution control equipment, sports and leisure products, analytical and scientific instruments, and defense industry equipment.

Number 11: Italy

1997 population. 57,534,088 (22).

Number of hosts as of July 1997. 279,353 (11).

1995–1997 host growth. 103 percent (53).

Hosts per 100,000 population. 486 (32).

Stage of Internet development. Ajar.

1998–2000 outlook. Italy will play catch-up with the rest of the continent in Internet development. By 2002, Telecom Italia plans to invest seven billion dollars to link ten million homes with fiber-optic cables. The project, known as "Project Socrates," will become the backbone for a future nationwide Internet and communications network.

Best trade prospects. Industrial chemicals, computer services, electrical power systems, computers and peripherals, medical equipment, airport and ground support equipment, industrial process controls, aircraft and parts, telecommunications equipment and services, franchising, computer software, pollution control equipment and services, laboratory scientific instruments, and electronic components.

Number 12: Norway

1997 population. 4,404,456 (114).

Number of hosts as of July 1997. 239,089 (12).

1995–1997 host growth. 77 percent (69).

Hosts per 100,000 population. 5,428 (2).

Stage of Internet development. Wide open.

1998–2000 outlook. Norway will further upgrade its already excellent Internet infrastructure and help wire other European markets. In September 1997, Oslo-based Telenor, the Norwegian Telecommunications Administration, introduced a pan-European satellite network in cooperation with EUNet, an Amsterdam-based ISP. The network will improve Internet reliability for users all over Europe.

Best trade prospects. Offshore oil and gas exploration equipment, pipeline equipment and services, telecommunications equipment, defense industry equipment, pollution control equipment, aircraft and parts, airport and ground support equipment, computers and peripherals, computer software, industrial process controls, laboratory scientific instruments, medical equipment, soybeans, wheat, and rice.

Number 13: New Zealand

1997 population. 3,587,275 (122).

Number of hosts as of July 1997. 185,917 (13).

1995–1997 host growth. 87 percent (60).

Hosts per 100,000 population. 5,183 (4).

Stage of Internet development. Wide open.

1998–1990 outlook. New Zealand business will continue to rush online. New Zealanders are typically early adapters, and new technology is quickly accepted both on and off the Net. According to *New Zealand InfoTech Weekly*, the number of New Zealand companies online was over 32,400 in 1996, an increase of 135 percent from 1995.

Best trade prospects. Computers and peripherals, medical equipment, telecommunications equipment, plastic materials and resins, books and periodicals, automotive parts and equipment, soybeans, grapes, and apples.

Number 14: South Korea

1997 population. 45,948,811 (26).

Number of hosts as of July 1997. 168,436 (14).

1995–1997 host growth. 119 percent (48).

Hosts per 100,000 population. 367 (37).

Stage of Internet development. Ajar.

1998–2000 outlook. South Korea will be one of the fastest-growing Internet and telecommunications markets in the world. Economic restructuring and telecommunications deregulation will create a wealth of opportunities for ISPs and suppliers of communications equipment and systems.

Best trade prospects. Electrical power systems, transportation services, aircraft and parts, construction and engineering services, computers and peripherals, telecommunications equipment, security and safety equipment, medical equipment, household consumer goods, pollution control equipment, computer software, drugs and pharmaceuticals, building products, education and training services, telecommunication services, beef, pork, poultry meat, cheese, citrus fruit, processed fruits, seafood, and ice cream.

Number 15: Denmark

1997 population. 5,268,775 (104).

Number of hosts as of July 1997. 161,368 (15).

1995–1997 host growth. 90 percent (58).

Hosts per 100,000 population. 3,063 (9).

Stage of Internet development. Wide open.

1998–2000 outlook. Telecommunications deregulation will permit the establishment of new privately owned, local, and nationwide telephone companies and ISPs. Growing wireless services will spur demand for satellite communications equipment.

Best trade prospects. Computer software, computers and peripherals, construction and engineering services, pollution control equipment, electrical power systems, oil and gas field machinery, medical equipment, telecommunications equipment, automotive parts and service equipment, plywood, hardwood for furniture and floor manufacturing, and wine.

Number 16: Switzerland

1997 population. 7,248,984 (91).

Number of hosts as of July 1997. 148,028 (16).

1995–1997 host growth. 52 percent (89).

Hosts per 100,000 population. 2,042 (13).

Stage of Internet development. Partially open.

1998–2000 outlook. Switzerland will upgrade its Internet infrastructure. The country will modernize its public networks in integrated services and digital networks, broadband communications, and mobile systems. The Swiss Federal Railroads will continue to upgrade its own fiber-optic digital networks, and the Swiss Military Department is also expected to invest in radio systems.

Best trade prospects. Computer software, computers and peripherals, telecommunications services, telecommunications equipment, aircraft and parts, medical equipment, pollution control equipment, laboratory and scientific instruments, analytic process control instruments, industrial process controls, renewable energy equipment, electronic components, security and safety equipment, sporting goods and recreational equipment, industrial chemicals, drugs and pharmaceuticals, and automotive parts and service equipment.

Number 17: Spain

1997 population. 39,244,195 (28).

Number of hosts as of July 1997. 121,823 (17).

1995–1997 host growth. 75 percent (71).

Hosts per 100,000 population. 310 (40).

Stage of Internet development. Ajar.

1998–2000 outlook. The dominance of Telefonica, a state-owned telecommunications operation, will be slowly eroded by several alternative ISPs. This will mean new opportunities to supply Internet-related hardware and support services to Spanish business.

Best trade prospects. Pollution control and water resources equipment, franchising, computers and peripherals, aircraft and parts, telecommunications services, electric power systems, medical equipment, building products, architectural and engineering services, telecommunications equipment, organic chemicals for the pharmaceutical industry, industrial controls, and textiles and apparel.

Number 18: Russia

1997 population. 147,987,101 (6).

Number of hosts as of July 1997. 119,467 (18).

1995–1997 host growth. 227 percent (28).

Hosts per 100,000 population. 81 (61).

Stage of Internet development. Ajar.

1998–2000 outlook. Hampered by a lack of installed lines, outdated switching equipment, and inadequate revenues to finance investment, the Russian Ministry of Communications will seek new joint ventures and financial partnerships with multinationals to upgrade the country's Internet infrastructure.

Best trade prospects. Chemicals, telecommunications equipment, medical equipment, pharmaceuticals, paper products, food processing equipment, clothing, construction materials, automobiles and light trucks, furniture, construction equipment, oil and gas equipment, mining, cosmetics, wine and beer, red meats, poultry products, and apples.

Number 19: South Africa

1997 population. 42,465,030 (27).

Number of hosts as of July 1997. 117,475 (19).

1995–1997 host growth. 69 percent (78).

Hosts per 100,000 population. 277 (41).

Stage of Internet development. Ajar.

1998–2000 outlook. Telecommunications deregulation will encourage more competition and further boost the already dramatic growth of the Internet. In October 1997, the South Africa Telecommunications Regulatory Authority ruled that Telkom, the main telecommunications provider, cannot have exclusive rights to Internet connections in South Africa. According to an October 1997 survey, some six hundred thousand users are already online in South Africa, and the customer base is growing 10 percent a month.

Best trade prospects. Airport and ground support equipment, telecommunications equipment, health care, petrochemicals, safety and security products, franchising, computer software, computers, educational books, apparel, pharmaceutical products, and packaging machinery.

Number 20: Austria

1997 population. 8,054,078 (86).

Number of hosts as of July 1997. 87,408 (20).

1995–1997 host growth. 47 percent (90).

Hosts per 100,000 population. 1,085 (20).

Stage of Internet development. Partially open.

1998–2000 outlook. Gradual liberalization of the Austrian telecommunications market will change the structure of the ISP market. As competition intensifies, innovation will become more important, and equipment and access prices will drop.

Best trade prospects. Computer and peripherals, computer software, pharmaceuticals, electronic components, aircraft and parts, medical equipment, industrial chemicals, telecommunications, travel and tourism, pollution control, and cotton.

Ten Markets to Watch

Although off to a slow start on the Web, a number of countries—all from the Asia-Pacific region, the Middle East, or Latin America—are poised to explode online.

Number 1: China

1997 population. 1,221,591,778 (1).

Number of hosts as of July 1997. 25,594 (33).

1995–1997 host growth. 400 percent (16).

Hosts per 100,000 population. 2.1 (140).

Stage of Internet development. Ajar.

1998–2000 outlook. Although Internet access is currently controlled—all packets go through government-controlled gateways, and access is limited to academics—the Chinese government will closely monitor developments in electronic commerce and possibly develop a number of Web-based pilot projects with selected multinationals in China.

Best trade prospects. Aircraft and parts, electric power systems, computers and peripherals, telecommunications equipment, automotive parts and service equipment, agricultural chemicals, industrial chemicals, plastic material and resins, pollution control, machine tools, metalworking equipment, oil and gas field machinery, medical equipment and dental equipment, mining equipment, building materials, electronic components, computer software, food processing and packaging machinery, pharmaceuticals, veterinary supplies, paper and paperboard, leasing services, agricultural machinery and equipment, security and safety equipment, biotechnology, wheat, corn, barley, cotton, poultry meat, hides and skins, soybeans, snack foods, fresh fruit, beef and pork variety meats, and dairy ingredients.

Number 2: India

1997 population. 967,612,804 (2).

Number of hosts as of July 1997. 4,794 (52).

1995–1997 host growth. 173 percent (35).

Hosts per 100,000 population. 0.5 (161).

Stage of Internet development. Ajar.

1998–2000 outlook. Telecommunications deregulation will create new Internet supply opportunities. In 1997, the Indian government privatized Internet access in the country, which previously had been the sole domain of VSNL—Videsh Sanchar Nigam Ltd. By the end of the decade, NASSCOM—National Association of Software and Service Companies—expects there to be 125 new ISPs in the country, while the Department of Telecommunications (DOT) anticipates some 1.5 million new Internet subscribers.

Best trade prospects. Telecommunications equipment and services, aircraft and parts, electric power generation, computers and peripherals, plastic materials and resins, industrial chemicals, iron and steel plant equipment and services, computer software, mining and mineral processing equipment, oil and gas equipment and supplies, food processing and packaging equipment, medical electronics, aviation equipment and services, urban mass transportation, hazardous waste management, broadcast, cable and satellite equipment, and book publishing.

Number 3: Indonesia

1997 population. 209,774,138 (4).

Number of hosts as of July 1997. 10,862 (43).

1995–1997 host growth. 258 percent (23).

Hosts per 100,000 population. 5.2 (121).

Stage of Internet development. Ajar.

1998–2000 outlook. Indonesia will continue to expand and modernize its telecommunications and online networks. The government of Indonesia plans to develop five million new telephone lines, privatize selected state-owned telecommunications services, deploy satellites, wire many rural areas, and enhance cellular lines and paging systems.

Best trade prospects. Computer systems and peripherals, construction equipment, building products, franchising, electrical power systems, pollution control equipment, medical equipment, architectural, construction and engineering services, food processing and packaging equipment, telecommunications equipment, pulp and paper industry equipment and technology, computer software, tourism, cotton, wheat, logs, corn, soybeans, vegetable oils, lumber and panel products, juices, beef and poultry, feed ingredients, frozen french fries, and hides and skins.

Number 4: Brazil

1997 population. 164,511,366 (5).

Number of hosts as of July 1997. 68,685 (23).

1995–1997 host growth. 144 percent (39).

Hosts per 100,000 population. 41.8 (75).

Stage of Internet development. Ajar.

1998–2000 outlook. The largest Internet market in Latin America, Brazil is preparing for an online boom. As part of its Recovery and Expansion Program of the Telecommunications and Postal Systems—a massive economic development initiative—the Government of Brazil plans to invest over $75 billion over the next seven years, some $10 billion a year, to modernize its telecommunications system.

Best trade prospects. Telecommunications equipment, computer hardware and peripherals, medical equipment and supplies, electrical power systems, oil and gas machinery and services, pollution control equipment, computer software, processed food, transportation equipment, machine tools, mining equipment, plastic production machinery, agricultural machinery, food processing and packaging machinery, port and shipbuilding equipment, aircraft and parts, cosmetics and toiletries, apparel, automotive parts and service, home furnishings, beer, and cheese products.

Number 5: Mexico

1997 population. 97,563,374 (11).

Number of hosts as of July 1997. 35,238 (30).

1995–1997 host growth. 105 percent (52).

Hosts per 100,000 population. 36.1 (78).

Stage of Internet development. Ajar.

1998–2000 outlook. The breakup of Telmex, the state-owned telecommunications monopoly, will create new opportunities to supply Internet-related equipment and services. In cooperation with foreign investors—mainly from the United States—the government of Mexico will spend fifteen to twenty billion dollars over the next five years to upgrade the country's telecommunications networks.

Best trade prospects. Automotive parts, auto maintenance, franchising, oil and gas equipment, water resource equipment and services, management consulting services, apparel, machine tools and metalworking equipment, electric power generation, building products, mining industry equipment, electronic components, security equipment, pollution control equipment, wheat, livestock, corn, oilseeds, oil meals, beans, meat and veal, swine, fresh apples and pears, whey, chicken, and turkey meat.

Number 6: Thailand

1997 population. 59,450,818 (18).

Number of hosts as of July 1997. 12,794 (41).

1995–1997 host growth. 127 percent (45).

Hosts per 100,000 population. 21.5 (91).

Stage of Internet development. Ajar.

1998–2000 outlook. A number of major Internet-related projects are planned or underway. These include the installation of 4.9 million fixed telephone lines, the launch of Thailand's third satellite (THAICOM 3), the launch of Thai-Laos joint venture satellites (L-Star 1 and L-Star 2), and the construction of satellite earth stations.

Best trade prospects. Cotton, wheat, soybeans, fresh fruit, temperate hardwood lumber, wine, processed foods, computers, telecommunications equipment, franchising, pollution control equipment, education, training services and supplies, medical equipment, laboratory scientific instruments, computer software, automotive parts and service equipment, electric power systems, defense industry equipment, architectural and construction services, food processing equipment and machines, packaging equipment, and electronics testing equipment.

Number 7: Turkey

1997 population. 63,528,225 (17).

Number of hosts as of July 1997. 22,963 (34).

1995–1997 host growth. 187 percent (33).

Hosts per 100,000 population. 36.1 (77).

Stage of Internet development. Ajar.

1998–2000 outlook. To promote private sector investment, Turk Telecom, the state-owned telecommunications provider, will seek revenue-sharing contracts with private firms as a way to provide new Internet and communication services. Major opportunities exist in supplying equipment to the value-added services market such as paging systems, data networks, billing systems, satellite earth stations and systems, and submarine cable and intelligent network systems.

Best trade prospects. Electrical power systems, telecommunications equipment, building products, telecommunications services, medical equipment, textile machinery and equipment, automotive parts and service equipment, electronic test equipment, construction and engineering services, pollution control equipment, food processing and packaging equipment, franchising, agricultural machinery and equipment, security services, management consulting services, defense industry equipment, wheat, soybeans, rice, live cattle, cotton, vegetable oils, and planting seeds.

Number 8: Poland

1997 population. 38,700,291 (29).

Number of hosts as of July 1997. 43,384 (28).

1995–1997 host growth. 66 percent (79).

Hosts per 100,000 population. 112.1 (60).

Stage of Internet development. Ajar.

1998–2000 outlook. The government of Poland plans to spend over $30 billion by the year 2010 to upgrade the country's telecommunication infrastructure. The Polish telephone network is estimated to grow at least 17 percent per year until the end of the decade.

Best trade prospects. Building products, computer software, computers and peripherals, sporting goods, recreational equipment, pollution control equipment, telecommunications, automobile parts and components, medical equipment, broadcasting equipment, wheat, corn, poultry meat, beef, veal and offal, beef cattle, wood paneling.

Number 9: Argentina

1997 population. 35,053,980 (31).

Number of hosts as of July 1997. 18,985 (37).

1995–1997 host growth. 141 percent (40).

Hosts per 100,000 population. 54.2 (70).

Stage of Internet development. Ajar.

1998–2000 outlook. Hundreds of thousands of telephone lines in Argentina are being modernized, and opportunities abound to supply Internet-related hardware and software and services, along with personal communications services, fiber-optic cables and accessories, software for management of telecommunications networks, and fixed cellular systems for rural telephony.

Best trade prospects. Electric power generation and transmission equipment, telecommunications equipment, computers and peripherals, medical equipment, computer software, airport and ground support equipment, franchising services, oil and gas field machinery, pollution control equipment, construction and building materials, plastics processing machinery, food processing and packaging equipment, water treatment equipment, aircraft parts and accessories, auto parts and service equipment, agricultural machinery and equipment, sporting goods, laboratory and scientific equipment, apparel, planting seeds, processed fruit and vegetables, dairy products, and breakfast cereals.

Number 10: Malaysia

1997 population. 20,376,235 (48).

Number of hosts as of July 1997. 40,533 (29).

1995–1997 host growth. 511 percent (14).

Hosts per 100,000 population. 198.9 (49).

Stage of Internet development. Ajar.

1998–2000 outlook. As part of an economic reform plan, the Government of Malaysia is developing Putrajaya, a so-called intelligent city equipped with state-of-the-art Internet and communications technologies, and the Multimedia Super Corridor, a 15 by 40 kilometer information technology park between the Kuala Lumpur City Center and the Kuala Lumpur International Airport.

Best trade prospects. Multimedia equipment and services, computer services, aircraft and parts, telecommunications services, management consulting and engineering services, pollution control equipment, electronics test equipment, medical equipment, electrical power systems, pulp and paper machinery, franchising, industrial chemicals, industrial process controls, oilseeds, corn, fresh fruit, and frozen french fries.

This mile-high view of the leading Net trends, top markets, and emerging hot spots provides a big-picture snapshot of cyber-markets around the world. The coming chapters explain how to transform this broad, strategic perspective into a bottom-line, tactical approach that will earn you new global business leads and results around the world using the Internet.

CREATING A TRADE RESOURCE CENTER ON YOUR DESKTOP

10

Whether you run a home-based business or a billion-dollar conglomerate, your first step in making a global mark on the Internet is the same: Get organized. Although it is packed with information, the Net—and the world itself—is often chaotic and overwhelming. Already, some twenty million servers are connected to the Net, each of which holds potentially thousands of Web pages. On top of that, some eighteen thousand new servers are added every day, about one every five seconds. Connected to all this is a world with some 260 countries and nearly six billion people. Tens of millions of users are now online, and thousands more pour onto the Net every hour. Without a plan of attack—a system for scanning and processing information—you will be hopelessly overwhelmed and lost in this exploding online universe.

How do you get organized? For cyber-traders, people who want to use the Internet to start or expand their international business, the key is to globalize your desktop and transform your computer into an international trade command post. This chapter shows you how. You'll learn how to get online, create your own virtual trade library and resource center, and set up a world business filing system using only a few simple techniques and bookmarks. With this as your foundation, you can achieve immediate cost savings and prepare for more advanced steps described later in the book.

Get WIRED

Before leaping into the digital ocean, you need to prepare. As originally suggested by Joel Maloff in a November 1996 article in *Internet World* magazine, your first step should be to appoint a Web/Internet Resource Executive (WIRE). The WIRE is not simply a Webmaster or a computer techie, but someone who knows marketing, international business, strategic planning, *and* the Internet. His or her job is to explore Net opportunities, develop cyber-strategies and tactics for your firm, and, ultimately, use the Net to make you money. If you work alone, congratulations— you're it. If you work in an organization, select a well-respected person who has leading-edge marketing and technology skills, plenty of global business experience, and a thorough knowledge of your firm's mission and direction. To be most effective, the WIRE should be a senior champion—someone with direct access to top executives and a high enough position in the organization such that employees and customers alike respect the position and know the Internet is a management priority. All will know who's in charge and who to contact with Internet questions and issues as they relate to your company. This will bring focus, legitimacy, and accountability to your Internet efforts.

If you haven't done so already, your next step should be to get on the Net. For that, you need three things: a computer, a modem, and an Internet service provider (ISP). Buy the best computer you can afford, preferably a Pentium system with at least 16 MB RAM and a 100 MB hard drive. The more powerful your computer, the better its performance will be online. Purchase at least a 28.8 modem, although a faster speed, say 33.6 or higher, is preferable. The faster the modem, the quicker your downloads will be on the Net. To shop for a computer and a modem, check out the newsstands for publications such as *Computer Shopper* magazine at http://www5.zdnet.com/cshopper/ and *Internet Shopper* magazine at http://www.internet-shopper.com/. Packed with information on the latest computer products, both can help you with your buying decision. For a list of ISPs in your area, review The List, a directory of over three thousand ISPs around the world, at http://thelist.internet.com/. Select a provider who offers the services that meet your needs and budget. At a minimum, you should get an email account and Internet access.

Once online, download a number of software programs—many of them are free—to enhance your Internet experience. The most important software program is your browser, your driving wheel in cyberspace. Browsers are available from Microsoft at http://www.microsoft.com and Netscape at http://home.netscape.com. Test drive the browsers and select the one you like best, or use both. Many people drive two or more automobiles, so why not use two browsers? You'll have more browsing options, keep up to date on the latest Web searching developments from both companies, and add more variety to your Internet experience. To hear newscasts, conferences, and other audio programming over the Internet, download RealAudio at http://www.realaudio.com. To sample other programs, visit Shareware.Com at http://www.shareware.com. The site contains thousands of Internet software programs you may download at no charge.

Create Your Own Trade Resource Center

After you've downloaded a browser and other software, the real fun begins. Select the Bookmarks or Favorites button on your browser. Create a new bookmark folder and name it the "Trade Resource Center." You might wish to personalize the folder and name it after yourself; for example, "Jane Smith Trade Resource Center." Within your Trade Resource Center folder, create three subfolders. Call the first "Search Engines," the second "Geographic CyberPorts," and the third "Virtual Trade Teams" (Figure 10.1). In the Search Engines folder, you'll place bookmarks that will help you gather information on global trade or any other subject in seconds. In the Geographic CyberPorts folder, you'll place bookmarks that provide geographic trade information—reports on a particular place, either a world region, individual country, or specific city. In the Virtual Trade Teams folder, you'll place bookmarks that provide functional trade information—reports that are normally obtained from a variety of export professionals such as a consultant, accountant, or lawyer. Now you're ready to fill each folder with bookmarks.

Search Engines Folder

Place all your search engine bookmarks in a separate folder, as shown in Figure 10.2. If you've already bookmarked some engines, move them here. Your search tools will all be in the same place, and you'll know exactly where to find the engines when you

Figure 10.1 Jane Smith Trade Resource Center folder with subfolders.

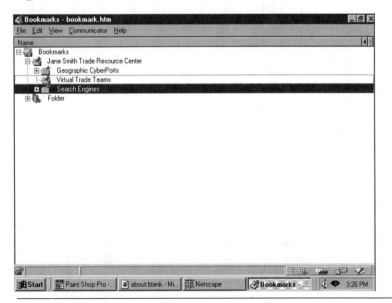

Figure 10.2 Bookmarks.

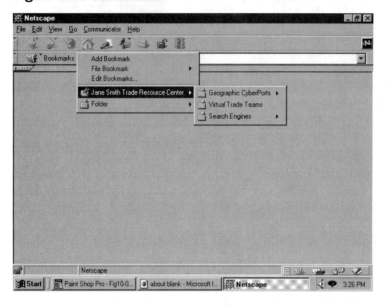

need them. This also eliminates the frustration of searching for engines that may be buried in long lists of bookmarks or scattered throughout different folders.

Along with any personal favorites, you should bookmark the following engines, all of which are top-notch search tools. The act of bookmarking these and the other tools may take some time—a few hours or so—but it's an important exercise. You'll learn more about what's on the Net and where and how to find information related to international trade.

All-in-One (http://www.albany.net/allinone/). This site is a compilation of various Internet search tools.

AltaVista (http://www.altavista.digital.com). Developed by Digital Equipment Corporation, AltaVista is renowned as the most comprehensive of all Web search databases, and it performs thorough scans of the entire Net.

Dogpile (http://www.dogpile.com). Strange name, but what a tool. This multiengine search program allows you to query twenty search engines at the same time—including AltaVista, Infoseek, and Yahoo.

Excite (http://www.excite.com). Of all the engines, Excite is among the best at finding current information, particularly mainstream topics that are widely discussed.

HotBot (http://www.hotbot.com). The engine of Wired magazine, Hot-Bot allows searches to be limited by domain (such as .com, .edu, and .org), geographic region, and date last modified.

The Informant (http://informant.dartmouth.edu/). A free online search agent, this scans the Internet for keywords that you designate and notifies you when new or updated Web pages are found.

Infoseek (http://www.infoseek.com). Although it does not have the most powerful Web page database, Infoseek has proved to be the best at consistently finding the most relevant Web sites in search engine tests.

Lycos (http://www.lycos.com). Covering more than one hundred million URLs (universal resource locators or Internet addresses), Lycos includes a "Top 5%" feature, which is a directory of Web site reviews. Lycos staffers scan the Web and rate sites based on content and design. The best sites are awarded a Top 5% review.

Northern Light (http://www.nlsearch.com). A recent arrival on the Net scene, this not only searches the entire Web but also information from over eighteen hundred journals, books, magazines, databases, and news wires not available on any other search engine.

Webcrawler (http://www.webcrawler.com/). A popular Internet search service, the site began as a University of Washington research project in Seattle. Webcrawler was sold to America Online in 1995, which in November 1996 sold the site to Excite, Inc.

Yahoo (http://www.yahoo.com). Developed by two electrical engineering students at Stanford University, Yahoo is the single largest guide in terms of traffic, advertising, and household reach on the Internet and is one of the most recognized brands associated with the Internet.

Geographic CyberPorts Folder

Place bookmarks for Geographic CyberPorts in a separate folder. These are Web sites usually developed by a nation's embassy or consulate, trade promotion department, or local economic development authority or by an international trade consultant or student interested in promoting business opportunities in his or her country to a global audience. The sites generally provide background information on the culture, history, and economy of the country and may include a list of leading exporters, trade-related government programs and assistance, trade matching services, and links to leading business Web sites in the country.

In the Geographic CyberPorts folder, create six subfolders, one for each major region of the world, as shown in Figure 10.3. Name the first folder "North America," the second "Latin America," the third "Western Europe," the fourth "Eastern Europe and Newly Independent States," the fifth "Middle East and Africa," and the sixth "Asia Pacific." This order corresponds to the west-to-east position of these regions on a world map. If you've already bookmarked Web sites that fit the description of a geographic cyberport, move them into the appropriate regional folder. For example, if you've bookmarked a site that discusses trade opportunities in Taiwan, move that bookmark into the Asia-Pacific folder. A site that reviews trade opportunities in the Netherlands should go into the Western Europe folder. A site on Brazil would be transferred to the Latin America folder, and so on. If your information is organized by global region, you'll find geographic reports quickly and easily.

Within the Geographic CyberPorts folder, bookmark the geographic cyberports in each of the regional folders described in the following sections. This list is by no means complete or exhaustive: the sites represent only a microscopic sampling of online international trade resources. These particular sites were selected based on my informal but extensive survey between January 1996 and April 1998

Figure 10.3 Geographic CyberPorts folder.

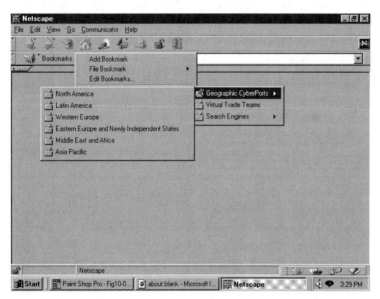

of over three thousand Web pages related to global business. Among all the sites reviewed, these offer the most and best business content, connect to key decision makers and organizations, are relatively easy to use, offer extensive links to other related sites, and are generally free to access. Even then, past performance is no guarantee of future quality, especially on the highly fluid Web. By the time you read this, some of the sites may have deteriorated or been discontinued, or they may have been eclipsed by superior sites. Still, the pages provide starting points and an information base from which you can retrieve global trade information by region and country.

North America Subfolder

For resources on Canada, bookmark the following sites:

Canadiana (http://www.cs.cmu.edu/Unofficial/Canadiana/). This links to all things Canadian on the Web, from business to culture to government.

CanadExport On-Line (http://www.dfait-maeci.gc.ca/english/news/ newsletr/canex/). Updated daily, this trade Webzine features Canadian trade news and business opportunities from around the world.

Department of Foreign Affairs and International Trade (DFAIT) (http://www.dfait-maeci.gc.ca/english/menu.htm). The flagship of Canadian trade promotion, DFAIT organizes outgoing trade missions from Canada and incoming trade missions from around the world. On trade missions, both outgoing and incoming, teams of businesspeople from a particular country visit another country in search of trade and investment opportunities.

Revenue Canada Importing and Exporting (http://www.rc.gc.ca/menu/EmenuHLA.html). Canada's tax collection and customs agency, Revenue Canada explains the trade rules and paperwork north of the forty-ninth parallel.

Strategis (http://strategis.ic.gc.ca/engdoc/main.html). Developed by Industry Canada, this is a mammoth online business library that includes company profiles, sector reports, microeconomic research and statistical analysis, business support, marketplace laws and regulations, human resource materials, and consumer information.

For resources on the United States, bookmark the following sites:

U.S. Embassy in Ottawa (http://www.usis-canada.usia.gov/). This report on Canada-U.S. trade reviews American government and business and links to dozens of top U.S. resources.

International Trade Administration (ITA) (http://www.ita.doc.gov/). The leading trade promotion agency for the U.S. government, the ITA provides an archive of global business information and export support services online. These include country commercial guides, trade statistics, industry profiles, and market analysis services.

Trade Compass (http://www.tradecompass.com/). Based in Washington, D.C., this site features export news feeds, shipping schedules, trade leads, trade statistics, market reports, cargo tracking, a trade show database, and company directories.

U.S. Trade and Development Agency (http://www.tda.gov/). A little-known unit of the U.S. federal government, the agency funds feasibility studies, orientation visits, specialized training, and business workshops for American exporters.

United States Trade Representative (USTR) (http://www.ustr.gov/). The leader on U.S. trade policy, the USTR posts reports on foreign trade barriers, future free trade area negotiations, and World Trade Organization (WTO) implementation.

Latin America Subfolder

For resources on Latin America in general, bookmark the following sites:

Latin American Network Information Center (http://info.lanic .utexas.edu/). Based at the University of Texas Institute of Latin American Studies in Austin, the Center provides the latest Latin links by country and subject.

Foreign Trade Information System (http://www.sice.oas.org/). Developed by the trade unit of the Organization of American States (OAS), this site offers articles and statistics on Latin American trade.

Inter-American Development Bank (IDB) (http://www.iadb.org/ ENGLISH/index_english.html). Based in Washington, D.C., the site highlights projects being considered for possible financing by the IDB throughout the Americas.

For resources on Caribbean and Central American countries, bookmark the following:

CubaWeb (http://www.cubaweb.com/eng/index.html). An online business library, this site reports on U.S. laws and legislation dealing with Cuba and Cuban foreign investment laws.

Dominican Republic One (http://209.41.4.222/). Based in Santa Domingo, this site reports on Dominican Republic politics, culture, trade, and travel.

Export Jamaica (http://www.exportjamaica.org/). Sponsored by the Jamaica Exporters Association, this site lists leading companies and sector reports from the Caribbean nation.

Costa Rica Development Board (http://www.cinde.or.cr/). Available in English and Spanish, this site spotlights Costa Rican companies, government agencies, and business associations.

El Salvador Online Resources (http://www.nortropic.com/el_salvador/index.html). Available in four languages—English, German, Italian, and Spanish—this site provides links to everything from Salvadorian art to schools to companies.

Trade Point Guatemala (http://www.tradepoint.org.gt/indexe.html). A directory of reports and links, this site profiles leading companies, products, and decision makers in Guatemala.

Honduras Resources (http://www.honduras-resources.com/). A gateway to scores of links, this site connects to leading banks, government agencies, and newspapers.

Mexico Information Center (http://www.mexico-trade.com/). Developed by Bancomext, a leading Mexican bank, this site includes a directory of exporters, business opportunities, trade shows, government agencies, universities, and news sources in Mexico. The Web site has the best content and design of any based in Latin America.

Panama: Crossroads of the Americas (http://holly.colostate.edu/~panama/panama.html). Developed by a Ph.D. student at Colorado State University, this site reports on Pananamian culture and business.

For resources on South American countries, bookmark the following sites:

Externa (http://www.externa.com/). Using a server based in the United States, this site provides an index of Argentine companies and products.

Bolivia Business Online (http://www.boliviabiz.com/index.htm). A directory of Bolivian companies and business associations, this site includes a picture gallery and tips on hotels and places to visit.

Brazil Exporters (http://www.brazilexporters.com/). Along with profiles on leading Brazilian traders, this site offers business news, product catalogs, and a sourcing Webzine.

Chile Trade (http://www.chiletrade.cl/). A searchable import/export database, this site includes a monthly newsletter published by the Trade Commission of Chile.

Colombian Trade Bureau (http://www.coltrade.org/). Based in the Colombian Embassy in Washington, D.C., this site highlights economic news and trade shows in the South American republic.

EcuaNet (http://www3.ecua.net.ec/). A directory of Ecuardorian provinces, cities, and companies, this site includes a list of leading exporters and hotels nationwide.

Peru Online (http://www.peruonline.com/). Available in English and Spanish, this site features online shops and a directory of leading government agencies, schools, and companies.

Embassy of Uruguay (http://www.embassy.org/uruguay/). Located in Washington, D.C., this site includes briefs on tourism, business, and regional trade agreements in Uruguay.

Trade Venezuela (http://www.trade-venezuela.com/). An online business matchmaking service, this site spotlights Venezuelan companies seeking investment and trading partners in a diverse range of product and service areas.

Western Europe Subfolder

For resources on Western Europe in general, bookmark the following sites:

Europages (http://www.europages.com/). Available in five languages, this site is a searchable database of 150,000 companies throughout Western Europe.

Europa (http://europa.eu.int/index-en.htm). A service of the European Union, this site explains the role and responsibilities of European institutions in economic and foreign policy matters.

EBN Interactive (http://www.ebn.co.uk/). Wired with audio broadcasts and a ticker tape window, this online service reports on European business news.

For resources on European countries, bookmark the following:

How to Do Business in Austria (http://www.wk.or.at/aw/aw_intl/business/home.htm). Prepared by the Austrian Foreign Trade Organization, this site covers business laws, import regulations, and taxation issues in Austria.

Belgian Foreign Trade Board (http://www.obcebdbh.be/en/obce/index.html). A primer on the Belgian economy, this includes exporter profiles and travel tips.

Export Directory of Denmark (http://www.krak.dk/export/uk.htm). Hosted by the Danish Chamber of Commerce and the Confederation of Danish Industries, this site is a searchable database of Danish exporters.

Finnish Top 100 Companies (http://www.nedecon.fi/top-100/). An online company catalog, this site profiles leading Finnish operations in seventeen industries ranging from foodstuffs to retail to construction.

French Embassy (http://www.info-france-usa.org/). A virtual handbook on French industry and culture, this site features business and trade.

Facts about Germany (http://www.bundesregierung.de/ausland/index_e5.html). An archive of economic studies and statistics, this site profiles German sectors and labor markets.

Hellenic Ministry of Foreign Affairs (http://www.mfa.gr/). A fact sheet on Greek foreign policy, this site includes reports on the Greek economy, press, and consulates abroad.

Irish Trade Web (http://www.itw.ie/). A virtual library of international business information, this site spotlights Irish exporters and trade shows.

Welcome to Italy (http://www.italyemb.nw.dc.us/italy/index.html). A service of the Embassy of Italy in Washington, D.C., this site features Italian economic reports and tips for travelers.

Survey of Luxembourg (http://www.restena.lu/gover/index_english.html). Available in English, French, and German, this site explores the history, geography, and economy of Luxembourg.

Malta External Trade Corporation (http://www.u-net.com/metcowww/). An online business directory, this site lists exporters and trade services in Malta.

Royal Netherlands Embassy (http://www.netherlands-embassy .org/). Posted by the Dutch Embassy in Washington, D.C., this site discusses technology and transportation in the Netherlands.

Norway Online (http://www.norway.org/). A searchable archive of Norwegian information, this site includes fact sheets on business, tourism, and government services.

Welcome to Portugal (http://www.portugal.org/pageindex.html). An economic overview of Portugal, this site includes briefs on foreign trade trends by region and product.

Si, Spain (http://www.docuweb.ca/SiSpain/english/index.html). Sponsored by the Spanish Foreign Ministry, this site examines the culture, politics, and trade of Spain.

Sweden Online (http://www.swedentrade.com/). Developed by the Swedish Trade Council, this site features Swedish business news and an interactive marketplace.

Britain in the USA (http://britain.nyc.ny.us/). Posted by the British Embassy, this site reports on the British business, trade, and investment.

Eastern Europe Subfolder

For resources on Eastern Europe in general, bookmark the following Web sites:

REESWeb (http://www.pitt.edu/~cjp/rees.html). Developed by the University of Pittsburgh's Center for Russian and East European Studies, this site is an index of electronic resources on Eastern Europe and the former Soviet Union.

BISNIS (http://www.itaiep.doc.gov/bisnis/bisnis.html). The home page of the U.S. Commerce Department's Business Information Service for Newly Independent States, this site includes country reports, bulletins, and statistics on trade between the United States and new states in the former Soviet Union.

Central Europe Online (http://www.centraleurope.com/). An electronic news service, this site covers events in Central and Eastern Europe and includes a daily video broadcast.

For resources on Eastern European countries, bookmark the following sites:

Baltics Online (http://www.viabalt.ee/). A primer on Estonia, Latvia, and Lithuania, this site reviews the Baltic culture and economy.

Bulgaria.Com (http://www.bulgaria.com/). Featuring audio feeds and a chat room, this site links to Bulgarian business, government, and university information.

Czech Information Center (http://www.muselik.com/czech/frame .html). Updated daily, this site includes fact sheets on the Czech economy and an export/import bulletin board.

Hungarian Home Page (http://www.fsz.bme.hu/hungary/homepage .html). Wired with an interactive map that highlights the ISPs throughout the country, this site provides background reports and news on Hungary.

Welcome to Kyrgyzstan (http://www.kyrgyzstan.org/). This site features quick facts and general information about Kyrgyzstan, one of the newly independent states.

Poland Now (http://sarnow.com/poland/BUSINESS/). A Polish business Webzine, this site offers company guides, city profiles, and law and tax reports.

Romania Business Economics (http://www.romaniabusiness.com/). A searchable database of Romanian companies, this site includes business and political briefs and a free advertising service.

Business Collaboration Center (http://www.cbi.co.ru/). A U.S.-Russian business matching service, this site features an electronic library, events calendar, and yellow pages directory.

Russian Business and Trade Connections (http://www.publications-etc .com/russia/business/). A Russian trade Webzine, this site profiles Russian companies, business proposals, and trade shows.

Russia Today (http://www.russiatoday.com/). A daily news service, this site reports on politics and business in Russia and the Commonwealth of Independent States.

Slovenia Chamber of Commerce (http://www.gzs.si/eng/index.htm). A compendium of Slovenian business and economic data, this site includes news brief and cultural fact sheets.

Ukraine: FAQ Plus (http://www.std.com/sabre/UKRAINE.html). A country business guide, this site features Ukrainian economic analysis and company reports.

Middle East and Africa Subfolder

For resources on the Middle East and Africa in general, bookmark the following sites:

Middle East/North Africa Home Page (http://www.ita.doc.gov/mena/econof.html). Presented by the U.S. Commerce Department's Office of the Near East, this site highlights business news and trade opportunities in the Middle East and North Africa.

ArabNet (http://www.arab.net/welcome.html). A compendium of Arab world resources, this site reports on twenty-two countries including Algeria, Kuwait, Morocco, and the United Arab Emirates.

For resources on Middle Eastern countries, bookmark these sites:

Egypt's Business Center (http://163.121.10.42/amman/main/). A primer on doing business in Egypt, this site features economic indicators, company profiles, and product directories.

India Online (http://indiaonline.com/biz.html). An online business matching service, this site offers a searchable database of Indian buyers, sellers, and joint venture opportunities.

India World (http://indiaworld.co.in/). Featuring the latest Indian news and business headlines, this site has banking reports, book reviews, and television guides.

Salam Iran (http://www.salamiran.org/IranInfo/). Developed by the Iranian Embassy in Ottawa, this site profiles the Iranian government, economy, and culture.

Israel's Business Arena (http://www.globes.co.il/cgi-bin/Serve_Arena/level/English/1.1). A searchable online newspaper, this site includes editorials, economic projections, and price comparisons.

Turkey Business and Economy (http://www.mfa.gov.tr/GRUPC/GRUPC.htm). Using data from the State Institute of Statistics, this site provides Turkish economic reports, foreign trade briefs, and tourism bulletins.

Top 100 Saudi Companies (http://www.arab.net/saudi100/welcome.html). Compiled by Arab News, this site lists leading Saudi operations in a variety of manufacturing and service industries.

For resources on African countries, bookmark these sites:

Africa Online (http://www.africaonline.com/). A gateway to African electronic information, this site features regional news, business analysis, and travel tips.

Kenya Web (http://www.kenyaweb.com/economy/economy.html). Prepared by the Central Bank of Kenya, this site reports on Kenyan trade, markets, and World Bank projects.

Welcome to South Africa (http://www.southafrica.net/). Presented by the Embassy of South Africa in Washington, D.C., this site spotlights South African trade opportunities, business assistance programs, and travel destinations.

South African Business Directory (http://os2.iafrica.com/w3/ bus_dir.htm). This site profiles South African companies in industries ranging from architecture to food processing to retail.

Asia-Pacific Subfolder

For resources on Asia Pacific in general, bookmark the following sites:

InAsia (http://www.inasia.com/). A searchable database of Asian companies, this site features country reports, business news, and a trade show calendar.

ASEANWeb (http://www.asean.or.id/). The home page of the Association of South East Asian Nations (ASEAN), this site has economic reports on Brunei, Indonesia, Laos, Malaysia, Myanmar, the Philippines, Singapore, Thailand, and Vietnam.

Asia Inc. (http://www.asia-inc.com/index.html). The electronic counterpart to Asia Inc. magazine, this site includes business headlines, conference rooms, and a reference library.

Asian Development Bank (http://www.asiandevbank.org/). The home page of the Manila-based financial institution, this site posts Asian Development Bank contract tenders, business seminars, and job openings.

For resources on Asia-Pacific countries, bookmark these sites:

Business in Brunei (http://jtb.brunet.bn/homepage/bus_com/ brubusin.htm). A primer on the Bruneian economy, this site reports on the nation's agriculture, construction, and oil and gas sectors.

Chinese Embassy (http://www.china-embassy.org/). Developed by the

Chinese Embassy in Washington, D.C., this site reports on the Chinese economy and development plans.

China Council (http://www.ccpit.org/). Developed by the China Chamber of International Commerce, this site offers Chinese trade news and a business matching service.

World Trade Database (http://www.wtdb.com/). An online trade network, this site offers Chinese credit reports, business profiles, and market studies.

Hong Kong Trade Development Council (http://www.tdc.org.hk/). A government trade promotion service, this site features Hong Kong product catalogs, design galleries, and trade matching services.

Access Online Indonesia (http://www.accessindo.com/). A virtual gateway to the island nation, this site covers Indonesia business, travel, and culture.

Japan Information (http://www.mofa.go.jp/jpn_inf.html). Developed by the Ministry of Foreign Affairs of Japan, this site links to a diverse range of Japanese online resources from company directories to kids' Web sites.

JETRO (http://www.jetro.go.jp/index.html). Prepared by the Japan External Trade Organization, this site highlights Japanese trade programs and business opportunities.

Business in Korea (http://korea.emb.washington.dc.us/business/). Created by the Korean Embassy in Washington, D.C., this site profiles Korean trade organizations, investment incentives, and companies.

Malaysia Electronic Publication (http://www.asiaep.com/my/malays.htm). A primer on Malaysian business, this site has a product catalog, export/import center, and an international buyers list.

Philippine Embassy (http://www.sequel.net/RPinUS/WDC/). Developed by the Philippine Embassy in Washington, D.C., this site highlights Philippine business and trade opportunities.

Singapore Government (http://www.gov.sg/). An overview of Singaporean Ministries, this site includes press releases and biographies on leading government officials.

Trade Point Taiwan (http://tptaiwan.org.tw/). Developed by the

China External Trade Development Council and the Taipei World Trade Center, this site reports on export and import opportunities in Taiwan.

Royal Thai Embassy (http://www.thaiembdc.org/). Hosted by the Royal Thai Embassy in Washington, D.C., this site has general information on Thailand, a press center, and a Thai resource directory.

Welcome to Vietnam (http://www.vietnamembassy-usa.org/). The home page of the Vietnamese Embassy in the United States, this site provides general news and background reports on Vietnam.

For resources on the countries of Oceania, bookmark these sites:

Australia World Direct (http://www.austrade.gov.au/). A database of Australian exporters, this site includes trade statistics and an online product category.

New Zealand Embassy (http://www.emb.com/nzemb/). A tutorial on setting up a business in New Zealand, this site covers key immigration, taxation, and international trade issues.

Virtual Trade Teams

In the Virtual Trade Teams folder, create sixteen subfolders. Give them the following names: Trainer, Researcher, Consultant, Reporter, Pollster, Rainmaker, Banker, Accountant, Lawyer, Diplomat, Customs Broker, Travel Agent, Shipper, Translator, Employment Counselor, and Webmaster. Collectively, they are a so-called trade team because they offer functional information, reports, and advice normally derived from a firm or team of professional service providers in that particular specialty. Although no substitute for professional advice, this collection is the next best thing. It's like having your own in-house trade staff always ready to provide trade intelligence twenty-four hours a day—at no charge—with a few clicks of the mouse.

The trade teams will help you augment internal capabilities, save fees for selected export services and information, scope out terms of reference for professional service outsourcing, comparison shop, negotiate improved terms, and find answers and solutions after business hours or in an emergency. If you've already bookmarked sites that match any of these descriptions, move them into the appropriate subfolder. A site that discusses any of the legal implications of international trade, for example, should be placed in the Lawyer folder. A financial site that covers global trade finance should be moved to the Banker folder, and so on. Organizing sites by export function allows you to retrieve key professional information in seconds. As with the geographic cyberports, these represent only a tiny share of what's available online in these areas. They were selected as the top sites in my trade Web page survey based on comparisons of content and design. Now, go get the bookmarks!

Trainer Subfolder

For your Trainer subfolder, bookmark the following Web sites:

Small Business Guide to Exporting (http://www.sbaonline.sba.gov/gopher/Business-Development/ International-Trade/Guide-To-Exporting/). A U.S. Department of Commerce primer on international business, this site explains everything from developing a global business to transporting goods internationally to identifying foreign investment opportunities.

Export Source (http://exportsource.gc.ca). Developed by Industry Canada and the Department of Foreign Affairs and International Trade, this site provides a series of export tutorials including how to bid on international projects, how to prepare for trade shows and business trips, and how to respond to an unsolicited order.

Take a World View (http://strategis.ic.gc.ca/SSG/sc01071e.html). An introduction to the export of services, this site is a three-phase, twelve-module system that walks an aspiring services exporter through the global trade process, from assessing export readiness to expanding into new markets.

Researcher Subfolder

Bookmark the following pages for your Researcher subfolder:

The World Factbook (http://www.odci.gov/cia/publications/ nsolo/wfb-all.htm). Prepared by the U.S. Central Intelligence Agency, this site is a compendium of political facts and economic statistics on countries around the world.

City.Net (http://www.city.net/). A searchable database of some five thousand locations, this site includes interactive maps, business links, and weather information for cities all over the world from New York to Nairobi to Tokyo.

International Business Resources (http://ciber.bus.msu.edu/busres .htm). Developed by the Michigan State University Center for International Business Education and Research, this site reviews hundreds of top trade-related sites on the Net in a variety of news, country, and event categories.

World Class (http://web.idirect.com/~tiger/). A free guide to the Web's best global business sites, this site includes a daily news feed and monthly awards for the most innovative trade pages.

Trade Data Online (http://strategis.ic.gc.ca/sc_mrkti/tdst/engdoc/ tr_homep.html). An electronic archive of U.S. and Canadian trade data, this site allows a user to prepare custom trade reports on over five thousand commodities and five hundred industries by country, Canadian province, and U.S. state.

InfoSpace (http://www.infospaceinc.com/). A searchable database of phone and fax numbers and email addresses, this site includes business and city guides, classifieds, and e-shopping.

Consultant Subfolder

For your Consultant information file, bookmark the following sites:

Country Commercial Guides (http://www.state.gov/www/about_state/ business/com_guides/index.html). Prepared by U.S. embassies and consulates, these guides provide political and business situation reports on countries around the world.

International Comparisons (http://strategis.ic.gc.ca/sc_mrkti/ ibin/compare.html). A custom trade report service, this site allows users to build their own international business comparisons of countries and sectors.

Market Research (http://strategis.ic.gc.ca/sc_mrkti/ibinddc/engdoc/ 1a1.html). A library of international market reports, this site provides trade facts and statistics for hundreds of industries and dozens of countries around the world.

Stat-USA Export and International Trade (http://www.stat-usa.gov/ BEN/subject/trade.html). An archive of trade leads and market research reports, this site includes export yellow pages and a list of international market reports and trade leads.

Reporter Subfolder

For your Reporter information subfolder, bookmark the following site:

MediaINFO Links (http://www.mediainfo.com/emedia/). A gateway to thousands of online newspapers, radio stations and television networks, this site includes background reports on news organizations and publications from around the world

Pollster Subfolder

For your Pollster subfolder, bookmark this site:

DejaNews (http://www.dejanews.com/). The source for Internet discussion groups, this site allows a user to keyword search, post messages, and browse groups.

Rainmaker Subfolder

Bookmark the following sites for your Rainmaker subfolder:

Procurement Assistance Jumpstation (http://www.fedmarket.com/ international.html). This site links to hundreds of purchasing agencies and procurement offices in government agencies across the United States and around the world.

International Trade Leads (http://ciber.bus.msu.edu/busres/ tradlead.htm). This site reviews the leading online trading networks in a variety of geographic and sectoral areas.

Expo Guide (http://www.expoguide.com/). A searchable directory of trade shows, this site provides background and contact information for thousands of international business events around the world.

Trade Show Central (http://www.tscentral.com/). A virtual catalog of trade events around the world, this site allows you to request additional information on a particular show including schedules, costs, workshops, seminars, and keynote speakers.

Telephone Directories on the Web (http://www.contractjobs.com/ tel/). An index of phone books from around the world, this site includes detailed listings of online white pages, yellow pages, and fax directories.

Electric Postcard Links (at http://tor-pwl.netcom.ca/~skardber/ postcards.html). A directory of electronic postcard services, this site allows you to send free seasonal and personal greetings in a variety of languages.

Banker Subfolder

For your Banker subfolder, bookmark the following sites:

Financial Information Link Library (http://www.mbnet.mb.ca/ ~russell/). A directory of online financial resources, this site links to leading banks, venture capital firms, and other financial service operations around the world.

Trade Finance (http://infoserv2.ita.doc.gov/Tradebase/Finance.nsf). Developed by the U.S. International Trade Administration, this site is a searchable database of U.S. trade finance firms.

Credit Reporting Agencies (http://www.creditworthy.com/us/ providers/agency.html). A list of online credit reporting agencies, this site includes country- and sector-specific services from all regions of the world.

Global Business Forms (http://www.qualitylc.com/gbm.html). A directory of standard transaction forms, this site allows a user to download or print templates for a variety of export documents including a basic ordering agreement, purchase order, pro forma invoice, and letter of credit instructions.

Universal Currency Converter (http://www.xe.net/currency/). A foreign exchange conversion tool, this site allows you to convert the value of dozens of international currencies into other currencies.

Accountant Subfolder

Bookmark the following site for your Accountant subfolder:

Tax and Accounting Sites Directory (http://www.taxsites.com/ international.html). Developed by a University of Northern Iowa accounting professor, this site is a gateway to hundreds of international tax resources including tax treaties, legislative updates, and software.

Lawyer Subfolder

For your Lawyer subfolder bookmark this Web site:

International Trade Law Monitor (http://ananse.irv.uit.no/ trade_law/nav/trade.html). Developed by the University of Tromsö Law Faculty in Norway, this site links to scores of international law resources including international trade treaties, cross-border contract law, dispute settlement, and intellectual property.

Diplomat Subfolder

Bookmark the following site for your Diplomat subfolder:

Electronic Embassy (http://www.embassy.org/). A directory of online embassies and consulates from countries around the world, this site includes a searchable index and an international business center.

Customs Broker Subfolder

For the Customs Broker subfolder, bookmark the following Web sites:

World Customs Organization (http://www.wcoomd.org/). A directory of customs organizations around the world, this site reviews international customs rules and procedures.

Import/Export (http://www.customs.ustreas.gov/imp-exp/). Developed by the U.S. Treasury Department, this site lists a variety of U.S. customs rulings, publications, and reference tables.

Virtual Customs Office (http://207.6.23.164/english.htm). A Government of Canada prototype, this site explains exporting and importing procedures and customs and trade administration paperwork.

Travel Agent Subfolder

Bookmark the following site for your Travel Agent subfolder:

Travelocity (http://www.travelocity.com/). An electronic travel reservation service, this site allows a user to check airline schedules, compare prices, arrange trips, and book hotels online.

Shipper Subfolder

Bookmark the following sites for your Shipper subfolder:

Freightworld (http://www.freightworld.com). A directory of online transportation resources, this site links to the leading maritime, railroad, aviation, trucking, and logistic sites on the Internet.

Air Cargo Online (http://www.cargo-online.com/). A global cargo capacity database, this site enables a user to advertise or locate aircraft seeking cargo and cargo seeking aircraft. The site features a virtual showroom of aircraft for sale and lease.

Maritime Global Net (http://www.mglobal.com/). With links to over eight hundred maritime-related companies and organizations, Maritime Global Net is the online source for ocean carriers and cargo. The service includes the Broker's Exchange, a virtual marketplace of ocean vessels and equipment.

Electronic Shipping Guide (http://www.shipguide.com/). A database of container shipping schedules, this service allows a user to track the voyages of over sixty carriers into and out of Canada and the United States from destinations around the world. The voyages are searchable by departure port, by arrival port, and by carrier.

TruckNet (http://www.truck.com). A virtual library of trucking information, this site includes freight-locating and referral services as well as databases on truck dealers, repair facilities, new and used vehicles, parts, and employment opportunities.

Translator Subfolder

Bookmark the following site for your Translator subfolder:

Online Language Dictionaries (http://rivendel.com/~ric/ resources/dictionary.html). An index of online language resources, this site features free translation services, multilingual directories, and language software.

Employment Counselor Subfolder

Bookmark the following site for your Employment Counselor subfolder:

Riley Guide (http://www.dbm.com/jobguide/). Named after the site's creator, a Rockville, Maryland, Internet consultant, this site features a wealth of employment opportunities and job resources on the Internet.

Webmaster Subfolder

The following sites can be bookmarked for your Webmaster subfolder:

Web Marketing Info Center (http://www.wilsonweb.com/webmarket/). Featuring links to hundreds of articles and resources about Web marketing, this site offers a free triweekly email newsletter and advice on electronic commerce.

Internet World **(http://www.internetworld.com/).** The electronic version of the monthly Internet magazine, this site has new product reviews, interviews with Internet innovators, and full-length articles from the current issue and all back issues.

Use Your Global Business Filing System

Now that you've bookmarked all these sites (you have, haven't you?), pat yourself on the back. You've not only created a trade resource library, you've set up a global business information filing system. From now on, whenever you come across an international business site you wish to bookmark, place the bookmark in the appropriate folder. Discovered a great trade site on Italy? Swish, into the Western Europe folder. On Australia? Zip, into the Asia-Pacific folder. Found a great Web page on international airlines? Whoosh, into the Shipper folder. A language resource? Kerplunk, into the Translator folder. Having a place for everything and putting everything in its place means you access more electronic trade resources in less time with less effort.

Look for Immediate Benefits and Savings

Put this system to work right away. On a piece of paper or spreadsheet, make two columns. Title the left column "International Trade Activities." Title the right column "Opportunities for Benefits and Savings." Under the left column, make a list of all your organization's international trade activities. For example, this could include collecting trade data, sending letters overseas, preparing international marketing reports, seeking legal or tax advice on a cross-border deal, finding a list of customers in another country, using a travel agent to arrange a foreign trip, translating documents, recruiting employees from other countries, or shipping a product overseas. Each organization is different, and your list will be unique. An example list is shown in Figure 10.4. Keep in mind that your organization may not necessarily have to export or import goods and services to conduct an international trade activity. Your product research, for example, may involve productivity comparisons with other countries. Your vice president may attend an international conference overseas. Your customer service department may respond to questions about products or suppliers in other markets. Note all such activities and transactions, whether or not you export or import goods or services.

Figure 10.4 Sample Benefits and Savings list.

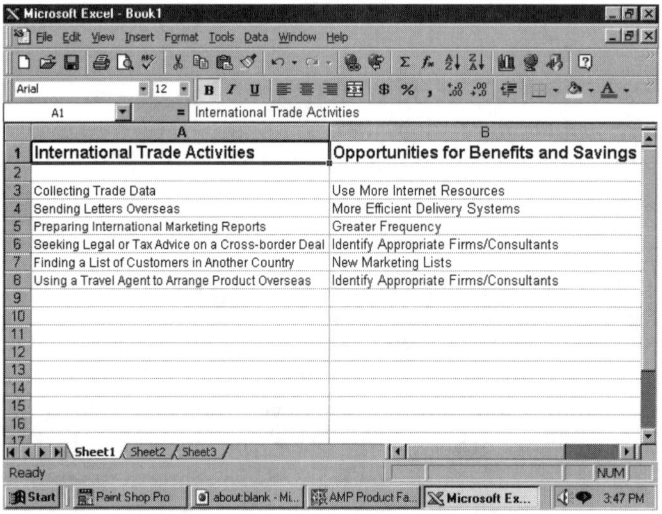

International Trade Activities	Opportunities for Benefits and Savings
Collecting Trade Data	Use More Internet Resources
Sending Letters Overseas	More Efficient Delivery Systems
Preparing International Marketing Reports	Greater Frequency
Seeking Legal or Tax Advice on a Cross-border Deal	Identify Appropriate Firms/Consultants
Finding a List of Customers in Another Country	New Marketing Lists
Using a Travel Agent to Arrange Product Overseas	Identify Appropriate Firms/Consultants

Review the list of your organization's trade activities in the left column, and see which trade activities could be complemented, improved, or replaced, however modestly, using any of the search engines, geographic cyberports, and virtual trade teams resources. If you see a potential fit, make a note of it in the Opportunities for Benefits and Savings column. Also note whether the activity is one that could be handled internally or if it should be outsourced. If delivered internally, contact the staff members who provide the service, and let them know about the appropriate resource. The site(s) may help your colleagues save time and money when conducting international training, research, marketing, and other global business activities. If the activity is outsourced, approach your supplier. Opportunities may exist to negotiate faster or better service, lower prices, or more competitive terms. The bottom line is this: Why pay for international trade information or services that can be obtained for free or at a huge discount on the Net? Use the resources as electronic leverage to augment internal capabilities, comparison shop, save fees for selected export services and information, arrange improved deals, and find answers and solutions in an emergency. You may win big.

With your trade resource center up and running, it's now official—your desktop is globalized, and you're ready for anything. Almost. In the next chapter, we explore how to roll out this trade resource center and use it to find new international business prospects online.

DEVELOPING GLOBAL BUSINESS LEADS USING THE INTERNET

11

From government procurement notices in Tokyo and patent registrations in Stockholm to job openings in Mexico City, the Internet offers a huge harvest of international business information. Unfortunately, the cyber-waters are deep and murky and finding this material can be a real challenge. Pounded by tidal waves of data and tossed around in whirlpools of links, cyber-traders can easily lose their bearings and crash into the digital rocks. Like a treasure map that leads to buried riches, this chapter shows you how to navigate through these hazards and find the hidden gems. Using your desktop trade resource center as a platform, you'll learn how to set targets, search effectively, and prowl the leading hotspots for the latest and best global trade opportunities.

Set Targets

Try this exercise: Get a blank sheet of paper and title it "My Internet Targets." Under the heading, make two columns. Title the left column "Who Buys What I Sell." Title the right column "Who Sells What I Buy."

In the left column, profile your ideal customer. Be as specific as possible. If you sell to industrial markets, list the industries. Are your ideal customers, for example, residential building contractors? Greeting card publishers? Recreational vehicle parks? If you're not sure, visit North American Industry Classification System at http://www.census.gov/epcd/www/naics.html for hundreds of standard industrial codes (SICs) that you can review to identify the precise industries you want to reach. Once you've established what these are, consider what type of company in each industry you want to approach. Are they a manufacturer? Distributor? Dealer? What size are they—less than 50 employees, between 50 and 250 employees, between 250 and 1,000 employees, or larger? How often do they buy what you sell—every day, once a month, once a year? Are they more interested in price, quality, or service? Typically, who in the organization makes the decision to buy what you sell—the president, the vice president, a corporate buyer, or a manager? If you sell to consumer markets, profile your typical customer: What age group? Lifestyle? Gender? Income level? Education level? Personality type? Preparing this buyer profile focuses your thinking, precisely identifies the type of companies and people you want to target online, and helps you create an effective plan. The more you know about your customers, the easier they will be to find in cyberspace.

In the right column, jot down a list of your key suppliers and the major offerings you buy from each. Briefly describe the items and services. Preparing this supplier profile helps you key in on a potentially lucrative but often overlooked part of the electronic commerce equation: The Internet can be used not only to sell to the world but also to buy from it. Start thinking of global business leads from both the demand and supply sides. A lead can mean both an opportunity to market and boost revenue and also an opportunity to buy smarter or cheaper and cut costs or improve efficiency.

Now, the second exercise. Take another blank piece of paper and title it "Hot Lead List." Under the title, draw ten blank spaces down the page and number them. Starting today (yes, today) and over the next few days, fill in those spaces with the names and addresses of ten people who match your profile, two each from Western Europe, Eastern Europe, the Middle East, Asia Pacific, and Latin America. These should be individuals who could potentially partner with you, buy what you sell, or sell what you buy. Don't worry if you know little or nothing about delivering your product or service overseas or importing a product in your country. We'll cross that bridge later. For now, just focus on compiling that list of ten names.

Effective Searching Tips

You've completed the profile and know which companies and individuals you want to target. What's the next step?

Before zeroing in on specific sites, you need to adjust your thinking about information gathering. You're in a new electronic age, not your old public library, and some new attitudes and tactics are required to take full advantage of the hyperlinked, speed-of-light Internet medium. Some key tips are as follows:

Search offline. Start your searches off first at the newsstand, bookstore, and library. Look for trade magazines and books that focus on the "Top 100 Web sites." PC Magazine, for example, has a Top 100 Web sites issue, the electronic version of which is at http://www.zdnet.com/pcmag/special/web100/_open.htm. You'll tap the expertise of Net specialists who scan the Web full time for the best online information.

Ask colleagues. Ask your colleagues, customers, and suppliers for a list of their favorite business Web sites. They'll be flattered that you want their input, and you'll benefit from their experience.

Budget time. Budget four hours a week—preferably an entire morning or afternoon—to conduct Internet searches. Based on experience, you'll get better results in a focused, block session, as opposed to a series of ad hoc, shorter sessions.

Decide: Work or play. Before each of your Internet sessions, ask yourself: What is the purpose of this session? Do I want to work or play? If the answer is play, surf away. This is your private time, and you do as you please. If the answer is work, view your online sessions as a serious and legitimate business development activity. Think of online sessions as being similar to exhibiting at a trade show or making a sales presentation to a customer. Time is money, and you'll maximize your time investment if you focus on business results.

Write down goals. Before you log on, write down your session goals on paper, don't use a word processor. Online, you are constantly bombarded with hyperlinks, banner ads, and other cyber-invitations. Written goals will help you stay on track and minimize time-wasting detours. Place this paper next to your computer and refer to it often to keep you on track.

Set quotas. For every hour online, set of goal of finding at least four new leads—one every fifteen minutes—from the Internet. The repetition will improve your Internet game. You'll gain experience, develop new skills, and—most important—achieve specific, measurable outputs from your online sessions.

Set time limits. Stories abound of Internet users who have become so absorbed in their online sessions that they lose track of time and neglect other activities. Don't overdo it. If necessary, put an alarm clock next to your computer and have it ring after a set time, for example, four hours. Heed the advice: "Moderation in all things."

Be disciplined. When online, you're always one click away from countless distractions. Learn to resist amusements and temptations during work sessions, and save that for play sessions. When working, you'll be more productive. When playing, you'll have a clear conscience.

Use a word processor. When online, run your word processor along with your browser. When you spot useful information online, copy the material from your browser using the Select, Edit, and Copy commands. Then paste the material into your word processor using the Edit, Paste command. You'll maintain a complete and orderly record of your Web scanning.

Open more browser windows. Use two or more browser windows at the same time. When downloading a file, don't wait around. Open a second or third browser window using the File, New Window command. As long as you don't log off, you can continue searching the Internet as usual in one window, while other windows download Internet files.

Use cold, warm, and hot searching. Be aware of the various searching "temperatures." Cold searching is using search engines like Yahoo and Infoseek to scan the entire Internet. This approach is quick, easy, and sometimes useful, but the results are often unpredictable and unreliable. The engines will return tens of thousands of documents that match your query, but none may have the information you really want. Warm searching is using link sites—Web pages like International Business Resources at http://ciber.bus.msu.edu/busres.htm and WorldClass at http://web.idirect .com/~tiger/ that offer a collection of links on a particular subject, for example, global trade.

In general, the links are prescreened by specialists and connect you to the best sites in a particular field. This saves you the time and trouble of searching for information yourself, although the links are sometimes incomplete or out of date. Hot searching is scanning content-concentrated sites—such as company Web sites—that provide background information and answers. While they may provide links to other sites, they mostly provide content. These sites provide key insights and contacts, although the credibility of the information may be suspect in some cases. Example: A particular company may offer a critical review of a competitor's product. Although the criticism may be valid, always consider the source and inherent biases of the organization and person providing the information. They may have a hidden agenda. When scanning for information online, use a combination of all three search strategies to hunt for information. All three have strengths and weaknesses, so experiment and choose a search mix that works best for you. Just remember: Your ultimate goal on the Internet is not to search for information but to retrieve it.

Expect limitations. No search engine is perfectly accurate or comprehensive. The Internet is ever expanding and evolving, and even the best engines can only give you a piecemeal snapshot of what's online. The engines are especially poor at finding very recent material—particularly material on news sites and other daily updated pages. Even when a Webmaster submits a site to an engine, it can take as long as three or four months before the page is indexed and appears in a search. The reason is that the Internet is so huge and fluid. Engines take months to sweep the millions of pages in cyberspace. By the time one sweep is completed, Web content has already changed significantly. Moral: Expect to encounter difficulties when tracking down the latest updates and content using search engines.

Anticipate frustrations. If you find a useful site one day, it may not be there the next, or the information may be different. Many sites take a long time to download, are confusing to navigate, or are poorly designed with excessive graphics. Other are crash-prone, filled with typing mistakes, or offer sparse or questionable content. Be patient. The Web as we know it is still in its infancy, and, like any new system, many bugs have to be worked out.

Avoid the online rut. According to a May 5, 1997, Business Week/ Harris Poll, 57 percent of Internet users go to the same sites repeatedly rather than moving from one site to the next. While you should spend time on tried-and-tested sites, always seek out new and better information and pages. You'll expand your networking circle, and uncover new business prospects.

Use double quotes. When doing keyword searches, use double quotationa marks for phrases or words in exact sequence. For example, if you're looking for information on Santo Domingo, type "Santo Domingo" (with the quotes) in the search engine text box, not Santo Domingo (without the quotation marks). With the quotation marks, the engine will find the pages with that exact phrase. Without them, the engine will get the pages that contain any of the search words, even if they're in different paragraphs.

Use the Edit, Find command. Use the Edit, Find command on a browser to search for keywords within a page. You'll save time scanning and scrolling, especially in long documents.

Search in other languages. Some search engines allow you to scan for documents in a particular language. AltaVista, for example, allows a user to search for documents in over twenty languages including Chinese, German, and Spanish. To access this feature, click the down arrow next to "for documents in" (any language) on the search engine window and select a language from the list. While an estimated eight out of every ten Web sites are in English, non-English speaking sites should not be overlooked. They may provide additional information in the local language of a particular international market.

Capitalize names. Capitalize names of people and places. The engines treat capitalized words as a single name or title, while uncapitalized words are treated like any other group of words. Example: "Rock Hudson" would be treated as a single name, while "rock hudson" would include sites about rock climbing, rock music, and the Hudson River.

Use commas. To search for several names or titles, use commas to separate them. If a comma is not used between names, it will be treated as one long single name. To find sites that mention Bill Clinton and Boris Yeltsin, for example, type "Bill Clinton, Boris Yeltsin."(Remember to use double quotation marks for phrases that include full names and to capitalize the names.) If a comma is not used between names, the search terms will be treated as one long single name, and a search may not find information about either individual.

Use a plus sign. Use a plus sign (+) in front of a word to identify must-have words or phrases. This will require that a word appear and will increase the precision of your search. For example, using "+Transcona" would return documents that include the word Transcona. Be sure not to leave a space between the plus sign and the word that must appear, or this must-have feature will not work

Slash after the slash. Occasionally, when you try to access a particular Web site you may receive a "File Not Found" prompt. When you do, move your cursor to the end of the URL in the location window. Delete the URL from this point back to the first backslash (/) you encounter. If nothing happens, delete that portion of the URL to the next backslash (/). Keep repeating until you access the site or delete the entire URL. If you delete the entire URL but the domain and you still get the "File Not Found" prompt, move on. The Web site has been moved. If you do access the Web site, it means the particular page within the site you sought has moved, not the entire site. Now, scan the site. Often, you'll find the page in a new spot.

Search Usenet. Many engines search not only the Web but also Usenet newsgroups, which are Internet-wide discussion groups. To access this feature, click the down arrow next to "Search" (the Web) and select "Usenet."

Cut your losses. If you can't find what you're looking for on a site within sixty seconds, leave and search elsewhere. Don't waste time on sites that lead you in circles or make promises they don't keep. Chances are, if the site architecture is poor the information is too.

Walk away. If you spend more than an hour searching for information on a particular topic without success, either move on to a different subject or shut off the computer and head to your local library. Don't assume the Internet has all the answers and information. It doesn't. As big as the Internet is, it represents only a fraction of human knowledge. Even if the information is online, poor Web site design, indexing, and registration may make the information virtually impossible to find.

Don't neglect other information sources. The Internet is merely one power tool on a vast information-gathering workbench. Don't neglect other resources such as public libraries, bookstores, archives, government records, transcripts, interviews, focus groups, research papers, surveys, and many other materials and forums. A sound search strategy uses a careful mix of all of these elements, not just the Internet, to gather bits and pieces of information and assemble a complete intelligence picture.

Scanning for Trade Leads

With an understanding of searching basics, you're now ready to jump online and track down your targets. In a perfect world, the Internet would have a site called "The Definitive Place for International Trade Leads." There, you would find all the trade opportunities from every country and organization in the world. In the real world, it's more chaotic. The Net is overflowing with trade prospects, but they're not clearly marked, and you have to know where to look. In my experience, the best trade lead hotspots are in six online areas—sweepers, directories, periodicals, organizations, events, and professionals.

Sweepers

Trade lead sweepers refer to search engines and other online information retrieval tools. These aren't actual trade leads but they are a resource to scan the Internet for the target customers and suppliers you identified in your profile. The prime sweepers are the following:

Search engines. You've already bookmarked the leading engines such as Excite, Infoseek, Northern Light, and Yahoo in your Search Engine folder. Use *all* these engines, not just one or two, when hunting for trade lead possibilities. Each search engine has its own indexing system, and the same keywords will return different results on different engines. Another tip: Refer to your target customer profile when scanning for information. Every term on your profile represents a potential keyword. Try out the names of industries, companies, suppliers, competitors, job titles, products, geographic areas, senior executives, equipment, trade shows, and advertising slogans. Experiment with different words and phrases in different combinations and use double quotation marks, commas, the plus sign, and capital letters in your searches. You'll uncover a wider range of material from a variety of angles.

Metaengines. Metaengines are multiengine search tools that scan dozens of different engines at the same time. The leading metaengines include All-in-One at http://www.albany.net/allinone and Dogpile at http://www.dogpile .com, both of which are bookmarked in your Search Engines folder. These tools can help you search more of the Net in less time.

Regional search engines. Make use of regional search engines or the international editions of the popular engines such as AltaVista Australia, Infoseek Japan, and Yahoo! Germany. These engines focus on Web sites in a specific region or country and provide a more thorough scan of Web pages in countries other than the United States. For a list of regional search engines—including a list of the international editions of popular engines—visit "Virtual International Search Engines" at http://www .dreamscape.com/frankvad/search.international.html.

Specialized engines. These engines focus on a specific field or industry such as "Legal Resources" at http://www.findlaw.com and "HealthAtoZ" at http://www.healthatoz.com. Use these engines to search for information within disciplines and sectors around the world.

Informant. Available online at no charge, the Informant at http://informatn.dartmouth.edu is a search robot. You enter keywords in the robot and it will automatically sweep the Net for you at regular intervals looking for those keywords. The service allows you to pick one of four search engines—Lycos, AltaVista, Excite and Infoseek—to conduct the automatic scanning. Every few weeks, alternate the search engines to keep your searches fresh. Also, change keywords and incorporate double quotation marks, commas, the plus sign, and capital letters in the phrases when appropriate. Your searches will be more accurate.

Directories

Directories refer to sites that provide collections of links, reports, ads, and opportunities directly related to international trade. The top directories are the following:

Trade link sites. Trade link sites are a collection of Web page links that have been prescreened by trade researchers and professionals. In your Research subfolder, you've already bookmarked two of the best: International Business Resources at http://ciber.bus.msu.edu/busres.htm and WorldClass at http://web.idirect.com/~tiger/. Both are frequently updated and link to the latest and best global business sites on the Internet. Start your searches here, and you'll save yourself hours of search time.

Industry- or subject-specific link sites. Link sites have been developed on virtually all subjects, not just trade. Check out the WWW Virtual Library at http://vlib.stanford.edu/Overview.html for a catalog of links on hundreds of business and academic subjects. Scan this list for link sites in your target industries. You'll tap the experience and expertise of specialists who scan for information in a particular area on a regular basis.

Geographic CyberPorts. Virtually all the sites bookmarked in your Geographic CyberPorts folder offer international trade contacts and opportunities. Email two of them with a brief note about your business and the type of business alliances you're seeking in that country. Many of these sites offer free matchmaking services that will refer you to a suitable partner. Another tip: When communicating with foreign trade officials, never say you want to export to their country. Instead, say you're seeking a joint venture, strategic alliance, or bilateral selling relationship. The officials will be more responsive. Whether or not they admit it, many trade officials discourage importing into their own countries and are reluctant to help those only interested in selling in their market.

Trade lead services. Trade leads are offers posted by exporters and importers to buy or sell products internationally. For a list of the leading online trade lead services, check your Rainmaker folder for International Trade Leads at http://ciber.bus.msu.edu/busres/tradlead.htm. Widely divergent in size, style, and quality, some are free to access while others are subscription based. Some cover many different industries in many countries, while others focus on one industry in one country. Experiment with several services that cover your industry and test drive at least one that offers the best features and benefits for you. A word of caution: Subscribing to these services often results in a flood of email, which grows quickly tiresome. Ensure that any leads you receive from these services are prescreened and provide information only on your specific industry and target market. If they aren't, select another service or quit altogether. When selecting a trade lead service, also insist on quality, not quantity. Better to receive one credible trade lead every three months that you can act on than one hundred marginal trade leads a day every day, which congest your inbox, consume your time, and divert your attention from pursuing legitimate export opportunities.

Market research reports. Market research reports are studies prepared by consultants or specialists on opportunities in a particular sector in a particular country. Look in your Consultant subfolder and check out two sites—the Department of State's Country Commercial Guides at http://www.state.gov/www/about_state/business/com_guides/index.html and Industry Canada's Market Research at http://strategis.ic.gc.ca/ sc_mrkti/ibinddc/engdoc/1al.html. Both are packed with hundreds of free reports that provide key background information and contacts. Just because they're free, don't take them for granted. The information in just one of these reports would typically cost you thousands of dollars from an average management consultant.

Telephone directories. Telephone directories provide lists of names, addresses, and telephone and fax numbers for firms and potential customers in a particular area. Look in your Rainmaker subfolder and select "Telephone Directories on the Web" at http://www.contractjobs.com/tel/. Scan two directories, and use the search functions to compile as detailed list as possible of your target group—for example, dental offices in London. You'll zero in on exactly the people you want to reach, and have a "hot lead" list of prime prospects.

Patent databases. Patent offices issue exclusive rights to authors and inventors for their writings and discoveries. View Patent Web sites at http://www.uspto.gov/web/menu/other.html for a list of patent office Web sites around the world. Scan the sites for new inventions and discoveries. You may be able to partner with the inventor to develop the product or process. Also, be on the lookout for patents that are scheduled to expire shortly or expire because of nonpayment of maintenance fees. You may gain access to an innovative product or technology at virtually no cost.

Technology databases. Technology databases are listings of new products and processes that are available for commercialization. Cold search for databases in your industry. Use these directories to seek new products, and find new partners in your technology area. For an example, visit the National Technology Index at http://www.cisti.nrc.ca/programs/ indcan/nti/engindex.html. The database provides a searchable index of commercialization opportunities in Canada. Scan the index for potential contacts and partnering ideas.

Business school cases. Business school cases are reports by university professors and students on particular industries, markets, companies, and products. Cold search for business schools across the country and around the world. Email two and inquire if any cases have been prepared in your product or service area. If so, request a copy. You may receive a wealth of free information and contacts—material that would cost thousands of dollars from a consultant.

Press releases. Press releases are announcements that publicize a new initiative, product, or other development to the general public and media. Visit Business Wire at http://www.businesswire.com and PR Newswire at http://www.prnewswire.com for a list of the latest corporate press releases from around the world. At least once a week, search the database for press releases and breaking news in your industry. This may alert you to new selling, strategic alliance, and subcontracting opportunities. Watch for individuals who receive major promotions, particularly those in organizations you could potentially supply. These are precisely the people you want to target—the rising stars and top decision makers who have the clout and cash to buy what you sell.

Classified ads. Classified ads are notices to buy or sell a product or service. Visit Free Classified Sites at http://www.magpage.com/~rispoli/free .html for a list of Web sites that allow you to read and post online ads at no charge. Scan two sites for leads in your industry. Like all classified ads, they're a mixed bag of offers, but good deals can be found. Post your own ad—they're free after all. Describe what you offer and the business partners you're seeking. You may connect with a valuable business partner.

Career and help wanted ads. Help wanted and career ads list employment opportunities with all types and sizes of organizations. Visit Opportunities for Employment at http://www.dbm.com/jobguide/ jobs.html for a listing of job Web sites online. Review the resources that feature job opportunities in your industry and other countries around the world. Look at which organizations are hiring, what skills and experience they are seeking, and how many positions are they filling. This provides key indicators about where the organizations are headed and what kinds of products and services they wish to develop and market. For example, software company A posts an ad for ten computer game programmers. This suggests that company A is building a game development team. Knowing this, anticipate future needs and supply opportunities. The new hires will need new workstations, equipment, and training. The game will need a paper booklet, CD-ROM, and cardboard packaging. It will have to be tested with focus groups, distributed to dealers, and promoted to consumers. Ask yourself: Where along this business chain could I provide a value-added product or service? If you see a fit, pitch a proposal to company A. The lesson to be learned is that behind all job ads are at least two opportunities: an opportunity to supply and train the new hires and an opportunity to provide inputs and assistance to design, package, distribute, and promote whatever new or enhanced product or service they've been hired to deliver.

Resume databases. Look in your Employer Counselor subfolder and scan the Riley Guide at http://www.dbm.com/jobguide/. Check its resume databases for individuals who work in your industry and either still work or have worked for organizations you're targeting as customers or partners. Email selected individuals and seek their advice on who best to approach and how business is really done inside a particular organization or market. While you should caution them not to reveal any proprietary information, many will provide surprisingly frank and valuable insights based on their unique knowledge and experience. These insights can give you the edge when developing business and pitching deals.

Net broadcasts. Using RealAudio and RealVideo software available at http://www.realaudio.com, you can listen to radio stations, watch television stations and videos, and catch concerts, games, and events from around the world—all live—on your computer. Check out Timecast at http://www.timecast.com/ for a list of stations, videos, audio, and live programming available on the Net. Look for stations in markets where you'd like to find customers or suppliers and business programs that discuss your industry or market. Tune in—these stations and shows may alert you to new opportunities and contacts.

Periodicals

Periodicals refer to discussion groups and publishing sites that are frequently updated and monitor a particular industry or market. The leading periodical sites are the following:

Newsgroups. Newsgroups are online discussion groups that bring together Internet users from around the world to share information and communicate about common interests. For a list of the over twenty thousand Internet newsgroups, visit DejaNews at http://www.dejanews.com. Bookmarked in your Pollster subfolder, the site includes a searchable database of newsgroup transcripts and instructions on how to join a group. Search for the groups that discuss your industry and products and pick the one your clients and prospects frequent the most. Monitor the discussion and offer free advice. You'll pick up valuable feedback, gain recognition, and earn credibility with the key decision makers you're targeting.

News networks. News networks refer to news syndicates and newspapers that report on current affairs in a particular area. Check your Reporter subfolder and visit **MediaINFO Links at http://www.mediainfo.com/ emedia/** for a list of thousands of newspapers and other news networks-online around the world. View two newspapers and scan the headlines. Look for key terms such as "major expansion," "privatization," "sell-off," "purchase," and even "cutbacks." All signal change and potential buying and selling opportunities for you.

Newspaper ads. Study the online ads of the newspapers. Examine their content, design, and tone. Are they graphics-rich? Text-heavy? Do they promote quality? Service? Price? Any testimonials? This will give you insight into the nuances of that market and how to sell there online. Also consider the advertisers—the fact they're advertising on the Internet suggests they're innovative and open to new ideas. They may be a potential partner for you.

Business editors. Email the business editors from two of these online newspapers. Ask for contacts and tips on how to operate in the local market. The editor has the inside scoop on the major business personalities and stories in that area.

Magazines. Magazines are weekly, monthly, or quarterly publications that provide news and opinions on a particular area, industry, or lifestyle. Visit the Electronic Newsstand at http://www.enews.com/ for information and links to some three thousand magazines online. Review two publications in your industry. Look for articles that profile businesspeople and projects in other countries. You may spot a useful contact or opportunity or information that could lead to a contract or opportunity.

Magazine writers and columnists. If you find a valuable magazine about a person or project, email the author and request additional information. Because of space and time constraints, many published articles contain only a fraction of the research that was conducted for the writing assignment. Ask the author for more, and he or she may be able to provide an avalanche of additional material and contacts.

Journals. Journals are publications that publish research reports by academics or industry specialists. Visit E-Journal at http://www.edoc.com/ ejournal/ for a list of online journals, and scan at least two related to your business. Hunt for new products, processes, techniques, breakthroughs, and contacts that you can use to boost your business around the world. You'll keep up to date on the latest developments in your industry and keep a fresh perspective.

Organizations

Organizations refer to selected companies, government agencies, and associations involved in procurement and international trade. The premiere organizations for trade leads are the following:

Existing customers. Look for ways to solidify and expand your business with existing customers using the Internet. Check out the Web sites of your customers, and review all corporate plans, executive biographies, and product profiles. You may be surprised what you don't know about your own clients, and new supply opportunities may be apparent. If you have a Web page, offer to post a link on your site to their home page if they post a link on their page to your site. Your customer's customers and contacts may represent new business opportunities for you.

International units of existing customers. Through the Web or a phone call, inquire if your existing customers have units or alliances in other countries. If so, pitch proposals to these international units, and use your existing customer as a reference. Other members of a corporate family may be interested in your offerings, especially if you have a proven track record with one of their own.

Company sites. Company Web sites are those posted by individual firms and organizations. Cold search for organizations that fit your customer profile. Scan their Web pages closely and return regularly for updates. The sites provide a bonanza of information such as a list of products made, equipment used, services offered, and executives in charge that you can use to qualify the prospect. Also check out company directories such as these:

- **Europages (http://www.europages.com/)** for a list of European companies
- **InAsia (http://www.inasia.com/)** for Asian companies
- **Companies Online (http://www.companiesonline.com)** for United States companies
- **Canadian Company Capabilities (http://strategis.ic.gc.ca/ sc_coinf/ccc/engdoc/homepage.html)** for Canadian companies

All provide corporate and product profiles on thousands of firms around the world.

Procurement agencies. Procurement agencies are the purchasing arms of governments. They buy billions of dollars of goods and services everyday. Visit your Rainmaker folder and select the Procurement Assistance Jumpstation at http://www.fedmarket.com/ to check out the major procurement agencies online in the United States and offshore. Many of these organizations post requests for proposals on their sites and allow you to bid online. Also look out for recent contract awards and a list of winning bidders on the procurement sites. If you see a potential fit, email the contractor and suggest ways you could be a resource or supplier on the project. Subcontracting opportunities may be available.

Federal and national governments. Although roles vary by country, federal or national governments around the world generally procure goods and services related to national defense, agriculture and food, scientific research, the environment, transportation, communication, international trade, pensions, consumer safety, statistics collection, weather monitoring, search and rescue, immigration, taxation, corrections, national parks and wildlife protection, and other activities. Visit City.Net at http://www.city.net/ for a list of federal and national governments on the Net in your target market. Review the press releases and What's New sections of federal government Web sites and look for major announcements such as these:

- new environmental regulations that require businesses to upgrade their pollution control standards

- new policy initiatives that require research or consulting services
- plans for new infrastructure such as airports, rail, power, and telecommunications
- bidding opportunities for a major international event such as the Olympics, a G-7 Summit, or the Rio Summit
- natural disasters that require rebuilding
- the closing of military bases or weapons depositories

All are leads to new supply and partnering opportunities.

State, provincial, and regional governments. Subnational levels of government generally procure goods and services related to health, education, road and bridge construction and maintenance, driver licensing, vital statistics, child and family services, job training, natural resource management, tourism, health development, business registrations, and other activities. Visit City.Net at http://www.city.net/ for a list of state and provincial governments on the Net in your target market. Check out the press releases and What's New sections of these subnational government Web sites and look for major announcements such as the following:

- new social policies on literary development or lifelong learning
- new curricula being introduced in universities, community colleges, high schools, and junior and elementary schools
- the provision of emergency services in rural and remote areas
- the privatization of heath care systems
- trends toward deregulation, privatization, or right-sizing
- new tourism initiatives or national parks or areas

All have business potential.

Local and civic governments. Local and civic governments generally procure goods and services related to fire and police protection, ambulance services, water supply, garbage collection and disposal, recycling, traffic control, sewage treatment, building permits and inspections, plumbing and gas permits, libraries, parks and recreation, zoning and development, and chemical spills and pollution control. Scan the press releases and What's New sections of these subnational government Web sites and look for major announcements such as these:

- new recycling programs

- privatization or subcontracting of fire, police, and garbage-collection services
- new water treatment or pollution control initiatives
- construction or maintenance of roads and bridges
- traffic congestion studies
- new industrial parks
- new civic reorganization, quality standards, or downsizing

All have business development possibilities.

International financial institutions. International financial institutions or IFIs refer to organizations such as the World Bank, the Inter-American Development Bank, and the Asian Development Bank. Every year, these agencies provide billions of dollars to finance infrastructure and other economic development projects, largely in developing countries. Visit IFI Net at http://www.dfait-maeci.gc.ca/ifinet/menu-e.htm to learn more about IFI procurement and capital project opportunities around the world.

Foreign embassies in the United States. Foreign embassies and consulates in the United States provide a wealth of information on their respective countries and can assist you with business networking. Check your Diplomat subfolder for Electronic Embassy at http://www.embassy.org. The site links to foreign embassies in the United States and Canada. Email two and request a list of business contacts in their country in your industry. Opportunities may be apparent from the lists you receive.

U.S. embassies. U.S. Embassies monitor local economic conditions and identify business opportunities for U.S. firms in foreign markets. Visit the U.S. Department of Commerce Commercial Service at http://www .ita.doc.gov/uscs/forweb.html for a list of the U.S. embassies and trade offices around the world. Email two offices and ask for the names of the biggest buyers and suppliers in their market that match your profile. The trade commissioners will give you frontline intelligence on local business leaders and trends. Just as with foreign trade officials, never tell U.S. trade officials that you want to import into the United States. Again, that may be precisely what you want to do, but keep that to yourself. Instead, say you're interested in international procurement, bilateral sourcing, or cross-border linkages. These are key buzzwords that trade officials like to hear, and you'll get faster and better service if your describe your plans in these terms.

U.S. industry associations. U.S. industry associations promote the interests of American companies and businesspeople in a particular sector. Cold search for local and national associations in your product or service area. Email two of them and inquire whether any international marketing reports or initiatives have been developed on behalf of your industry. Many associations have full-time staff or contractors who track business opportunities in your industry around the world. Tap into this expertise—you're paying for it with your membership dues. If your association hasn't developed any international business reports or plans, demand that it start. To truly promote and protect your interests in this global economy, your association should constantly monitor global business trends on behalf of your firm and industry.

Foreign industry associations. Cold search for industry associations in other countries. If possible, become a member and offer to serve as a virtual volunteer on one of their committees. You wouldn't attend any meetings in person but would stay in the loop using email. You'll instantly make contacts and win friends with key industry decision makers in other countries. At the very least, monitor the Web sites of relevant industry associations around the world. You'll learn who the leading players are and get the inside track on industry needs and developments in other regions.

Chambers of commerce. Chambers of commerce promote business development in a particular city or county. Look in your Researcher subfolder and select CityNet at http://www.city.net/. The site lists commerce chambers and other economic development authorities in over five thousand locations around the world. Select two chambers and email both. Request a list of potential partners in their community that meet your profile. Chambers know all the local movers and shakers and can direct you to the appropriate businesspeople. Whenever possible, focus on smaller, regional centers (such as Birmingham, United Kingdom) as opposed to larger national or international centers (such as London). Economic development authorities in larger centers are often more bureaucratic and impersonal when responding to requests for information. By comparison, authorities in smaller centers are generally more personable and flexible and have a try-harder attitude. The lesson is that you shouldn't overlook the first-class opportunities and capabilities of many so-called second-tier or rural communities.

Foreign trade zones. Foreign trade zones are special areas and enclaves in which goods may be imported for processing or storage and subsequently exported duty-free. Cold search for foreign trade zones in your target market or visit the National Association of Foreign Trade Zones at http://imex.com/naftz.html. Email a foreign trade zone in your target market and inquire if any trade zone user matches your customer, supplier, or partner profile.

Utilities. Utilities are agencies that provide public services such as water, gas, and power. Cold search for utilities Web sites around the world or visit Utility Companies at http://www.yahoo.com/Business_and_Economy/ Companies/Utilities/, a listing of utility organizations online. Email two of them and ask for a list of organizations in their service area that meet your target profile. Although they don't like to advertise this, all utilities conduct extensive studies of their users—both business and residential— to forecast demand. They can lead you to leading firms in the area, provide a status report on their operations, and alert you to projects just started and major developments in the works.

Events

Events refer to international trade-related meetings and special initiatives. The best events are these:

Outgoing trade missions. Hundreds of outgoing trade missions are organized every year in the United States by federal, state, and local government trade promoters. On these missions, teams of U.S. companies from a particular industry visit a foreign country to explore new business opportunities. For a list of upcoming trade missions planned in your industry, review the U.S. Trade Events Calendar at http://infoserv2.ita .doc.gove/epc.nsf. If an outgoing mission interests you, consider going: Many events offer subsidized travel and meetings with leading deal makers that would be impossible to arrange on your own. If you can't make the event, email the mission organizers a few weeks or so after the event, and request a copy of the mission report. You'll find out all the contacts made and deals struck on the trip. Scan the list of foreign contacts, and email those that interest you. Note in your communication that you were unable to attend the event but still wish to pursue opportunities there. Don't underestimate this approach: businesspeople who don't go on missions but follow up will often reap more rewards than businesspeople who go but don't follow up.

Incoming trade missions. On incoming missions, teams of foreign firms visit the United States to find business partners in the States. Check the

U.S. Trade Events Calendar for any incoming missions in your industry. If any international delegations in your industry are scheduled to visit your area, invite the delegation to tour your plant or office. Offer to host a reception or request meetings with members of the group. You'll lead international buyers literally right to your door at minimal expense.

Trade shows. Trade shows are industry exhibitions that showcase new products and services. Thousands are held every year around the world in virtually all sectors. Tap this network without leaving your office. Look in your Rainmaker folder and select ExpoGuide at http://www.expoguide.com and Trade Show Central at http://www.tscentral.com. Search these online trade show directories and identify the three top trade shows in your industry and then obtain the contact information for each event. Email or fax show organizers and request a list of the event exhibitors, attendees, and proceedings. Although some lists are free and others are available for a modest fee, all provide fresh information about what's hot and who's buying in your industry.

Export awards. Numerous government agencies at the federal, state, provincial, and local level in countries around the world have an "Exporter of the Year" or similarly named initiative that recognizes excellence in international trade. These include the Canada Export Award Program at http://www.dfait-maeci.gc.ca/english/trade/award-e.htm and the Queen's Award for Export Achievement at http://www.open.gov.uk/qawards/export.htm in the United Kingdom. Cold search the Web for these award programs and note the winners in recent years, particularly in your target market. Acclaimed by peers, these organizations are generally high-growth and outward-looking operations that are keen to explore new cross-border alliances and business opportunities.

Professionals

Professionals refer to companies and specialists who provide international trade support services. They are key intermediaries who can direct you to leading buyers, sellers, and partners in a particular industry or market. The foremost trade professionals are the following:

Banks and venture capital firms. Banks and venture capital firms are establishments that lend money and review business plans and loan applications. Select your Banker subfolder and visit the Financial Information Link Library at http://www.mbnet.mb.ca/~russell/ for a list of leading moneylenders online from around the world. Email two and request a list of their clients that match your target profile. Although most banking information is confidential, moneylenders know the leading businesspeople and the pending deals in the area. If your product or service offers a potential benefit to their clients, they may be keen to pass along names and arrange introductions.

Credit services. Credit services do credit checks on companies around the world. Visit Credit Reporting Agencies at http://www.creditworthy .com/us/providers/agency.html and check out those services that specialize in your target market and product area. Email the Webmasters to inquire about opportunities and contacts in a particular location and segment. They have a wealth of information on thousands of companies and may be able to qualify and screen prospects for you.

Accountants. Accountants manage financial and taxation issues. Check out International Tax Resources at http://www.taxsites.com/international .html for a directory of accountants online. Email accountants in your target market for information on leading prospects and opportunities.

Customs brokers. Customs brokers clear goods through customs. Cold search for customs brokers in your target market and visit FABNet at http://www.tradecompass.com/fabnet/ for a list of leading customs brokers in the United States. The brokers know who's moving what across the border, where, and to whom, and may be able to direct you to potential customers and partners.

Freight forwarders. Freight forwarders prepare documents and arrange various transactions related to the international distribution of goods. Scan Freightworld at http://www.freightworld.com/ and search for forwarders in your target market. Email a few and ask for the names of companies that match your profile. The forwarders are well connected in the export community, and know most of the leading players.

Couriers. Couriers provide local delivery services and are an underrated source of business intelligence. Cold search for couriers in your target market and request a list of organizations that meet your profile. Couriers are in constant contact with the busiest firms in an area and may direct you to prime prospects.

Motor carriers. Motor carriers provide truck transportation services within and between countries. Check Trucking and Motor Carriers Worldwide at http://www.freightworld.com/truc_geo.html for a list of trucking operations online around the world. Email several operations in your target market and seek their advice on who to call and how to do business in their particular area.

Seaport Business Development Managers. Seaport business development managers promote port and harbor operations. Visit Transportation and Logistics Ports and Harbors at http://www.freightworld.com/port_geo.html for a list of seaports worldwide. Email the leading port in your target market and ask the business development manager to pass along contacts and information. That's their job.

Ocean carriers. Ocean carriers transport goods around the world on waterborne vessels. Visit the Electronic Shipping Guide on the Web at http://www.shipguide.com/ for a list of container shipping schedules of over sixty ocean carriers for voyages in and out of the United States and Canada, including import, export, connecting, and feeder service. Email a carrier or two. Tell them about your business, and what type of deals you are seeking. They have a wide circle of contacts and may be able to identify potential customers and partners.

Rail Carriers. Rail carriers provide rail transportation services within and between countries. Visit Railroads Worldwide at http://www.freight-world.com/railroads.html for a list of railroads around the world on the Web. Zip off an email to the leading rail operations in your target market, and ask for names.

Airport Business Development Managers. Airport business development managers promote airport operations and air cargo facilities. Visit Airports of the World at http://www.freightworld.com/airptgeo.html. Email the leading airports in your target market and ask for referrals. The managers will be especially helpful if the customers or partners you are seeking are involved in the transport of time-sensitive or perishable goods.

Air Carriers. Air carriers provide air transportation services to international traders. Visit Airlines of the Web at http://www.itn.net/cgi/get?itn/cb/aow/index:XX-AIRLINES for a list of airline and cargo air services online. Email one or two that operate in your target market and ask for contacts. They know all the movers, shakers, and highflyers in their area.

Management consultants. Management consultants conduct a wide variety of research, evaluation, and strategy formulation assignments on a contract basis. They do business with a wide variety of clients from all sectors of the economy and often assist in the long-range planning of organizations. Visit the International Council of Management Consulting Institutes at http://www.mcninet.com/icmci/cmcHome.html and seek out management consultants who specialize in your target market, product, or service. Email one and ask for information about leading opportunities and contacts in a particular area. They may provide useful tips and contacts.

Lawyers. Lawyers advise clients on legal matters on everything from contracts to payments to dispute settlement. Visit International Trade Law Firms and Associations at http://ananse.irv.uit.no/trade_law/nav/law.firms.associations.html and search for lawyers that specialize in your target market and product area. Email a few and ask for referrals. Often, they're eager to oblige: If their clients win new business, so do they.

Translators. These professionals translate documents and speeches from one language to another. Review Online Dictionaries and Translators at http://rivendel.com/~ric/resources/dictionary.html and email one or two of the translation companies and services listed. Inquire if any of their clients might be interested in your offering or business proposal. They may be keen to pass on names in order to generate new translation work for themselves.

Advertising agencies. Advertising agencies develop promotional ads and campaigns for clients. Visit the International Advertising Resource Center at http://www.ou.edu/class/jmc3333/ and search for a list of advertising firms in your target market. Fire off an email or two and ask them to pass along the names of top accounts in their areas that match your profile. Advertising agencies are aware of major and planned promotions and can lead you to top media buyers in their respective territory.

Banner ads. Instead of exploring the Web for trade leads, get the trade leads to come to you. Find a high-traffic Web site that attracts the customers or partners you are seeking to reach and post a banner ad—a rectangular "click-through" online advertisement. The graphic could link to your Web site or the host site of the ad and provide details about your organization and the opportunity. For more information about advertising on the Net, visit the Internet Advertising Resource Guide at http://www.admedia.org/cgi-bin/bs3/bs3.pl?ts=878355813 and Web Site Banner Advertising at http://www.markwelch.com/bannerad.

Keyword ads. According to Linda Himelstein in her article "Web Ads Start to Click" (*Business Week*, October 6, 1997), keyword ads, featured primarily on Web search engines, link a specific ad to the text or search query a Web user may enter. Miller Brewing, for example, bought the word "beer" on Yahoo. Every time someone uses the word *beer* in a search, an ad appears for "Miller Genuine Draft Beer." Similarly, you could "buy" a word related to your business on a search engine. When a user types in that word—whatever it may be—an ad for your organization and opportunity would appear. For more information, contact the site administrators of the search engine sites such as Yahoo at http://www.yahoo.com, Infoseek at http://www.infoseek.com, and AltaVista at http://altavista.digital.com.

Business school professors. Business school professors conduct research on industries, markets, products, and companies. Scan business school sites and professor biographies for those who specialize in your target market, product, or service area. Email one and ask for tips on who to contact and how to do business in a country or market segment. They may offer useful pointers and referrals that could expedite your international marketing plans.

Each of these trade-lead areas provides potentially hundreds, if not thousands, of fresh cross-border contacts and opportunities every *week*. Over the next few days, take a morning or an afternoon to explore these sites in more detail. Be on the lookout for companies and business people that match your profile, and you should be able to gather your list of ten names in no time. That completed, you're now ready to master the final—and most important—step: how to use the Internet to transform this list of names into a new cross-border sale or international deal.

GOING ON VIRTUAL
TRADE MISSIONS

12

In the physical world, trade missions are one of the key tools used by individuals and companies to develop, market, and sell new international business. The organizer of the mission—usually a government trade promotion agency—arranges for a team of individuals or companies from a particular country to visit another country to explore trade opportunities. On the trip, businesspeople attend briefings, visit trade shows, and meet face to face with potential partners and customers to discuss their mutual business interests. The missions often produce spectacular results—new contacts, new sales, and new deals.

However, trade missions also take their toll. Some tours can last as long as two weeks or more, amounting to a huge investment in time for any businessperson. This can be especially difficult for those who run small companies with limited resources. Despite a glamorous image, overseas trade missions frequently involve lengthy travel times, jet lag, lost luggage, customs lines, tainted food or drink, contacts who don't show, and cultural or linguistic misunderstandings. Often, one trip is not enough. Many participants find themselves forced to return to a foreign market two, three, or even more times to work out details and reach a final agreement with potential business partners in other countries. Each time they travel, they also endure the rigors of the road.

Using the Internet wisely, you can now bypass all these challenges. Each day, you can go out on *virtual* trade missions—Web-based excursions that take you around the world in search of cross-border sales and deals. In much the same way you would prepare for a trade mission in real life, you'll need to learn what to pack, how to qualify prospects, and what deals to pitch. Eventually, you'll learn how to leverage the Internet to achieve everything you would on an overseas trade mission, without all the hassles, time, and expense.

Packing Your Digital Briefcase

As part of the work you did in Chapter 11, "Developing Global Business Leads Using the Internet," you should now have a list of ten key contacts you'd like to do business with in other countries. Your next task: Go out on your first virtual trade mission to contact all these individuals and begin a dialog about mutual business opportunities.

To start, you'll need to pack for your trip. On a real-life trade mission, you would prepare and pack such things as business cards, brochures, samples, and other marketing materials to support your global outreach. The same is true here—only this time, all of the following materials you prepare can be digitally transmitted rather than physically shipped.

Biography. Take time to prepare this vital electronic calling card. In any international business transaction, the most important element you'll be selling is yourself. To succeed in your trade mission, you must first prove your own credibility before any discussions or deals will flow. As in any biography or resume, highlight your education, work experience, affiliations, and hobbies. Don't be shy. Discuss your past accomplishments and your current professional goals. Provide substantive insights into your character and professional reputation.

To provide enough detail for a potential overseas business partner, your biography should be at least five hundred words in length. In some cases, depending on how much information you can include, it might be several pages longer. This is OK–your potential overseas partner will be seeking to find out as much as he or she can about you and your capabilities. Prepare your biography (and all other text files mentioned in this chapter) in plain text format. Computers and software programs vary widely around the world, and it's best to use a basic format that is readable by virtually all systems. That means that stylish fonts, bolds, and italics will not appear in the document and should not be used. When it is ready, name this file "Resume."

Company profile. In your company profile, identify basic information that you know will be important to a foreign company, such as corporate name, address, telephone, fax, and Internet numbers. Provide a brief history of the business to date, including current ownership, predecessor companies, and any other relevant information. List the names of all senior executives and directors at the company, including biographical information. Without revealing any proprietary information, indicate the number of people employed by your company and their major areas of activity. You may also wish to provide a summary of financial information, including sales by major product or business lines or by geographic area. Your profile should be at least five hundred words long to provide a minimum amount of background information. When it is ready, name this file "Organization" or "Org."

Brochure. On the Net, most global partners are looking for niche capabilities, not generalists. Insurance shoppers, for example, would not be overly interested in a firm that provides general insurance—thousands already do that—but they would be interested in a firm that provides insurance for plastics factories or shipping vessels. The narrower your focus, the easier it will be to attract more credible and targeted prospects.

Make sure your brochure covers all your products and/or services. Describe the features of each, including technical specifications, options, colors, and sizes. Provide a list of past customers, testimonials, and mini case studies describing how your product or service has produced results and added value. Be sure to emphasize your specialty. Write at least one hundred words for each product or service. When it is ready, label this file "Brochure."

Supplies. This is an inventory of all the major goods and services you buy. Describe the items you purchase and be as specific as possible: Identify your precise requirements relating to cost, color, shape, quality, durability, packaging, composition, mixture, quantity, delivery, and after-sales service. Include digital scans of product photos, or even blueprints if necessary. To attract reliable tenders from prospective suppliers, you need to provide as many details as possible about your needs. Write at least one hundred words for each major product or service. Name this file "Supplies."

Pictures. Using your own camera or photos already on file, take at least four pictures: one of yourself, one of your company headquarters, one of your products/services, and one of your service providers in action. Heed the old saying, "A picture is worth a thousand words." In this video era, people are more likely to believe what they see as opposed to what they read. The photos will provide added credibility to your proposal and make you seem more real to a prospect. Scan these pictures into digital files. A photo or print shop can do this for a modest fee, or you can use your own scanner. If you're using a photo or print shop, request that each of the photos is saved in a .jpg format—these should each be around 50K in size and no more than 100K. The smaller the file size, the faster it will transmit over the Net. Large files—anything over 100K—take quite a while to transmit and are annoying to download.

If you're using your own scanner, import your files into a graphics package such as PaintShop Pro, an image processing program available at http://www.jasc.com. Using the package, tinker with the color depth and the image size to minimize file size. When they are ready, label your photo "MyPhoto," the company shot "HQ," your image of your products/services "Product/Services," and your service providers "Service." If you have more than one product or service, get a photo for each and label each photo (for example, "Product1," "Product2").

Hometown profile. Go to City.Net at http://www.city.net/ and gather information about the city or community in which your business is located. On real-life trade missions, businesspeople from other countries are often interested in where and how you live and how life is different—or the same—compared to where they reside. Profile your community's history, economic base, population, tourist attractions, and claims to fame. This should be about one hundred to two hundred words in length. When it is ready, label this file "Hometown."

Hot links. From your Internet research, compile a list of at least twenty Web sites that provide useful information about your particular industry. This simple but effective service will be appreciated by your prospect and will show that you're Net literate and willing to share information. For each site, list the title of the Web page, its address or URL, and the name of the organization or individual responsible for posting the site. Also prepare a brief fifty-to-one-hundred-word description of each site. Describe the site's contents and why it is useful. In total, this document should be between one thousand and two thousand words in length. When it is ready, label this file "Hotlinks."

Assembling Your Briefcase

Once all these files have been prepared, it's time to ready your briefcase for the trade mission at hand. Instead of something made out of leather, however, you'll be using 3.5-inch computer diskettes instead. Get two diskettes—one plus a backup. Label the first diskette "Digital Briefcase #1" and the second "Digital Briefcase #1 (Backup)." Copy all of the files for your trade mission from your word processor and image processor onto the diskettes. Depending on the size of these files, you may need two or more diskettes to hold all the documents. In that case, get additional diskettes and name them "Digital Briefcase #2" and "Digital Briefcase #3" and so on, along with backup diskettes for each. You're now packed and ready for the next step.

Readying Your Online Jet

In the physical world, you climb aboard a high-powered jet that whisks you away to foreign lands. Online, you're the captain of an exponentially more powerful vehicle—so powerful, in fact, that it makes a 747 look like a moped. It's your browser and email, and it's sitting right there on your desk.

Think about it. To service and pilot a real airplane, you need dozens of highly trained professionals, ranging from mechanics to flight crews to air traffic controllers. One person—even a child—can pilot a browser and work email at virtually no cost. To reach a faraway destination on an airplane, you may have to travel eighteen hours or more, wait for connecting flights, and switch jets. With a browser and email you can leapfrog around the world in mere seconds and reach numerous locations simultaneously.

A real aircraft can only take you to the airport. You still need to get where you are going and hope that your contact is available as scheduled. Using a browser and email, the digital "you" whizzes through the heaviest midtown traffic, zips through the front door, and whooshes past the gauntlet of advisors and assistants who orbit any influential decision maker. You rush into the corner office and touch down on your prospect's desktop without an appointment and without regard for office hours or time zones. Not even a $12.5 million Gulfstream can do that.

These days, access to the Web and a basic email account are all you really need to conduct international business in many places around the world. While it's nice to have a Web page, this can come later. Your first few weeks and months in cyberspace should be focused on how to effectively search, extract information, and use email. These are underrated but critical skills that will deliver far more business results in a much faster way than building a Web site, especially if you're new to computing and the Internet.

For virtual trade missions, the following tips can make your browser and email even more powerful and efficient tools for achieving success.

Add Your Electronic "Signature" to Every Email

Consider adding a signature—an online business card—to the bottom of every email you send. This will help boost your organization's profile and name recognition on the Net and encourage follow-up from potential clients or partners. The signature should include your name, title, company, telephone and fax numbers, email address, Web address if you have one, and even a corporate slogan. To create an electronic signature, check the Help file of your browser. It's normally a simple, five-minute procedure depending on the type and version of your browser and well worth the modest time investment.

Create an Address Book

Just as you use an address book, a digital diary, or a Rolodex to organize your contacts on paper, you should consider creating an address book inside your email system that allows you to organize your virtual trade mission contacts online.

To do this, let's start by adding the ten names and email addresses identified in Chapter 11, "Developing Global Business Leads Using the Internet." Consult the Help file of your browser for instructions on how to add the name and contact information for each entry.

As you gather other global business leads online, add them to your address book, and be sure to include a brief description of each contact and whether he or she could be a potential customer, supplier, or partner for your firm. As the addresses pile up, tagging each entry with a brief profile will make them easier to find and sort.

Start Your Own Mailing Lists

As your list of contacts grows and you develop more confidence online, it's time to consider starting your own Internet mailing lists. Lyris at http://www.shelby.com/, an Internet mail shareware program, allows you to run your own open discussions, moderated forums, and announcement lists functions, along with document robots and auto-responders. You can use the program to create your own Internet marketing network at virtually no cost.

Develop an Email Traffic Control System

Just as a busy airport has a system for handling inbound and outbound aircraft, your email traffic needs to be properly routed and queued to make the most of your electronic messaging capability. Appreciate that your marketing success on the Net will be highly dependent upon your speedy and courteous response to incoming email. If you take too long to respond to someone's message or reply in a haphazard manner, you will lose goodwill and alienate potential business allies or customers.

For maximum efficiency, develop and follow an email response system each day. Check your email as much as possible (at least every day) and code incoming correspondence into one of three categories: "top priority," which you respond to immediately; "information required," which you respond to within a day; and "trash," which you delete immediately. When dealing with emails, remember that they are just like paper—only handle it once (OHIO). You'll save time and boost productivity.

Use Folders

Think of your email inbox as a runway that should be kept as clear and unclogged as possible. Like an airport, it should be a place where emails initially touch down, but then are quickly redirected to other "information hangars," or folders.

To handle these incoming messages, create a classification system that is easy to use and fits your needs. You might consider groupings by geography ("Asian business leads"), by industry ("Aerospace business leads") or by type of opportunity (such as "Sales leads" or "Purchasing leads"). Using this method will help promote a more organized and prompt response to incoming messages, while minimizing the likelihood that emails will be misplaced or forgotten.

Register

To help potential prospects find you, list your email address in a number of free online business directories. You might want to consider registering with Four 11 (http://four11.com), Whowhere (http://www.whowhere.com), or Infospace (http://www.infospace.com). Any of these online directories will allow you to post your company's name, email address, and regular mailing address at no charge.

Promote

Put your email address—and Web address, if you have one—on all your business cards, brochures, catalogs, Yellow-Pages ads, trade show displays, billboards, answering machines, samples, and any other promotional materials or signage. This is an easy way to let people from any country know where to find you online.

Develop an Internet Tip Sheet

Prepare an Internet tip sheet or a Frequently Asked Questions (FAQ), a one-page, hard-copy primer on the basics of the Internet. Naturally, the sheet should list your company's email address and other background information. You could also include some or all of the Web site reviews you prepared for the Hot Links file for your digital briefcase. Hand this sheet out at trade shows, insert it in company brochures and catalogs, and include it in mail outs to customers and suppliers. Despite all the hype surrounding the Net, the majority of Americans—57 percent according to a May 1997 *Business Week*/Harris Poll—do not use a computer, let alone the Internet. Preparing a simple tutorial on Web basics will be appreciated by those unfamiliar or new to the Net. When they finally do get online, your message—and company—will be remembered.

Set Up a Virtual Office

A number of offline services are available that extend the global business reach of your email. These include JFAX Personal Telecom at http://harvard.net/products/jfax.phtml. For about $13 a month, the service will set up a private phone and fax number for you in selected cities around the world. All the voice mails and faxes received are then forwarded to you by email. The benefit? Customers in other countries can reach you by a local phone or fax number—local to them, that is—and contact you via email even though they may not be online.

Use Free Translation Services

Use language resources such as Free Translation Services at http://rivendel.com/~ric/resources.dictionary-2.html#freetrans. This is a list of Web sites that offer—you guessed it—free translation. The sites will translate brief English messages into a variety of languages including Chinese, French, German, Italian, Portuguese, and Spanish.

Consult Colleagues

If you work in an organization, don't hoard information. Share your list of ten business leads, and other leads you gather in the future, with the appropriate sales or purchasing staff. Working together, decide who should take the lead in following up online with a particular prospect. You'll avoid turf wars and hurt feelings. Also ensure that whoever is assigned the lead—yourself included—may speak for the company. The person should be able to make decisions and commitments on behalf of the organization. If not, beware. A potential customer, partner, or supplier will become frustrated and uninterested because the individual does not have sufficient authority.

Cruising and Schmoozing Online

With your digital suitcase packed and your cyber-jet fueled, the trade mission preparations are complete. Now it's time to power up the throttle, take to the air, and soar through the skies at light speed. Your goal: Seek out and engage your ten targets.

On a real-life trade mission, one-on-one meetings would be arranged between you and your leading prospects from the other countries. Mission organizers would brief you on the businessperson's background and company. Normally, you would be formally introduced to the other party and have an hour or so together in a private conference area to talk business. Here, you would shake hands, exchange business cards, and get to know each other. You would chat about your respective organizations, seek out mutual interests, and explore ways you could possibly work together. If no opportunities were evident, you would shake hands and go your separate ways.

If opportunities were apparent, you would agree to meet or talk again shortly to continue the discussions. In some cases, you would be invited to your prospect's place of business to tour the operation and personally inspect the products, service, or project under consideration. In other cases, you would wait until you return home to continue the dialog.

After the mission, additional information would be exchanged using the telephone, mail, courier, and fax. As the negotiations intensify, follow-up face-to-face meetings may be scheduled. Either they would travel to meet you or you would venture again to the foreign country, although you would be on your own this time and not part of a mission. Ultimately, all this would lead to a proposed deal between you and the prospect, a deal that is either rejected or approved by the parties. If an agreement could not be reached, you would both move on. If accepted, your goal would be achieved, and new international business would be generated. This entire process—from first meeting to final deal—might take as little as a few weeks or as long as several years or more, depending upon the commitment of the parties and the nature of the opportunity.

On a virtual trade mission, you can conduct all these activities—or as many as possible—online in five key steps: introduce, qualify, pitch, negotiate, and manage. Just as a polished salesperson works a room or a trade show floor, this approach involves "working" the Net and using email as a forum to meet and greet others. A hybrid of traditional marketing, cross-border prospecting, and electronic networking, this system will help you zero in on needs, match your capabilities to opportunities, and cut deals the world over from your desktop in a fraction of the time and cost that would be required on a real-life trade mission.

Your next exercise: Using this five-step system, go on your first virtual trade mission and target your ten prospects.

Step One: Introduce

Just as you introduce yourself to an international prospect for the first time on a trade mission, you do the same thing online. You write an email that says who you are, what you do, and that you want to explore how the two of you could work together in the future. Some key do's include the following:

Keep it simple and short. Your first message should be straightforward and no more than three hundred words. Long, rambling emails tend to get deleted rather than read.

Be correct. Ensure your messages are free of spelling, grammar, or formatting errors. If you can't spot the mistakes, have someone else proofread your text or use a business writing guide. Error-filled emails suggest a lack of discipline and sloppiness, and you don't get a second chance to make a first impression.

Send message to a specific person. Whenever possible, address the email to the specific person you want to target—such as johnsmith@acme.com—as opposed to a general company address such as acmecompany@acme.com. The message will go directly to that person and not be bounced around or filtered through other members of the organization who may or may not pass along the note to its intended recipient. If you must use a general company address, request that the message be passed along to a specific individual. Without a name, the message may be perceived as junk mail. With a name, the message will be perceived as private and important correspondence.

Offer sincere compliments. Compliment your prospect's Web site—and do it sincerely. With the Net so new and fluid, many businesspeople are hungry for feedback on their Web investments.

Personalize your message. Some executives receive hundreds of emails daily, and you must customize your note to stand out from the crowd. Make the recipient feel important and special. Always look for biographical information on the prospect's Web site and make some reference, however brief, to the person's hobbies or recent successes. Your message will be noticed and appreciated.

Focus on one lead at a time. While the Internet connects you to millions of people and potentially millions of opportunities, the key to success is to focus on one prospect and one lead at a time. Select a few targets and then concentrate your efforts on building those relationships and deals, not on running after a bunch of things at once. Remember the old saying: Chase a hare, get one; chase two hares, get none.

Use inclusive language. As much as possible, use words like you, we, us, and our. This makes a message more personal and inclusive.

Ask questions. Encourage the recipients to talk about themselves and their organizations. This will encourage information exchange and may reveal needs and opportunities.

Be sensitive to international differences. Business deals can be jeopardized by a lack of attention to cultural nuances. European countries, for example, use the metric system. Latin America is predominantly Catholic. Canadians prefer British spellings. Keep these differences in mind when preparing messages. Also remember than time differences and international holidays can delay responses.

Share information. Direct a prospect to a useful Web site, refer them to a business colleague, and alert them to an opportunity. Share this and other information with them and they will often return the favor.

Say you were referred. Referrals are door openers. If someone referred you to particular prospect, name that person in the message. This may give you an inside edge.

Be positive. Try to be as upbeat as possible in your note. People are more receptive to enthusiasm than they are to dullness.

Some key don'ts include the following:

Don't broadcast. Don't send emails to multiple addressees, especially your first few messages to a prospect. People prefer to receive emails that were written especially for them and will be more likely to respond to a tailored message than a mass mailing.

Don't spam. Spam is sending junk mail. This is an annoying practice that could trigger an avalanche of angry messages back to you in response.

Don't be a wise guy. When talking face to face, gestures, tone of voice, and facial expressions are key to communicating. In email messages, these body and voice cues are not transmitted, and sarcastic comments may be misinterpreted or offensive, especially to prospects from more conservative cultures.

Don't be a know-it-all. Share your expertise, but be eager to listen and learn from others. No one likes to deal with people who are boastful or think they know everything.

Don't be a techno-snob. Appreciate that your prospects may be non-technical and not fully proficient in English. In your first correspondence at least, write simply and eliminate the techno-babble.

Don't use excessive jargon or acronyms. Don't assume your prospects know all the fancy buzz words and abbreviations. They may not. If you must use highly specialized words and phrases, spell out what they mean in plain English.

Don't capitalize entire words for stress. This is the email equivalent of shouting and may be considered offensive or inappropriate by some.

Don't hard sell. Pushy sales tactics don't work in cyberspace. In your first message especially, focus on starting a dialog, as opposed to making a sale. You'll pave the way for more detailed discussions later.

Here's an example of an introductory email message. Say you wish to write an introductory letter to Jose Santoya, Vice President of Marketing at Acme Corporation. You'd write the following:

> To: jsantoya@trinket.com *[List this one address and no others: this will show that the message is a targeted message, and not part of a mass mailing.]*
>
> Cc: hhuckleberry@direct.ca *[Only cc. yourself, not anyone else in your organization, especially in your initial message. Establish a one-to-one rapport first before bringing others into the loop.]*
>
> Subject: Great Web site, Acme Corp. Well done! *[Putting a sincere compliment in a subject header is an attention-grabber and screams to be read.]*
>
> Dear Mr. Jim Santoya, VP, Marketing *[State the person's name and job title in the first line of the message. This will make it clear exactly who the message is for.]*
>
> Just a quick note to say that you have a terrific Web site. The information is useful, the design is slick, and navigating is a breeze. I wish all of cyberspace were this good. My compliments to your company and the Webmaster. *[Starting off with sincere praise and an upbeat tone will make a positive first impression and encourage the prospect to read on.]*
>
> I was particularly intrigued by your product X, service Y, or process Z, and I would like to learn more. Exactly how do you market X? Do you use a local agent? A foreign rep? I ask this because my firm—company AA—is also interested in this niche. We manufacture custom products for customers in the United States, and we're always on the lookout for new opportunities in other countries. *[Asking questions will engage the prospect and encourage him or her to talk about him- or herself. Linking the prospect's activities*

with your capabilities shows you already see a possible fit, and you're eager to connect with and complement his or her operations.]

I have a few ideas on how we could possibly work together in the future. If you wish, I'll forward you more detailed information about myself, my company, our products, and our base of operations for your review. I also have a list of informative Internet links from our industry that I could pass along for your information. I'd also like to learn more about your operation and your upcoming plans in this and other niches in the United Kingdom and Western European markets. I look forward to your reply. *[Using soft-sell techniques, offers of free information, and inclusive language shows you're interested in starting a dialog and not just making a sale. Requesting more information about their business conveys that you're interested in their needs and looking for win-win situations.]*

Thanks ahead of time for your interest and prompt response. *[Positive thinking never hurts.]*

Regards,

Henry Huckleberry *[Don't assume the "From:" header identifies who wrote the letter. Net users may use a shared email account to send notes or use another person's account to forward this particular message. Writing you own name makes it clear you're the author.]*

P.S. I noticed in your online bio that you play chess. You might be interested to know that *Chess Today* at http://www.kasparov.com provides tons of great info about the game. Check it out, and let me know what you think. *[Adding a personal note at the end shows you took the extra step to learn more about the prospect and that you're interested in them as an individual, not just a walking wallet.]*

Henry Huckleberry
Vice President, Cropdusters Inc.
405 Crosstown Way
Hoosli, Illinois 60698
Tel: 312/555-1234
Fax: 312/555-4321
Email: hhuckleberry@trinket.com
[Adding an electronic signature—an online business card—will get your name out and boost your profile.]

After completing the email and proofreading for any spelling and grammatical mistakes, hit the send button and fire off the message. Now you wait. If the prospect hasn't replied within a week, send the note again. The recipient may have been too busy to reply, or the email may have been accidentally deleted, misdirected, or lost. Wait another week. The recipient may be on holidays or traveling or having computer, network, or email access problems. If there is still no reply, send one more, but that's it. Three times should be enough. Although people admire persistence, they don't like pests. If a prospect is interested, he or she will get back to you. Your time is valuable, too. If they don't reply, move on. If they do get back to you and say they're not interested, respect their wishes. No means no. Move on. Remember, the Net offers an abundance of contacts and leads, not just one. If the prospect does return your message and expresses an interest, you're ready for the second phase.

Step Two: Qualify

Like a private business meeting on a trade mission, the qualify stage moves beyond initial introductions into more detailed discussions. In follow-up emails, you and the prospect exchange specific details about your respective operations and your mutual business interests to see if there's a genuine fit.

From your digital briefcase, forward the prospect copies of your biography, organization profile, brochure, photos, hometown profile, and hot links as email attachments. Let them know more about your background and your organization's capabilities, plans, and needs. In some cases, sending a briefing package in the mail or by courier may be appropriate. No matter how proficient and comfortable a prospect may be in using the Internet, many still want physical evidence—a business card, brochure, product sample—to verify you're real and credible. This is particularly true if your prospect is located in Asia, Latin America, or Eastern Europe. In these areas, the Internet is still in an embryonic state, and many businesspeople there are still not yet fully comfortable working in cyberspace.

Likewise, you should seek out more information about the prospect in particular and the organization in general. Is the prospect in fact the appropriate contact in the firm? Does he or she have the authority to make decisions and commitments? If not, ask to be directed to the person who does. How about the organization? Is it credible?

If you're considering the prospect as a potential customer, consider the following facets of his or her organization:

• general needs

- buying process
- purchasing policies
- size of order
- frequency of purchase
- seasonal variations in purchase
- delivery requirements
- packaging needs
- training needs
- after-sales service needs
- financial strength
- payment policies
- credit history
- loyalty

If you're considering the prospect as a partner, investigate the following aspects:

- professional accreditation
- technical expertise
- knowledge of the host country
- size in sales, assets, and number of employees
- management depth
- financial strength
- partners, contacts, and networks
- sales force
- sales record
- geographic coverage
- product mix
- facilities and equipment
- marketing policies
- customer mix
- eligibility to bid on target contracts
- mobility of personnel

If you're considering the prospect as a supplier, evaluate the following criteria:

- delivery capability
- quality
- pricing
- repair service
- technical expertise
- performance history
- production facilities
- aid and advice
- control systems
- reputation
- financial position
- training aids
- packaging capability
- labor relations record

For answers to these and other questions, turn to the Internet. The following features of the Internet may be helpful as you investigate the prospect:

Virtual reference checks. Ask the prospect for a list of references, and email some or all with questions. How long have they worked with the prospect? Would they recommend working with the organization? Do any Web sites provide more information on any of their projects or collaborations? Also be prepared with a list of your own references in case someone requests them of you.

Search Web and discussion groups. Revisit the firm's Web page and look for a list of customers, partners, and suppliers, past and present. In your Search Engines folder, select engines such as AltaVista at http://www.altavista.digital.com and Dogpile at http://www.dogpile.com and scan the Net for information about these people and companies. Email a sample to inquire about their relationships and experiences with the prospect. Also search the Web and Internet discussion groups for information on the prospect and organization. You never know what might turn up. Look for things like press releases, promotions, new product announcements, and other good news stories associated with that individual or, in some cases, any bad news reports that may document business failures or problems associated with that organization and prospect. Conversely, expect that the prospect will seek out more information about your organization and you on the Internet. Using several search engines, look for Web pages and discussion groups that discuss you. If you're not listed, make an effort to actively participate in discussion groups that review your product or service. This will get your name out and boost your Internet profile.

Email chamber of commerce. In your Researcher folder, select City.Net at http://www.city.net and search for the city in which the prospect is located and track down the email address of the local economic development authority or chamber of commerce. These are key networking organizations that monitor business conditions and companies in a particular area, and know who's reputable—and who's not. Email this organization and ask what they know about the prospect and the organization and whether they would recommend them as business partners.

Review memberships. Ask the prospect if he or she is a member of any professional affiliations and if the organization is a member of any industry associations. These organizations may provide professional certification, accreditation, and other measures of competency or rankings that may provide further information about a particular organization and prospect. Request or search the Net for the Web and email addresses of these groups. Email them to verify that the prospect and the organization are, in fact, members in good standing.

Credit check online. In your Banker folder, select Credit Reporting Agencies at http://www.creditworthy.com/us/providers.agency.html. Choose the appropriate geographic or sectoral-based service and request a credit report on the organization.

Contact U.S. Commercial Service. Visit the U.S. Department of Commerce Commercial Service at http://www.ita.doc.gov/uscs/forweb.html for a list of the U.S. embassies and trade offices around the world. Email the U.S. Embassy or consulate in the city nearest to the headquarters of the organization and get their perspective on the prospect. They may have unique insights including whether the prospect has participated in any trade events in the area or has done business in the past with other U.S. firms.

Contact government commercial services from other countries. The United States is not the only country with embassies and consulates abroad. Numerous other countries have a network of offices around the world that provide trade information and services for a specific city or territory. While focused on helping exporters from their own country, the offices will also provide information and assistance to businesspeople no matter where they live, although sometimes begrudgingly. Email them for their perspective on a prospect and general tips and leads on doing business in a particular market. The leading online government trade networks include the following:

- Canadian Mission Web sites (http://www.dfait-maeci.gc.ca/english/missions.menu.htm)

- German Embassies Online (http://www.germany-info.org/g_sites/index.htm)

- Japan Ministry of Foreign Affairs (http://www.mofa.go.jp/embassy/index.html)

- Trade Commission of Mexico (http://www.bancomextdallas.com/links-nf.htm#Offices)

- U.K. Foreign and Commercial Service Online (http://www.fco.gov.uk/)

When you've verified that the prospect is legitimate and trustworthy and confirmed that you both have complementary interests, you can proceed to the next stage.

Step Three: Pitch

If business meetings go well on a trade mission, the participants from the host and visiting country make arrangements to communicate after the event and expand the discussions. The question on the table is no longer whether they should work together, but *how*. The same is true on the Web. If you and the prospect see opportunities in your email "talks" and you've determined the prospect is genuine based on your Net research, you start pitching ideas, offering proposals, and structuring a deal.

Pitches to Sell

If you're interesting in selling to a businessperson in another country, you generally have two options: *indirect exporting* and *direct exporting*. Indirect exporting is using an export intermediary to ship your products and get paid in the export market. A variety of intermediary firms provide a range of export services. Some of these export intermediaries include the following:

- **Commission agents.** These buy products on behalf of foreign firms.

- **Export management companies.** Specialists either by product or by foreign market or both, these export products on behalf of a client.

- **Export merchants.** These purchase products directly from a manufacturer, pack and mark the products to their own specifications, and sell the product overseas on their own.

- **Piggyback marketing.** This is an arrangement in which one firm distributes another firm's product or service, usually complementary to their own.

Direct exporting is selling directly to a foreign buyer. The sales are generally made through a variety of channels.

- **Sales representatives.** Under contract and working on commission, these representatives make sales on behalf of an exporter in a foreign market.

- **Distributors.** A buyer who purchases merchandise from an exporter and resells it at a profit, they also support and service the product.

- **Foreign retailers.** These purchase products, mostly consumer related, from manufacturers for resale in retail chains and outlets.

- **Direct mail.** This is selling to customers in a foreign market through the mail.

- **Direct sales.** This is selling directly to end-users in foreign countries.

- **Retail outlets.** This is purchasing an existing retail chain or creating a new one in the target market.

- **Greenfield investment.** Derived from the term for building a company from the ground—or "green field"—up, this refers to building a wholly owned subsidiary in the target market.

- **Foreign trade zones.** Well-defined and duty-free enclaves, these attract manufacturers and other companies to invest and operate in a foreign market with special conditions and incentives.

For a list of export-related agents, representatives, management companies, merchants, distributors, and retailers that can help you export directly or indirectly, visit "Company Listings, Directories, and Yellow Pages" at http://ciber.bus .msu.edu/busres/company.htm. Part of the Michigan State University International Business Resources site, it links to dozens of online directories that profile export professionals from Argentina to Russia to the United States.

Pitches to Partner

If you're planning to partner with a prospect in another country, you have several options:

Joint venture. Traditionally used to avoid foreign ownership restrictions, this is an independent business formed by two or more parent firms.

Licensing. This is an agreement in which a firm sells the right to the use of its products or services but still retains some control over the product or service.

Franchising. A more specific form of licensing, this is the granting by a franchisor to a franchisee of the right to use a manufacturing or service process, along with business systems or trademarks.

Cross-licensing. This is an arrangement in which two firms license products or services to the other.

Cross-manufacturing. This is a pact in which companies agree to manufacture each other's products.

Coproduction. Normally developed by companies with complex manufactured goods with diverse components and various stages of assembly, this is an agreement to share production of components or assembly functions.

Comarketing. This is an alliance in which companies cooperate to market or promote each other's products.

Export consortium. This is alliance of three of more companies engaged in some export venture.

Mergers and acquisitions. This is the integration of two operations using friendly or hostile means.

Technology transfer. This is selling a technology to a foreign company for a fee or royalty.

Joint research and development. A way to share costs and reduce risks on product innovation, this is working together on research and development.

For more information on strategic alliances and partnering, review "U.S. Strategic Alliance" at http://www.ustradecenter.com/alliance.html, a report posted by the Buffalo-based U.S. Trade Center. The study explains how to find a partner and highlights some key do's and don'ts of a strategic partnership.

Pitches to Source

If you're thinking about sourcing from a prospect in another country, you have a variety of issues to consider, such as the following:

Competitive bidding. How would the supplier be notified of procurement tenders and proposals and participate in the bidding process?

Inventory control. How would the foreign supplier help inventory cost, forecasting, replenishment, accuracy, and customer supply chains?

Quality control. What procedures does the foreign supplier have to test products, correct faults, and meet quality control standards?

Outsourcing. Could the foreign supplier be contracted to conduct internal work and processes beyond the core competencies of the firm?

Supply chain management. How would information be shared and exchanged between the foreign supplier and buyer?

Import regulations. Would any tariffs, quotas, or other nontariff measures or regulations impede the delivery—and increase the cost—of the foreign-procured product or service?

For more information on sourcing and the Internet, visit the *Journal of Internet Purchasing* at http://www.arraydev.com/commerce/jip/, a Webzine on electronic procurement, and the National Association of Purchasing Management at http://www .napm.org/, a leading organization of U.S. purchasing professionals.

Web-Based Pitches

Whether you're looking to sell to, partner with, or source from your international prospect, look for ways you can work together on the Web.

As an interactive, multimedia, and hyperlinked platform, the Internet offers a whole new generation of business models that are ideal for companies of all sizes seeking to extend their global reach. In consultation with your prospect, explore how one or some of the following models could be applied in your situation to form the basis for a cross-border deal or collaboration.

Virtual billboards. These don't sell products online but promote an organization and its offerings. An example is Spectrum Signal Processing at http:/www.spectrumsignal.com, a Vancouver-based electronics manufacturer. The site provides a company profile, press releases, technical support information, a product catalog, and a list of employment opportunities.

Banner ads. These are small, usually rectangular graphics that appear on many consumer Web sites. Increasingly animated and interactive, the ads normally link to the firm's Web page, which provides more detailed information about a product or service. According to an October 1997 report in Business Week, Web ads have recently replaced Toyota's 800 number as their number-one lead generator. Between June 1996 and May 1997, 152,000 Web users typed in their name and address and requested a brochure or video about the Japanese automaker's products. These cyber-leads led directly to the sale of 7,329 cars, a 5 percent conversion rate. Check out Website Banner Advertising at http://www.markwelch.com/bannerad/for explanations of key terms and lists of key players involved in online banner ads.

Online storefronts. These offer direct sales and services through an electronic catalog or other format. An example is Security First Network Bank at http://info.sfnb.com/. The site allows online consumers to open accounts, pay bills, and manage their finances on the Web.

Online malls. These are a collection of online storefronts, each of which may contain different categories of products and services. The provider charges rent in exchange for the virtual real estate and may provide other services such as advertising and site maintenance. An example is Cool Shopping at http://www.coolshopping.com/index.phtml, a cluster of online merchants.

International buying centers. These post "requests for proposals" or RFPs, hold competitive bids, and award contracts online. An example is the GE Trading Process Network at http://tpn.geis.com. A joint venture between General Electric and Thomas Publishing, the site enables a supplier to view GE RFPs, request more information such as drawings and other technical information, and bid on a proposal. Processing more than $1 billion in business annually, the site manages the bids as they are submitted, narrows down the proposals through successive bidding rounds, and notifies the ultimate winner and the other bidders of the outcome.

Global catalogs. These offer information in multiple languages on a wide range of products that can be ordered from and delivered to virtually anywhere on the planet. An example is AMP Connect at http://connect.amp.com, an electrical and electronics supplier. Available in eight languages, the site provides a searchable database of ninety thousand AMP products and includes descriptions, pictures, three-dimensional models, and comparative charts.

Export catalogs. Geographic or product specific, these showcase companies promoting goods or services for export. An example is the Canadian Exporters Catalog at http://www.worldexport.com/. Available in seven languages, the site provide a database of Canadian exporters searchable by product, service, company name, and province.

Referral networks. These pay commissions to people who generate sales for a firm using the Web. An example is Amazon Books at http://www.amazon .com, an online bookstore. The company's Amazon Associates Program allows people to make money by reviewing books on their own Web sites. If someone reads a review on an associate's Web page and clicks through to Amazon to buy the book, the associate receives a percentage of the sales.

Transaction brokers. These facilitate buying and selling of a particular product or service but aren't generally involved in the manufacture or distribution of the offering. An example is Auto-By-Tel at http://www .auto-by-tel.com. The site helps a Web user find dealers, compare prices, and arrange financing online for an automobile.

Aggregators. These attract an audience by providing a clearinghouse of information, news, and links on a particular subject or industry. Aggregators sell advertising and often charge for links to other sites. An example is Happy Puppy's Front Porch at http://www.happypuppy.com, a central point of information on Web games and computer games.

Virtual communities. These are built around a common interest, profession, or hobby. An example is Agriculture Online at http://www.agriculture.com. The site offers farm news, global positioning satellite (GPS) data, commodity prices, bulletin boards, and other information for agricultural professionals and enthusiasts.

Virtual trade shows. These provide information on exhibitors and participants at a real or online trade show and may include virtual presentations and discussion groups. An example is the Electronics Virtual Trade Show at http://www.vts.com/. The site includes a product directory and a searchable database of electrical manufacturers, suppliers, distributors, and representatives.

Virtual business matchmakers. Geographic or product targeted, these match up businesspeople with complementary interests. An example is the Swedish-American Interactive Marketplace at http://www.saim.com/. Users can search for American and Swedish companies in dozens of industries by company name, product, and location and participate in online discussion groups.

Virtual consultants. These offer consulting advice online on a particular subject or industry, sometimes for a fee, sometimes not. An example is AutoSage at http://www.ey.com/autosage/default.htm. Run by Ernst & Young, the site features industry news, benchmarking tools, online transactions, and advice for the automotive industry.

Virtual seminars. These conduct live conferences and seminars online. An example is NetSeminar at http://www.netseminar.com, which enables a user to hear live audio, view presentation presentations, and interact—real-time—with the presenter.

Webcasting. Instead of you having to search the Net for information, these deliver or "push" Web content right to your desktop in online channels, depending on what type of information you want. An example is PointCast at http://www.pointcast.com. The site offers an customizable and continuously updated desktop newscast that features the latest news, business, weather, stock market, entertainment, and lifestyle information from around the world.

Online support. These answer questions and provide assistance to users of a particular product or product, sometimes for a fee. An example is Microsoft Support at http://www.microsoft.com/support/, which provides problem-solving tools and technical information, some free, some not.

Online auctions. These hold online auctions. An example is Onsale at http://www.onsale.com. Users visit the site to look at pictures of products and make bids. After a set time, the auction is over and the product is sold. Generally, online auctions charge sellers to list a product and take a commission on the product sold.

Business chat. These are scheduled online discussions in which businesspeople share their experience and expertise with peers. Sometimes sponsored, the sites may offer celebrity chat events at which an audience gets to interact with a celebrity and matchmaker chat rooms where participants are matched according to their interests. Business chat sessions are also used for online team meetings, distance education, training sessions, product support, and help desks. An example is Richard Seltzer's Business on the WWW at http://www.web-net.org/seltzer-intro.html, a weekly business chat session on Internet business.

Fee-based databases or Webzines. These provide content that a user pays to access. An example is Britannica Online at http://www.eb.com./. A virtual encyclopedia, the site contains articles, yearbooks, illustrations, and biographies.

Sponsored databases or Webzines. These provide content that is supported by advertising. An example is Village Voice Worldwide at http://www.villagevoice.com/. The online counterpart to the New York counterculture newspaper, the site features entertainment news, features, personals, and classified ads.

Step Four: Negotiate

Once you and your prospect determine what type of business relationship best fits your needs—be it buying, partnering, or sourcing; be it terrestrially based, virtually based, or some mix thereof—you must negotiate the details. Although each situation is different, a number of considerations are key to any set of negotiations, especially when they are conducted online and involve businesspeople from different countries and cultures.

Record keeping. A great thing about email is that the communication takes place in writing. People may forget what they said or promised, but email provides a record of interactions. Make sure to keep copies of all emails exchanged between you and the prospect, especially in the critical negotiating phase. To be extra sure, make backup copies of all your correspondence and download them on diskettes for safekeeping. In the event of any misunderstandings, you may refer back to the emails to clarify exactly what was said.

Agreements. Formal written agreements are not essential to finalizing a deal with a prospect. I've completed numerous export deals with a simple email message or verbal agreement over the phone. Still, they are highly recommended, especially if you're dealing with a prospect for the first time and the dollar values of the proposal are significant. Getting the deal in writing will help clarify deliverables and protect your interests.

Letter of intent. A letter of intent is a relatively brief—one paragraph to ten pages or so—document that discusses the general nature and scope of the proposed negotiations. The document normally contains:

- a description of the companies involved

- a description of the products, services, and projects under discussion

- a nondisclosure agreement pertaining to proprietary technical information that may be discussed during the negotiations

- a schedule for the negotiating process including expected dates for the signing of various documents

In cooperation with the prospect, draft a letter of intent, however brief. The document will help identify the key issues, define objectives, and keep the negotiations focused on track.

Duties. Ensure that you and the prospect are clear on the division of labor and who will do what with which products or services.

Territory and exclusivity. Understand exactly where the activities of the deal will take place, and which parties are responsible for which areas. Also determine whether certain locations are off limits or exclusive to the parties. Certain partnership agreements, for example, may restrict the operations of a particular firm or office to a specific territory in which the firm has exclusive authority, and prohibit the company from doing business in another area.

Financing. Explore how much each party is committing to the deal—both in cash and assets—and whether external financing may be required.

Costs. Determine who pays for what. In some cases, a budget may need to be developed to pay for items such as travel and promotional programs.

Proceeds. Agree on how and when profits are to be determined and distributed between the parties.

Remuneration. Clarify remuneration packages and to what extent they are linked to sales or performance targets. Incentives may be included in the package to reward high achievers.

Management. Decide which person from each party will control the agreement and manage its day-to-day workings.

Product. Confirm whether the products in the deal need to be altered to meet local conditions or preferences or whether new products need to be developed.

Pricing. Verify how much one party will pay for a product or service and how much will be paid by final consumers or other end-users.

Packaging. Determine if product packaging has to be redesigned. Certain colors, pictures, and symbols used on products in one market may be inappropriate or even offensive in other markets where consumer tastes and values are different.

Promotion. If required, address how a product or service will be promoted and advertised in traditional media such as newspapers, magazines, television, and radio and in new media such as the Internet and CD-ROMs. Also establish what brochures and other product literature and signage need to be developed and how this will be funded and distributed.

Orders. Agree which party will solicit orders and which will take orders and agree on whether the other party needs to be informed of the order.

Customer relationships. Identify who will prepare, ship, and deliver orders to customers and who will pursue payment and act on delinquent accounts.

After-sales service. Establish a process for administering warranties and guarantees, processing products that are returned, and providing after-sales service.

Transportation options. Determine which mode of transport—truck, rail, air, or ocean—is best for shipping your product and whether the shipment will involve more than a single mode.

Service delivery. If delivering a service, verify the extent and reliability of telecommunications links, the frequency and convenience of air links, and what work permits or professional certification is required in the target market.

Packing of goods. Explore how best to pack the goods and what special temperature control or protection may be required to minimize damage and pilferage during handling, transit, and storage.

Marking. Confirm which markings are required on the shipping containers. Markings include the buyer's name, a product description, the point of entry, gross and net weights, the country of origin, the number of packages in the shipment, and warning or cautionary markings, if necessary.

Labeling. Ensure that products meet local labeling requirements. This may include local language or bilingual labeling, metric measurements, product details such as weight and ingredients, type of fiber and instructions for use, technical specifications, and certification of conformity to local technical standards.

Insurance. Determine what type of insurance is required to cover commercial risks such as the insolvency of the buyer, political risks such as conversion difficulties caused by currency policies of a government, and professional liability and other litigation.

Documentation. Verify that the products have the correct shipping documents, certificates of origin, import licenses, inspection certificates, and dock and insurance receipts.

Employees. Ensure that all employees—from the loading dock to the call center to the corner office—have been properly trained to receive, ship, use, and sell the product or service.

Term. Specify the term of the arrangement, methods of renewal and termination, and the penalties for wrongful withdrawal. Many contracts specify a certain term for the agreement—often one year—but allow for automatic renewal unless either party gives notice in writing of its intention not to renew.

Escape clauses. Include an escape clause that allows the parties to end the relationship quickly and cleanly if the agreement does not work out. Some contracts specify that either party may end the agreement with written notice thirty, sixty, or ninety days in advance.

Dispute settlement. Agree on what mechanisms will be used to settle possible future disputes in the deal. Options include the appoinment of a jointly agreed-upon third party to review and decide the issue or the appointment of a specific lawyer or accountant to resolve differences in a legal or financial area.

Legal issues. Clarify key legal issues such as which country's laws govern a contract dispute and verify that the deal adheres to all antitrust, consumer protection, environmental, contract, labor relations, intellectual property, and other laws.

Tax issues. Consider the tax liabilities and obligations of the cross-border deal and how to repatriate dividends, interest, and royalties from a target market.

Cultural considerations. Appreciate that businesspeople in other countries and cultures have different management styles and perspectives on delegation, control, loyalty, competition, protocol, and time that may be different from your own.

Don't get overwhelmed or intimidated by all these details. Not all are relevant in all cases. Your Virtual Trade Team—particularly the Trainer, Consultant, Banker, Accountant, Lawyer, and Shipper folders—contains a treasure of online resources that can help you address these issues or lead you to an export professional who can. Expert help is only one mouse click or email away.

Step Five: Manage

The ultimate goal of a trade mission is to develop new international business. Once a deal has been finalized, pat yourself on the back. The mission has been successful and you've hit your target, but don't celebrate too long. This marks a new beginning, not an end, to your trade efforts. Managing this business relationship is now the top priority. However simple or complex the deal and whatever the size or number of the organizations involved, a number of important issues need to be addressed to keep the agreement on track.

Champion. Appoint an individual from your firm to oversee the overall agreement. He or she should be responsible for championing the deal internally and coordinating and consulting with the partners and should have sufficient power and authority to make things happen.

Control. Ensure that what was outlined in the agreement is, in fact, being delivered. Verify that performance and sales target are being met, quality standards are being maintained, all expenses are accounted for, the proper documentation is provided, and all other elements of the relationship are functioning in accordance with the terms and conditions of the agreement.

Communication. Regularly inform partners on the deal's progress in weekly or biweekly email updates. If questions or problems arise, a procedure should be set up to provide answers and address concerns as quickly as possible. Delays will harm the relationship.

Decision-making. As much as possible, involve your partners in decisions that impact the agreement and relationship. This will help minimize unnecessary frictions.

Relationships. Encourage senior executives and working-level managers to build relationships with their international counterparts. Personal contacts and informal discussion will help troubleshoot problems at an early stage. Simple email networking will promote key information sharing. Also encourage executives and staff to visit the partners in their own countries as part of management and sales trips to keep in touch and have face-to-face contact.

Flexibility. Almost nothing ever goes exactly as planned. Assumptions about a market may have been overly optimistic or pessimistic. Circumstances change. New opportunities and challenges arise. New competition emerges. The unexpected happens, especially in a medium as dynamic as the Internet. Be prepared to scrap what's not working and improvise a new plan on the fly in response to changing conditions.

Electronic data interchange. Explore how the Internet can be used to share purchase orders, invoice, billing, and record-keeping functions with your international customers, partners, and suppliers. Online electronic data interchange or EDI offers considerable savings and benefits over nondigital methods. For more information, visit EC World at http://pwr .com/ediworld, a monthly magazine on electric commerce, and the Electronic Commerce World Institute at http://www.ecworld.org, an international e-commerce organization.

New trade agreements. Monitor the progress of trade initiatives such as the proposed Free Trade Area of the Americas, the expansion of the European Union, and the next round of World Trade Organization negotiations. By the year 2000, new global trade talks are scheduled in agriculture, services, foreign investment, competition policy, labor standards, and other areas. All these initiatives will rewrite the rules of international trade and impact, to a greater or lesser degree, your operating environment, and entire business chain. Visit the World Trade Organization at http://www.wto.org/ for updates on the latest multilateral and regional trade negotiations.

Internet commerce. Track developments related to the government regulation of global electronic commerce. A number of governments have proposed new policies to govern online activity. The U.S. plan, "A Framework for Global Electronic Commerce" at http://www.iitf.nist .gov.eleccomm.ecomm.html, calls for an open market approach and minimal government intervention in Internet transaction. This includes making the Internet a tariff-free zone and allowing the private sector to self-regulate privacy, security, content, and technical standards.

The other leading proposals—the European Union's "A European Initiative in Electronic Commerce" at http://www.ispo.cec.be/Ecommerce/, and Japan's "Towards the Age of the Digital Economy" at http://www.miti

.go.jp/intro-e/a228101e.html—are more interventionist in nature. These propose government standards and regulations on Internet content and security and do not rule out tariffs or taxes. All are works in progress, and a series of global treaties and agreements will be needed to make these proposals a reality. The Internet commerce negotiations, expected to start by the year 2000, will likely be as complex, comprehensive, and controversial as any of the past General Agreement on Tariffs and Trade (GATT) rounds and will have profound implications for online commerce.

Standards. Set the highest standards for yourself and your partners when using the Internet. Respect and protect any personal information gathered from Web users. Ensure that all financial transactions are completely secure and confidential. Provide fresh and high-quality content and do business with only those firms that do the same. You'll set an example and prove that an open market system for electronic commerce is both productive and responsible.

By packing your digital suitcase, turbocharging your browser, and following a five-step cruise-and-schmooze action plan, you can generate new business around the world from your desktop. At little or no cost, you can do virtually everything from your own office that you could do on any real-life trade mission.

Approach your ten targets using this simple strategy. The process will trigger new ideas, generate new leads, and may yield surprising bottom-line results. To consistently develop new international business over time, launch a new trade mission "round," say, every two weeks or month. During each round, spend one or two days looking for fresh global business leads, identify ten prime targets, and then engage them online. As you gain experience and confidence, you will leverage the abundant bounty of online trade resources to maximum advantage; find more and better leads faster; convert a higher proportion of these into new revenue, alliance, and saving opportunities; and truly conquer the world from your desktop.

THE EVOLUTION TO ELECTRONIC COMMERCE ON THE INTERNET

"There is no time like the present." Whoever said these words centuries ago could have been musing about electronic commerce and the real opportunity presented today to companies who are committed to making the most of change.

As you move your business into the new millennium, time is of the essence. The confluence of advances in technology together with the loosening of barriers to global trade have created an unprecedented era of opportunity. You have the ability to make history. For companies of all sizes, regardless of industry sector, global experience, or technological savvy, it is a new age in business, devoid of boundaries but subject to the race against time.

Electronic commerce—or e-commerce—is not a new concept, but it is now positioned at the cutting edge of fundamental change. Especially in the business-to-business market, where only a fraction of companies worldwide—less than 10 percent in the United States—are currently involved, total intercompany Internet commerce is expected to grow at least 85 percent annually to top $325 billion by 2002, according to "Cyber-Commerce: Internet Tsunami" (1997), a recent Goldman Sachs report citing Forrester Research. In the next five to ten years, this surge, or tsunami, will spawn hundreds of billions of dollars in new market capitalization worldwide from electronic-commerce related services. Forrester Research also reports that by far the lion's share of this megamarket will emerge in business rather than consumer spending, where volumes of as much as ten to one are expected to dwarf the mass consumer market.

What is driving these staggering expectations for growth? According to the Goldman Sachs report, Web-based standards have evolved in three short years to impact all levels of technology, acting as a sort of glue that connects the supporting information technology and telecommunications infrastructure. This allows businesses to seamlessly exchange information across a range of systems and platforms through the familiar point-and-click interface of the Internet. The remarkable pace of technology innovation—in fiber optics, wireless telecommunications and other bandwidth solutions, and hardware and software—has brought a mind-numbing proliferation of commerce-enabling products and services to the forefront, which are now en route to the desktop of corporate business.

Yet with all that the new digital technology and infrastructure offers, widespread acceptance of e-commerce in a myriad of everyday applications will, in the end, rest on a winning business strategy. The best e-commerce plan is inexorably linked to a solid business plan that is integrated throughout the organization to meet revenue goals and companywide objectives, enhanced by and implemented with new technologies. These powerful new tools are only as effective as your company's ability to harness them to drive your unique business case. All the age-old tenets apply: Increase sales and profits. Find new markets. Whatever we have to pay is too much. Beat the competition before it beats you. The customer is king. Be conscious of inefficiencies and waste. Keep it quick, simple, and streamlined. Time is money. Grow or die.

The e-commerce challenge is clear, even for companies that as yet have escaped the call, or the push, to compete globally. It is truly a global, electronic marketplace, where smaller companies have proved they can compete successfully against larger competitors and where speed in transactions, communications, and decisions takes on new meaning. If you haven't tested the waters, now is the time to dive in.

Introducing E-commerce

At its most basic level, e-commerce is the quick, paperless exchange of critical business information by electronic means. It takes the form of documents, as in purchase orders or letters of credit, or information, as in cargo inventories and product catalogs or in less tangible, yet integral functions such as customer service and supplier relationships. It is the intersection of people with technology to create more competitive business communities, linked by a common electronic language. E-commerce currently occurs both on private networks and the Internet and has both external applications to your company's trading partners and internal applications throughout your company.

E-commerce makes possible increased sales, productivity, distribution, and attention to customers and reduced operating costs, lead times, inventories, and errors. It offers blanket availability in the global marketplace without regard to distance or time zone but can be customized to an individual's or company's culture, language, preferences, and requirements. For the overwhelming majority of routine, but critical business exchanges, e-commerce simplifies the complex process of conducting business worldwide.

The specific implications for your business follow three general themes. First, e-commerce allows your company to address topline, or revenue, growth by accessing new global markets and by meeting the needs of a wider, geographically dispersed trading community. This community can include Fortune 500 multinationals down to smaller firms and even enterprising start-ups. Next, e-commerce reduces costs. These efficiencies, which impact the internal operating bottom line, are passed on to your customers and trading partners. Finally, e-commerce has enterprisewide impact, forcing a new perspective both on established business processes and on finding and retaining new customers that crosses department and functional lines. It is this dynamic, pervasive quality that promises to forever change the way that companies do business.

The EDI Backbone of E-commerce

To get inside e-commerce, one must first start with electronic data interchange (EDI). If e-commerce is akin to an evolving organism, then EDI might be considered its backbone. EDI is a standardized format for the electronic exchange of business documents that forms the framework for the bulk of e-commerce that occurs today. The term *EDI* is sometimes used as a narrow definition for electronic commerce because an estimated two-thirds of all electronic commerce follows EDI and similar formats, most often conducted over private EDI networks (as recently reported in *Data Communications* magazine). These few private networks, also called value-added networks (VANs), carry invoices, payments, purchase orders, and shipping notices or other data between trading partners with a high degree of security and guaranteed by the inherent privacy of a closed network.

EDI technology has been in use for over thirty years. It was first adopted by the transportation industry to help reduce the voluminous paperwork required to document and track cargo shipments. Though its impact and cost effectiveness have proved to be significant, EDI acceptance has been steady but slow, moving in the past twenty years into major industries such as health care, pharmaceuticals, automotive, chemicals, finance, and retail. Today, EDI facilitates mission-critical transactions for these industries, yet some sources say it nevertheless is still limited to as little as two to three percent of the total data exchanged between businesses in the United States and involves only an estimated 338,000 companies worldwide (according to IDC Research, as cited in the 1997 Goldman Sachs e-commerce report). Large manufacturers, transportation companies, and banks have invested heavily in EDI networks, encouraging their suppliers to adopt the EDI standard as well (or mandating EDI acceptance, as in the case of the automotive industry in 1984). In fact, in many industries EDI has become a requirement for suppliers who want to stay competitive serving their largest, EDI-enabled customers—a requirement enforced by financial penalties to move the vendors quickly into the fold.

EDI's Trade and Transportation Infrastructure

EDI's capabilities are a particularly good fit for transactions involving the transport of goods. Now used by half of all companies shipping products internationally via ocean or air transportation, EDI is expected to grow to 90 percent acceptance within two years for maritime and air document exchange, according to a recent survey conducted by *American Shipper* magazine. Building on its well-established roots in the transportation industry and the fundamental customer need to know delivery times and track cargo shipments, EDI's growth in transport will likely mirror trends in the air cargo industry, particularly air express. Air express is expected to grow by 18 percent a year in the near term, eventually capturing over a third of the international air cargo market by 2015, according to DHL official Andy Tseng (as reported in the *Journal of Commerce*). Inevitably, more goods will ship faster via planes, creating a larger volume of shipments that will make EDI's swift documentation and immediate tracking capabilities a necessity.

The global EDI infrastructure that facilitates worldwide trade is well on its way to linking the world's major players in shipping: freight forwarders, airlines, ocean carriers, ports, airports, and trucking companies. EDI growth on a global scale, which is bolstered by effective regional systems supported by these key players in transportation, reflects the overriding need to eliminate repetitive paperwork in an industry that thrives on duplicative transactions. Some say that the same data about a shipment may be input up to ten or more times during the process of moving the goods, which introduces an extremely high margin for error. That challenge, along with customer demands for "just-in-time" distribution for manufacturing and component sourcing on a global basis, requires the highly reliable tracking capabilities of EDI.

In the past ten years, electronic systems enabling international communications based on EDI and electronic funds transfer (EFT) have been implemented in regional and country projects that are expected to yield a more complete—if not totally global—EDI infrastructure within a few years.

The cargo community systems concept (CCS) is a good example of this trend. Patterned after the London Airport customs system and first launched as ICARUS (Irish Community AirCargo Realtime Users System), CCS now facilitates the electronic transfer of documents for air cargo shipments via independent systems in several European countries. Each CCS functions as a network hub linking local freight forwarders to the airlines serving that region. Similar systems are in place for the ocean shipping industry, spearheaded by steamship lines and ports.

The Advantages of EDI

EDI delivers a host of benefits for companies that can afford the upfront expense of becoming EDI-enabled. Most stem from a single key starting point: data input.

Because data is entered just once, errors are kept to a minimum, and the entire process is streamlined, saving paper and time and improving accuracy and order fulfillment for customers. Of course, the overall benefit impacts expenses way beyond the costs of paper and mailing. In addition to data entry, other labor-intensive, manual processing tasks, such as typing invoices, sealing envelopes, and affixing postage, are dramatically reduced or eliminated. People are used more effectively, increasing productivity. Inventories are used more efficiently because EDI provides speedier, more accurate information on both the customer and supplier sides, reducing inventory costs and lead times.

In the long run, the investment in EDI delivers dramatic cost savings as well as the opportunity to do business within a wider, more global EDI-enabled trading community.

EDI Technology and Infrastructure

The EDI backbone of e-commerce is being transformed to accommodate a fundamental evolution in the organism. Will the organism walk or fly? The dawn of the Internet has shed new light on EDI's possibilities and potential in a new era of electronic commerce.

To understand this transformation, let's first examine EDI's defining characteristics. Historically, EDI has been characterized by three basic factors: (1) its common standards, (2) its point-to-point data transmission through legacy mainframe systems, and (3) its reliance on closed, private networks.

EDI Standards

EDI uses a common set of standards formats, principally defined as data codebooks that enable companies, through EDI software translators, to interpret business

---

applications. Then documents and data are converted into one of several commonly accepted formats.

Although several EDI standards exist—spawning numerous hybrids customized for specific industries—two have gained more universal acceptance: ANSI 12X (also called ASC X.12) in North America, introduced by the American National Standards Institute, and EDIFACT in Europe, from the United Nations Economic Commission.

A global standard has yet to be endorsed, although EDIFACT is seen by some as the likely contender. Companies looking to integrate global plans face the harsh reality that there is no global standard but a wide range of accepted implementations, no specific sets of standards geared to a sphere of trading partners or to one industry. The slow and hindered process of standards harmonization, with competing standards vying for more universal global market acceptance, means a fragmented and complex range of preferred standards for companies to implement. Mid-size or smaller suppliers trying to accommodate their largest customers, each requiring their own preferred form of EDI implementation, may face the challenge of dealing with several—some say as many as twenty—different EDI implementations of ANSI or EDIFACT. And this does not take into account the range of different standards and implementations necessary to serve customers outside Europe and North America.

EDI's Data Transmission

EDI data travels via point-to-point transmission. Data transmitted in a closed network follows a direct route, moving as the crow flies from one computer to another's database. Most companies have many suppliers, requiring several discrete EDI connections in order to move data along the supply chain to all members of the trading community. Connectivity is a costly and complicated proposition and a limiting factor for many mid-size and smaller firms, according to highlights of a recent Grant Thornton survey reported in *Export Today* magazine.

Point-to-point transmission accommodates large volumes of data, or batches, in a quick and reliable fashion, ensuring verifiable delivery that is well suited to the needs of high-volume, just-in-time manufacturing operations and their tightly managed inventory requirements. Yet while EDI traditionally has relied on point-to-point transmission through mainframe legacy databases, companies are moving toward integrated solutions that distribute information across the entire enterprise using client/server network systems, making it necessary that adaptations be made in the way data are exchanged as well.

Within a closed EDI network, EDI data moves along a proprietary, dedicated connection, often utilizing VANs that function as mailboxes, which in conjunction with EDI software help to translate the information from one computer to another. VANs guarantee a level of security, through limited access—trading partners must use the same VAN—and through services that authenticate the sender and recipient, verify that the data was received and was not changed en route, and provide an audit trail from sender to recipient.

These guarantees all occur in the context of lagged, store-and-forward delivery, making EDI via VANs most efficient when huge databases of proprietary information subject to security risks are involved, as in the case of financial networks, cargo reservation systems, and retail sales operations.

Where EDI Falls Short

EDI over private networks has proved its value time and again for an impressive range of EDI-capable industries and companies. Yet the fact remains that EDI technology is inaccessible to the vast majority—some say 80 percent—of the world's trading partners. Upfront costs and complicated implementation are most often the mitigating factors, especially for mid-size and smaller companies caught outside the sphere of larger EDI-enabled trading communities. To participate in this closed world, smaller companies must pay for the VAN or the dedicated connection. They must assimilate, implement, and stay current on a broad range of agreed-upon requirements for the transfer of EDI data, which vary by industry and are in continual negotiation and flux.

In addition, while EDI automates the order process, it is not linked in real time to the accounting and distribution processes, thus requiring duplication of effort that costs time and money—scarce resources at smaller companies. So although the largest companies with high-volume, business-to-business transactions for mission-critical information have embraced traditional EDI, a wide arena of business opportunities are simply out of reach for most mid-size and smaller companies under the traditional EDI model. The stage is set for a new form of e-commerce.

EDI Moves to the Web

The Internet's cataclysmic, nearly spontaneous impact on EDI has scrambled the basic building blocks of e-commerce, transforming an organism developed over the course of thirty years. With the Internet, e-commerce evolves to a new level of existence—certainly to a higher, more interactive form—and a realm of new possibilities.

Recent attention has focused on the depth and meaning of this change: Can traditional EDI coexist with Web-based commerce? What is the role of VANs in this new world? Is Web-based EDI a reality for business-to-business e-commerce? And most important, how do companies evaluate their e-commerce options given this new environment of competing agendas?

Web-based EDI appears on the scene concurrent with a vastly expanded vision of electronic commerce in general. For business-to-business commerce, there are essentially three schools of thought:

- Web-based EDI will eventually replace traditional EDI.
- Web-based and traditional EDI will settle into a somewhat tenuous, yet symbiotic coexistence of undetermined outcome.
- EDI, on or off the Web, is a minor player in the much more complex e-commerce realm of the future.

As in most debates, there is likely some truth in each perspective. But the real answer probably lies in a combination that favors the Web, suggesting a paradigm in which distinctions between the two EDIs are blurred and multiple e-commerce options coexist. Only time will tell.

In the few years since Web-based EDI first appeared on the horizon, the pace of adoption has been slow, shedding very little light on its path to an expected brilliant future. Although some of the most aggressive growth scenarios for Web-based EDI may be fueled by enthusiastic industry supporters pitching their Internet EDI products, the fact remains that there is plenty of room in the e-commerce market for a more affordable, more interactive, and more flexible solution than traditional EDI.

Web-based standards, technology, and security are advancing, creating fewer and fewer barriers to widespread acceptance. The question seems to be more a matter of when, rather than why not. How will this phase of the evolution take shape? No one knows for sure, but some of the best clues are revealed in the fundamentals that define EDI over the Internet.

Web-Based EDI Technology and Infrastructure

What is being called "Web-based EDI" is a developing form of business-to-business e-commerce that uses the Internet for information exchange, allowing non-EDI-enabled companies to electronically execute mission-critical transactions—shipping documents, purchase orders, inventory reports—with each other as well as with their EDI-based trading partners.

As a term, *Web-based EDI* may soon outgrow its definition, abandoning the notion of EDI for a much broader context. In this larger sense, the term refers to several possible types of e-commerce conducted over the Web, incorporating, but not limited to, traditional EDI's functions and capabilities and assuming EDI-like standards adapted for the Web.

Unlike traditional EDI's closed networks, Web-based EDI theoretically functions in the wide-open space of the Internet, redefining the private network underpinnings of EDI, its basic technology requirements, and its infrastructure.

Standards and Protocols

Like traditional EDI, Web-based EDI must rely on a common language that recognizes standardized formats of the exchanged information. Just as the underlying language and standards of all Internet communications such as Hypertext Markup Language (HTML), Transmission Control Protocol/Internet Protocol (TCP/IP), and Hypertext Transport Protocol (HTTP) set the rules for the creation of data links and transfer, there are Web-based standards and protocols specifically for e-commerce.

For example, Secure Electronic Transaction (SET), which is in use for secure payments over the Internet, and Open Trading Protocols (OTP), which is in development for a range of online purchasing transactions, both address the inherent security issues of payments over the Web, particularly for the business-to-consumer market. In addition, the ICE (Information Content and Exchange) protocol, which is now in its formative stages, is intended to help retailers glean inventory data from their suppliers' servers and to automate several routine business processes between merchants and their vendors. One of the most promising Internet business-to-business standards on the drawing board is OBI (Open Buying on the Internet), which recognizes EDI formats as part of a purchasing process that sets standards for how suppliers' online catalogs link to buyers' purchasing systems.

Surely some elements of EDI as we know it will endure on the Web because years of negotiations have hashed out some commonly accepted, if not universal, standards that form the foundation for all EDI-based interactions. Will a handful of universal standards suitable for all Web-based commerce emerge as well or is the current patchwork process a forerunner of a larger crazy quilt to come?

Many industry experts agree that in order for Web-based EDI to become viable in an EDI-entrenched marketplace it needs to be made easily compatible with existing EDI standards through a transition that reaches out to the untapped smaller and mid-size companies not yet served by traditional EDI. According to standards industry officials quoted recently in *ec/edi Insider*, the ideal for this next-generation, beyond-EDI standard would link old with new by recognizing a range of new technologies and methods while building on the ANSI 12X model—the established North American EDI standard.

This may sound too good to be true, at least in the short term. In their race to launch new products in a commerce-crazed marketplace, competing vendors may hinder support for a consistent standard, leaving a gap between those using traditional EDI and those using the Internet.

Data Transmission over the Internet

Although traditional EDI data follows a direct route from point to point, data released into the Internet's open contours follows a less prescribed regimen. This can be a blessing disguised as a curse, or vice versa. Data may take a circuitous route, causing delays and mishaps, depending on Internet traffic volume at the time of the transaction. On the other hand, the Internet allows an unsurpassed level of connectivity. From a company's centralized database, data can flow to one supplier and another, then on to several customers, back to the database, and so on. Imagine a childhood game where you connect all the points on a piece of paper without lifting your pencil. This is the powerfully diffusive nature of the Internet's open network, which allows unlimited access to trading partners, and the trading community theoretically encompasses the world. For the purposes of e-commerce, the open network of the Internet is nothing short of revolutionary.

The Role of VANs in Web-Based Transactions

One point of debate is how central VANs will be in e-commerce scenarios of the future. VANs, which are widely used in traditional EDI to help interpret messages between trading partners, assume a critical role in early Web-based EDI models.

Teamed with Web EDI software, the VAN facilitates the communications, interpreting EDI data for the Web and then interpreting it from the Web back into EDI format. However, industry insiders and VAN users recently quoted in *Electronic Buyers News* predict a rocky road ahead because of interoperability issues. Like traditional EDI—where both trading partners must use the same VAN—Web-based EDI via VAN requires agreement on both ends of the transmission over how the data will be exchanged, including some similar standards for the exchange of information over the Internet

Although VAN providers have embraced Web-EDI as an option for their customers, its adoption within trading communities has been piecemeal, reflecting uneasiness over the absence of a common standard and, in a larger sense, underlying uncertainty about EDI solutions in a fast-changing, cost/benefit-driven marketplace.

VANs are expected to continue to dominate the EDI landscape, at least in the short term, in both Web-based and traditional EDI. As reported in *Electronic Buyers News*, an input study forecasting a year 2000 scenario projects a robust EDI market of $385 billion, based on the total value of traded goods and services, at the turn of the century, including 71 percent from traditional EDI through VANs and 18 percent from Web-based EDI through VANs.

This whopping 89 percent share illustrates the expected control of the market by VAN-based alternatives in the next few years. The emerging paradigm is one still dominated by traditional EDI via VAN, while Web-based EDI—both with and without VAN—establishes a significant foothold.

Yet the most dramatic predictions in the input study fall outside the realm of EDI, off or on the Internet. An annual growth rate of 250 percent for the value of Internet-traded goods and services, as compared to a 32 percent rate for all forms of EDI, suggests a much wider context for Internet commerce in the future, in which EDI will have to share its limelight with a host of new approaches.

E-commerce beyond EDI

Electronic commerce on the Internet, or e-commerce, reaches far beyond EDI. It places unprecedented emphasis on the concepts of openness and interactivity while emphasizing the Web's all-inclusive nature. The goals of e-commerce are to enable low-cost availability to small and large companies alike and to enhance connectivity and unlimited access to worldwide trading partners twenty-four hours a day. Ultimately, e-commerce is designed with the flexibility to work with other software and to interface across an entire enterprise, while allowing dynamic, responsive, and immediate communication between customers and suppliers.

With this new era comes an enlightenment. The power of the personalized electronic commercial relationship is thrust to the fore, prompting a rediscovery of customer service, a new perspective on global sales and sourcing, and an expanding portfolio of practical business applications beyond the corporate Web site. The great unknown in this brave, new, unrestricted world—and the creative challenge for forward-thinking managers—is how to assemble the pieces into a cost-effective and long-term investment, one that adapts easily as e-commerce evolves.

A short while ago, a corporate Web site was the new frontier and was considered a must for companies who wanted to promote their wares while projecting a sufficiently enlightened digital image to established customers and the Web's worldwide audience of prospects. But confronted by Web surfers' indifference many have experienced an Internet version of the age-old social nightmare: "What if I gave a party and nobody came?"

Although the corporate Web site can be an effective public relations tool, today's hurdles and expectations are much higher. To help drive new sales, reduce churn, and increase profits, Web efforts must be intrinsically linked to revenue-enhancing and cost-reducing objectives. This is an area in which company size is of little consequence because the benefits are universal, and smaller companies can leapfrog the learning curve from the experimentation phase into immediately viable Web business programs.

A recent survey conducted by *CIO* magazine and Morgan Stanley concludes that, while 22 percent of large companies now have e-commerce programs for transactions on the Web, another 20 percent are in implementation stages and still another 43 percent are either planning to purchase or are evaluating e-commerce programs. This activity reflects the natural progression of these companies from Web sites to a range of business practices that link the Web's interactive capabilities with sales and service.

Extranets and the Cooperative Web Business Community

The emergence of virtual private networks (VPNs) counters the most serious impediment to growth in e-commerce via the Internet: security issues.

The VPN is the Web's VAN, enabling companies to create levels of private access to information between business partners that are differentiated by the nature of the transaction and the business relationship. These private communities—commonly called extranets, or extended intranets—are an outgrowth of a company's internal network that is specifically geared to suppliers and external partners.

Extranets combine security with the Web's ubiquity to redefine commonly held notions of cooperation, community, and efficiencies between companies. On a basic level, the extranet allows for routine transactions via the Internet within a trading community, assuring security through built-in measures appropriate to the user and task at hand. A much broader perspective envisions collaborative communities where partnering companies readily share data, knowledge, systems, goals, and leadership electronically to maximize market competitiveness and efficiencies along the supply chain.

Online Sales through Malls, Storefronts, and Electronic Catalogs

The Internet's global reach, coupled with developments in online purchasing protocols, processes, and security, elevates the sales function to an electronic plane.

Although in many cases there is no substitute for a personal sales call and no replacement for a customized sales presentation, the explosion in technologies and practices that focuses the interactive qualities of the Web on sales is enough to give pause to even the purists among global sales managers.

For retailers and business-to-business operations alike, the Web is an interactive, twenty-four-hour-a-day, worldwide shopping extravaganza that functions in tandem with online company catalogs, storefronts, or leased mall space as a surrogate salesman and customer service rep, point-of-purchase display, and order and payment processor.

Web Sales Efforts Have Top-line and Bottom-line Impact

Linked to warehouse inventories—in some cases virtual inventories that suppliers keep replenished through extranet access—the Web storefront or catalog extends the sales effort to far-flung markets without the standard costs associated with more staff, travel, marketing materials, and administration.

Perhaps the most dramatic potential savings are on the distribution side. By directly linking the point of sale to the supplier, electronic sales operations eliminate the need for companies to stockpile warehouses in multiple worldwide locations. On the purchasing side, buyers sourcing materials for product manufacturing benefit from a burgeoning base of product information and new ways to find suppliers, which in theory (and deference to Adam Smith's model of market-driven, pure competition) fosters more competitive prices from an expanded global supply network. Savings in price and distribution, when passed on, help companies keep existing customers, so their primary focus can be on developing new business prospects and global markets.

These Web-driven, cost-revenue synergies demonstrate that there is a reinforcing cycle of positive impact that affects both ends of the sale, both parts of the income statement, and internal processes throughout the enterprise.

New Heights in Customer Service

Customer service, historically a reliable barometer for sizing up a company's basic character, transcends the confines of traditional customer relationships to occupy a well-deserved, multidimensional status in Web commerce.

Internet pundits, especially attentive to the dynamics of this change, are quick to welcome the Web into the bowels of every company's most basic internal/external interfaces. (See the commentary in such magazines as *Infoworld* and *InternetWeek*, among others.) Because of its speed, interactive qualities, and ability to be customized or personalized to suit customers' preferences, culture, language, and currency, the Internet reinvents customer service possibilities and expectations for all companies, irrespective of their size or technological inclination. In the immediate time frame of the Internet, every customer's dossier of critical information and inputs creates the ultimate niche-marketing and product development environment.

In addition to making possible online order entry, inventory management, and product spec checking—as well as instantaneous account management and the real-time tracking of shipments—the invaluable feedback gained by conducting customer service on the Web acts as a catalyst that leads to more focused marketing efforts and quickly executed product improvements.

The E-commerce Imperative for Your Business

In the end, the most relevant perspective on e-commerce is the one that works for your business. The first decision is whether any of the new technologies and electronic applications—from basic browsers and email (sometimes called the poor man's EDI) to extranets—will survive a rigorous cost/benefit analysis to support your company's major revenue and operating goals.

Any e-commerce action plan needs to be rooted in terms of tangible return on investment in addition to more amorphous factors such as opportunity cost, competitive advantage, and the most critical driver of the Internet age, time. In fact, it is the exaggerated pace of time—in the speed of transactions, the immediacy of the medium, and the unbelievable rate of technology change—that is forcing companies, with almost primal vigor, into a Web-induced quest to survive.

When all is said and done, the consequences may be less draconian than survival. And there may be more time than it might appear. Yet the imperative is nonetheless clear. When upfront cost is eliminated as a barrier to entry and the leapfrog adoption of new e-commerce applications is possible even for technologically inexperienced companies, then there is no time like the present to deploy a new arsenal of e-commerce capabilities.

The second decision, regarding the scope of what to deploy, is based on an evaluation of your business processes, your trading partner preferences and requirements, and your growth plans in the context of available and soon-to-launch solutions. The technology tools you deploy should support your people, processes, and business philosophies without themselves becoming the primary focus. And because the pace of change makes the full spectrum of possibilities impossible to predict, your e-commerce program should allow ample room for ongoing growth and scalability to a larger, more complex plan yet to be crystallized.

Drilling Down to the Key Considerations

From EDI through all the current forms of Web-based commerce, a company's viable options are in large measure determined by its needs. Yet sorting through these options often yields answers that are not always either black or white.

Although traditional EDI offers security and compliance with large trading partners, its closed network, rigid format and standards, and static database-to-database exchange of information are best suited to repetitive, standardized transactions and documents. EDI standards ensure operability with other EDI-capable companies but limit the types of interactions and partners to predetermined sets. The costs and complexity of EDI setup and the establishment of VAN connections are generally serious barriers to entry for most smaller companies.

Of course, your own decision to implement EDI may be driven more by the competitive environment in your industry and the requirements of your suppliers, which therefore reduces your decision down to the question of Web-based versus traditional EDI implementation.

The Web's reach and open network allow global desktop-to-desktop access—including spontaneous exchanges between potential trading partners—as well as customized interactions but may also require an increased attention to security issues in the short term. VPNs can help bolster comfort levels as the relationship matures from new contact to trading partner by offering various levels of access, but given the nature of the Internet they are not as fundamentally secure as the VANs. Web-based solutions offer a more flexible, dynamic, immediate context for the customer interface at the front end as well as links from the Web point-of-sale back through the enterprise, but implementing coordinated technologies is challenging and not always cost effective.

The Brighter Side of Risks and Obstacles

En masse, companies' decisions are determining the pace and direction of the e-commerce movement. At the micro level, they must weigh the rewards against the risks. Lack of sufficient bandwidth to carry the increasing volume of Web communications was recently seen as the most serious threat to widespread adoption of Web-based commerce. Recently, however, a number of major telecommunications industry developments, while not reversing the trend, have helped put some distance between the bandwidth problem and Web commerce. These include the deployment of fiber (for both the local loop and the Internet backbone), improvements in the use of copper wire (such as cable modems and a technology known as ADSL), and new wireless services.

On the security front, although progress has been swift with encryption technology—which verifies the authenticity of electronic communications by using digital signatures—concerns remain about the degree of security necessary for commercial payments to flourish on the Net. According to *Network VAR* magazine, insiders claim that firewalls and payment standards like SET have mitigated the risks and that the problem to be overcome now is a feeling of insecurity no longer rooted in fact. For business-to-business financial transactions, especially within extranet communities, one likely solution lies in new payment transaction systems based on wire transfers and direct debit accounts with suppliers, methods familiar today to even the most paper-based businesses.

Finally, the quagmire of standards for data exchange and developing protocols offers little hope for a quick resolution, leaving managers to speculate over which will take hold and endure long term. Once again, a quantum leap in technology may supplant the whole issue. Recent developments in software enable the exchange of application-specific data over the Internet with links to the legacy EDI system on the back end, enabling a freer flow of communications between the Web and existing systems. According to *ENT Magazine*, in the larger arena of application development, technology is moving toward standardized component solutions that allow for entire legacy applications to be encapsulated, or wrapped, in a standard interface, such as Java, and then exchanged over the Internet.

Working in conjunction with smart middleware, which performs the translation of the interface, this type of solution eliminates the need for elaborate standards that specify how pieces of data are to be formatted.

Cyber Implications for Global Trade

The explosive $4 trillion market in global trade, which has doubled in the past ten years, will likely follow a similar course into the next millennium, perhaps doubling again in the next decade. Although fundamental changes in trade policy and regional dynamics have driven this astonishing rate of growth in recent years, the trend going forward will in large measure be impacted by digital and related technologies as well as global technology infrastructure. Fundamental improvements in global EDI infrastructure on every continent coupled with the inevitable cross-pollination of EDI and the Internet, will accommodate substantially larger volumes of trade, connecting even the most distant corners with electronic capabilities.

The recently launched Bolero project exemplifies the major efforts being undertaken to develop an e-commerce framework geared specifically to global trade. Bolero is a new initiative in trade facilitation, a joint project of banks, shipping companies, and members of the world trade community to serve the global community of exporters, importers, and freight forwarders. Through a system of standardized document formats; a legal framework that governs the exchange of electronic documents, security and support services; and a title registry database, Bolero provides an administrative foundation for critical cross-border trade documentation, including electronic financial transactions. Endorsed by major financial institutions, the Bolero project has widespread implications for both financial EDI and trade over the Internet.

The Future Is Electronic Business

The evolution continues. The future is now. Will the e-commerce organism walk or fly? The answer is both—and more.

As in the exponential leap from EDI to Web-based commerce, the concept of electronic business redefines the basic parameters of the organism once again. Electronic commerce, as we know it, becomes just one element incorporated within an expansive, more powerful vision: electronic business. Electronic business focuses on the entire enterprise within the context of trading communities, operating within a global framework of contacts and new global infrastructure. It places emphasis on the electronically enhanced business relationship, not just on the transaction or function-specific applications or single solutions.

The integration focus that has occupied so much thought in current enterprise paradigms is extended outward to suppliers, industries, and worldwide communities of interest. Electronic business uses what we today define as e-commerce as a means to this end rather than as an end in itself. Most of all, electronic business foresees that much of its potential is still unknown.

How close is the future? And the future's future? In the rush of Internet time, probably sooner than we think. In the context of your business, the future begins when you decide to act. There is no time like the present.

GLOBAL INTERNET MARKETS SURVEY

Regional and Country Rankings

RANKINGS			POPULATION		
Regional Rank	Regions/ Countries	Global Rank	1997 Population	Share of Global Population	Share of Regional Population
GLOBAL COMPOSITE			5,852,220,266	100.000%	-
NORTH AMERICA					
REGIONAL COMPOSITE			297,077,961	5.076%	100.000%
1	US	1	267,954,767	4.579%	90.197%
2	Canada	5	29,123,194	0.498%	9.803%
LATIN AMERICA					
REGIONAL COMPOSITE			495,920,344	8.474%	100.000%
1	Brazil	23	164,511,366	2.811%	33.173%
2	Mexico	30	97,563,374	1.667%	19.673%
3	Chile	36	14,508,168	0.248%	2.926%
4	Argentina	37	35,053,980	0.599%	7.068%
5	Colombia	45	37,418,290	0.639%	7.545%
6	Peru	48	24,949,512	0.426%	5.031%
7	Venezuela	53	22,396,407	0.383%	4.516%
8	Costa Rica	55	3,534,174	0.060%	0.713%
9	Bermuda	63	62,569	0.001%	0.013%
10	Ecuador	66	11,690,535	0.200%	2.357%
11	Uruguay	67	3,261,707	0.056%	0.658%
12	Guatemala	71	11,558,407	0.198%	2.331%
13	Nicaragua	73	4,386,399	0.075%	0.884%
14	Honduras	76	5,751,384	0.098%	1.160%
15	Bolivia	77	7,295,421	0.125%	1.471%
16	Trinidad and Tobago	82	1,273,141	0.022%	0.257%
17	Panama	85	2,698,477	0.046%	0.544%
18	Jamaica	87	2,615,582	0.045%	0.527%
19	Paraguay	100	5,651,634	0.097%	1.140%
20	El Salvador	105	5,934,611	0.101%	1.197%

APPENDIX

HOSTS			INDICATORS			
1997 Number of Hosts	Share of Global Hosts	Share of Regional Hosts	1995-1997 Growth in Hosts	1995-1997 Net Change in Hosts	Hosts Per 100,000 Population	Digital Market Access
19,540,325	100.000%		72%	12,898,784	333.9	Ajar
10,290,724	52.664%	100.000%	64%	6,463,650	3,464.0	Wide open
9,379,266	48.000%	91.143%	64%	5,884,811	3,500.3	Wide open
911,458	4.664%	8.857%	66%	578,839	3,129.7	Wide open
173,709	0.889%	100.000%	120%	137,704	35.0	Ajar
68,685	0.352%	39.540%	144%	57,109	41.8	Ajar
35,238	0.180%	20.286%	105%	26,856	36.1	Ajar
19,168	0.098%	11.035%	70%	12,504	132.1	Ajar
18,985	0.097%	10.929%	141%	15,715	54.2	Ajar
6,905	0.035%	3.975%	82%	4,830	18.5	Ajar
6,510	0.033%	3.748%	321%	6,143	26.1	Ajar
4,679	0.024%	2.694%	134%	3,826	20.9	Ajar
4,259	0.022%	2.452%	103%	3,230	120.5	Ajar
1,648	0.008%	0.949%	73%	1,098	2,633.9	Partially open
1,078	0.006%	0.621%	70%	706	9.2	Ajar
1,024	0.005%	0.589%	94%	751	31.4	Ajar
882	0.005%	0.508%	*	882	7.6	Ajar
743	0.004%	0.428%	255%	684	16.9	Ajar
590	0.003%	0.340%	*	590	10.3	Ajar
538	0.003%	0.310%	*	538	7.4	Ajar
423	0.002%	0.244%	*	423	33.2	Ajar
390	0.002%	0.225%	75%	263	14.5	Ajar
349	0.002%	0.201%	85%	247	13.3	Ajar
239	0.001%	0.138%	*	239	4.2	Ajar
200	0.001%	0.115%	*	200	3.4	Ajar

RANKINGS			POPULATION		
Regional Rank	Regions/ Countries	Global Rank	1997 Population	Share of Global Population	Share of Regional Population
21	Antigua and Barbuda	109	66,175	0.001%	0.013%
22	Guadeloupe	115	412,614	0.007%	0.083%
23	Puerto Rico	116	3,825,932	0.065%	0.771%
24	Aruba	119	68,031	0.001%	0.014%
25	Netherland Antilles	121	211,093	0.004%	0.043%
26	Saint Lucia	125	159,639	0.003%	0.032%
27	Anguilla	126	10,785	0.000%	0.002%
28	Cuba	127	10,999,041	0.188%	2.218%
29	Dominica	129	83,226	0.001%	0.017%
30	Guyana	131	706,116	0.012%	0.142%
31	Bahamas	132	262,034	0.004%	0.053%
32	Virgin Islands (US)	137	97,240	0.002%	0.020%
33	Turks and Caicos Islands	143	14,631	0.000%	0.003%
34	French Guiana	144	156,946	0.003%	0.032%
35	Dominican Republic	146	8,228,151	0.141%	1.659%
36	Belize	147	224,663	0.004%	0.045%
37	Barbados	148	257,731	0.004%	0.052%
38	Saint Kitts and Nevis	157	41,803	0.000%	0.008%
39	Cayman Islands	158	36,153	0.000%	0.007%
40	British Virgin Islands	165	13,368	0.000%	0.003%
41	Martinique	172	403,531	0.007%	0.081%
42	Saint Vincent	191	119,092	0.002%	0.024%
43	Grenada	192	95,537	0.002%	0.019%
44	Montserrat	194	12,800	0.000%	0.003%
45	Haiti	205	6,851,313	0.117%	1.382%
46	Suriname	220	443,446	0.008%	0.089%
47	Antarctica	233	4,115	0.000%	0.000%

WESTERN EUROPE

REGIONAL COMPOSITE			388,424,430	6.637%	100.000%
1	Germany	3	84,068,216	1.437%	21.643%
2	United Kingdom	4	58,610,182	1.002%	15.089%
3	Netherlands	7	15,653,091	0.267%	4.030%
4	Finland	8	5,109,148	0.087%	1.315%
5	France	9	58,211,454	0.995%	14.987%
6	Sweden	10	8,946,193	0.153%	2.303%
7	Italy	11	57,534,088	0.983%	14.812%
8	Norway	12	4,404,456	0.075%	1.134%
9	Denmark	15	5,268,775	0.090%	1.356%
10	Switzerland	16	7,248,984	0.124%	1.866%

HOSTS			INDICATORS			
1997 Number of Hosts	Share of Global Hosts	Share of Regional Hosts	1995-1997 Growth in Hosts	1995-1997 Net Change in Hosts	Hosts Per 100,000 Population	Digital Market Access
165	0.000%	0.095%	8%	23	249.3	Ajar
127	0.000%	0.073%	*	127	30.8	Ajar
114	0.000%	0.066%	17%	31	3.0	Ajar
101	0.000%	0.058%	*	101	148.5	Ajar
84	0.000%	0.048%	*	84	39.8	Ajar
74	0.000%	0.043%	*	74	46.4	Ajar
71	0.000%	0.041%	321%	67	658.3	Partially open
67	0.000%	0.039%	*	67	0.6	Ajar
62	0.000%	0.036%	*	62	74.5	Ajar
57	0.000%	0.033%	*	57	8.1	Ajar
54	0.000%	0.031%	*	54	20.6	Ajar
35	0.000%	0.020%	*	35	36.0	Ajar
29	0.000%	0.017%	*	29	198.2	Ajar
27	0.000%	0.016%	*	27	17.2	Ajar
25	0.000%	0.014%	-4%	(2)	0.3	Ajar
24	0.000%	0.014%	*	24	10.7	Ajar
20	0.000%	0.012%	100%	15	7.8	Ajar
12	0.000%	0.007%	*	12	28.7	Ajar
12	0.000%	0.007%	-46%	(29)	33.2	Ajar
7	0.000%	0.004%	*	7	52.4	Ajar
6	0.000%	0.003%	*	6	1.5	Ajar
1	0.000%	0.000%	*	1	0.8	Ajar
1	0.000%	0.000%	*	1	1.0	Ajar
1	0.000%	0.000%	*	1	7.8	Ajar
0	0.000%	0.000%	*	0	0.0	Closed
0	0.000%	0.000%	*	0	0.0	Closed
0	0.000%	0.000%	-100%	(4)	0.0	Closed
5,275,886	27.000%	100.000%	70%	3,443,339	1,358.3	Partially open
1,508,370	7.719%	28.590%	65%	957,448	1,794.2	Partially open
1,094,019	5.599%	20.736%	74%	734,460	1,866.6	Partially open
395,976	2.026%	7.505%	61%	243,295	2,529.7	Partially open
380,880	1.949%	7.219%	74%	254,804	7,454.9	Wide open
345,879	1.770%	6.556%	62%	214,887	594.2	Partially open
335,414	1.717%	6.357%	65%	212,571	3,749.2	Wide open
279,353	1.430%	5.295%	103%	211,887	485.5	Ajar
239,089	1.224%	4.532%	77%	162,971	5,428.3	Wide open
161,368	0.826%	3.059%	90%	116,696	3,062.7	Wide open
148,028	0.758%	2.806%	52%	84,233	2,042.1	Partially open

RANKINGS			POPULATION		
Regional Rank	Regions/ Countries	Global Rank	1997 Population	Share of Global Population	Share of Regional Population
11	Spain	17	39,244,195	0.671%	10.103%
12	Austria	20	8,054,078	0.138%	2.074%
13	Belgium	21	10,203,683	0.174%	2.627%
14	Ireland	32	3,555,500	0.061%	0.915%
15	Greece	35	10,583,126	0.181%	2.725%
16	Portugal	38	9,867,654	0.169%	2.540%
17	Iceland	40	272,550	0.005%	0.070%
18	Luxembourg	56	422,474	0.007%	0.109%
19	Malta	72	379,365	0.006%	0.098%
20	San Marino	74	24,714	0.000%	0.006%
21	Liechtenstein	78	31,461	0.000%	0.008%
22	Greenland	84	58,768	0.001%	0.015%
23	Monaco	95	31,892	0.000%	0.008%
24	Faroe Islands	97	43,057	0.000%	0.011%
25	Andorra	111	74,839	0.001%	0.019%
26	Gibraltar	114	28,913	0.000%	0.007%
27	Isle of Man	149	74,504	0.001%	0.019%
28	Guernsey	156	63,731	0.001%	0.016%
29	Vatican City	160	1,000	0.000%	0.000%
30	Jersey	174	88,510	0.002%	0.023%
31	Corsica	221	258,967	0.004%	0.067%
32	Saint Pierre and Miq.	231	6,862	0.000%	0.002%

EASTERN EUROPE

REGIONAL COMPOSITE			409,769,580	7.002%	100.000%
1	Russia	18	147,987,101	2.529%	36.115%
2	Czech Republic	26	10,318,958	0.176%	2.518%
3	Poland	28	38,700,291	0.661%	9.444%
4	Hungary	31	9,935,774	0.170%	2.425%
5	Slovenia	39	1,945,998	0.033%	0.475%
6	Slovakia	42	5,393,016	0.092%	1.316%
7	Ukraine	44	50,684,635	0.866%	12.369%
8	Croatia	46	5,026,995	0.086%	1.227%
9	Estonia	47	1,444,721	0.025%	0.353%
10	Romania	49	21,399,114	0.366%	5.222%
11	Bulgaria	50	8,652,745	0.148%	2.112%
12	Latvia	51	2,437,649	0.042%	0.595%
13	Bosnia and Herzegovina	58	2,607,734	0.045%	0.636%
14	Lithuania	59	3,635,932	0.062%	0.887%
15	Kazakhstan	64	16,898,572	0.289%	4.124%

HOSTS			INDICATORS			
1997 Number of Hosts	Share of Global Hosts	Share of Regional Hosts	1995-1997 Growth in Hosts	1995-1997 Net Change in Hosts	Hosts Per 100,000 Population	Digital Market Access
121,823	0.623%	2.309%	75%	81,904	310.4	Ajar
87,408	0.447%	1.657%	47%	46,712	1,085.3	Partially open
86,117	0.441%	1.632%	91%	62,411	844.0	Partially open
33,031	0.169%	0.626%	82%	23,090	929.0	Partially open
19,711	0.101%	0.374%	88%	14,136	186.2	Ajar
18,147	0.093%	0.344%	44%	9,399	183.9	Ajar
14,153	0.072%	0.268%	44%	7,353	5,192.8	Wide open
3,854	0.020%	0.073%	59%	2,338	912.2	Partially open
785	0.004%	0.015%	*	785	206.9	Ajar
734	0.004%	0.014%	*	734	2,970.0	Partially open
479	0.002%	0.009%	242%	438	1,522.5	Partially open
417	0.002%	0.008%	921%	413	709.6	Partially open
258	0.001%	0.005%	618%	253	809.0	Partially open
253	0.001%	0.005%	-27%	(218)	587.6	Partially open
155	0.000%	0.003%	*	155	207.1	Ajar
138	0.000%	0.003%	*	138	477.3	Ajar
19	0.000%	0.000%	*	19	25.5	Ajar
13	0.000%	0.000%	*	13	20.4	Ajar
10	0.000%	0.000%	*	10	1,000.0	Partially open
5	0.000%	0.000%	*	5	5.6	Ajar
0	0.000%	0.000%	*	0	0.0	Closed
0	0.000%	0.000%	*	0	0.0	Closed
323,130	**1.654%**	**100.000%**	**120%**	**256,123**	**78.9**	**Ajar**
119,467	0.611%	36.972%	227%	108,300	80.7	Ajar
49,104	0.251%	15.196%	82%	34,262	475.9	Ajar
43,384	0.222%	13.426%	66%	27,692	112.1	Ajar
33,818	0.173%	10.466%	73%	22,520	340.4	Ajar
17,055	0.087%	5.278%	125%	13,674	876.4	Partially open
10,959	0.056%	3.392%	135%	8,967	203.2	Ajar
10,513	0.054%	3.253%	180%	9,174	20.7	Ajar
6,705	0.034%	2.075%	82%	4,670	133.4	Ajar
6,566	0.034%	2.032%	65%	4,163	454.5	Ajar
5,998	0.031%	1.856%	159%	5,107	28.0	Ajar
5,515	0.028%	1.707%	194%	4,876	63.7	Ajar
5,184	0.027%	1.604%	134%	4,234	212.7	Ajar
2,943	0.015%	0.911%	*	2,943	112.9	Ajar
2,761	0.014%	0.854%	221%	2,493	75.9	Ajar
1,136	0.006%	0.352%	916%	1,125	6.7	Ajar

RANKINGS			POPULATION		
Regional Rank	Regions/ Countries	Global Rank	1997 Population	Share of Global Population	Share of Regional Population
16	Belarus	80	10,439,916	0.178%	2.548%
17	Macedonia	81	2,113,866	0.036%	0.516%
18	Armenia	89	3,465,611	0.059%	0.846%
19	Georgia	90	5,174,642	0.088%	1.263%
20	Moldova	107	4,475,232	0.076%	1.092%
21	Uzbekistan	112	23,860,452	0.408%	5.823%
22	Kyrgyzstan	117	4,540,185	0.078%	1.108%
23	Azerbaijan	122	7,735,918	0.132%	1.888%
24	Turkmenistan	184	4,225,351	0.072%	1.031%
25	Serbia	201	10,017,394	0.171%	2.445%
26	Tajikistan	206	6,013,855	0.103%	1.468%
27	Montenegro	218	637,923	0.011%	0.156%

MIDDLE EAST AND AFRICA

RANKINGS			POPULATION		
REGIONAL COMPOSITE			**2,252,428,190**	**38.488%**	**100.000%**
1	South Africa	19	42,465,030	0.726%	1.885%
2	Israel	24	5,534,672	0.095%	0.246%
3	Turkey	34	63,528,225	1.086%	2.820%
4	India	52	967,612,804	16.534%	42.959%
5	Kuwait	57	2,076,805	0.035%	0.092%
6	United Arab Emirates	60	3,189,385	0.054%	0.142%
7	Cyprus	61	752,808	0.013%	0.033%
8	Egypt	62	64,791,891	1.107%	2.877%
9	Lebanon	65	3,858,736	0.066%	0.171%
10	Pakistan	68	132,185,299	2.259%	5.869%
11	Bahrain	69	603,318	0.010%	0.027%
12	Morocco	70	30,391,423	0.519%	1.349%
13	Sri Lanka	75	18,762,075	0.321%	0.833%
14	Kenya	79	28,803,085	0.492%	1.279%
15	Namibia	86	1,727,183	0.030%	0.077%
16	Qatar	88	560,057	0.010%	0.025%
17	Saudi Arabia	91	20,087,965	0.343%	0.892%
18	Ghana	92	18,100,703	0.309%	0.804%
19	Senegal	93	9,403,546	0.161%	0.417%
20	Zimbabwe	94	11,423,175	0.195%	0.507%
21	Zambia	96	9,349,975	0.160%	0.415%
22	Cote d'Ivoire	98	15,150,258	0.259%	0.673%
23	Swaziland	99	1,031,600	0.018%	0.046%
24	Botswana	101	1,500,765	0.026%	0.067%
25	Mauritius	104	1,154,272	0.020%	0.051%

HOSTS			INDICATORS			
1997 Number of Hosts	Share of Global Hosts	Share of Regional Hosts	1995-1997 Growth in Hosts	1995-1997 Net Change in Hosts	Hosts Per 100,000 Population	Digital Market Access
451	0.002%	0.140%	850%	446	4.3	Ajar
429	0.002%	0.133%	826%	424	20.3	Ajar
332	0.002%	0.103%	158%	282	9.6	Ajar
298	0.002%	0.092%	*	298	5.8	Ajar
168	0.000%	0.052%	332%	159	3.8	Ajar
153	0.000%	0.047%	130%	124	0.6	Ajar
108	0.000%	0.033%	*	108	2.4	Ajar
81	0.000%	0.025%	800%	80	1.0	Ajar
2	0.000%	0.000%	*	2	0.0	Closed
0	0.000%	0.000%	*	0	0.0	Closed
0	0.000%	0.000%	*	0	0.0	Closed
0	0.000%	0.000%	*	0	0.0	Closed
224,592	1.149%	100.000%	87%	160,063	10.0	Ajar
117,475	0.601%	52.306%	69%	76,146	276.6	Ajar
61,140	0.313%	27.223%	83%	42,917	1,104.7	Partially open
22,963	0.118%	10.224%	187%	20,173	36.1	Ajar
4,794	0.025%	2.135%	173%	4,149	0.5	Ajar
3,555	0.018%	1.583%	114%	2,779	171.2	Ajar
1,994	0.010%	0.888%	1,246%	1,983	62.5	Ajar
1,973	0.010%	0.878%	248%	1,810	262.1	Ajar
1,894	0.010%	0.843%	197%	1,680	2.9	Ajar
1,128	0.006%	0.502%	3,259%	1,127	29.2	Ajar
959	0.005%	0.427%	1,164%	953	0.7	Ajar
896	0.005%	0.399%	*	896	148.5	Ajar
888	0.005%	0.395%	*	888	2.9	Ajar
611	0.003%	0.272%	*	611	3.3	Ajar
457	0.002%	0.203%	2,038%	456	1.6	Ajar
350	0.002%	0.156%	*	350	20.3	Ajar
345	0.002%	0.154%	*	345	61.6	Ajar
293	0.001%	0.130%	303%	275	1.5	Ajar
275	0.001%	0.122%	642%	270	1.5	Ajar
275	0.001%	0.122%	642%	270	2.9	Ajar
272	0.001%	0.121%	269%	252	2.4	Ajar
255	0.001%	0.114%	381%	244	2.7	Ajar
248	0.001%	0.110%	809%	245	1.6	Ajar
240	0.001%	0.107%	*	240	23.3	Ajar
238	0.001%	0.106%	*	238	15.9	Ajar
211	0.001%	0.094%	*	211	18.3	Ajar

RANKINGS			POPULATION		
Regional Rank	Regions/ Countries	Global Rank	1997 Population	Share of Global Population	Share of Regional Population
26	Jordan	106	4,324,638	0.074%	0.192%
27	Albania	118	3,293,252	0.056%	0.146%
28	Cameroon	124	14,677,510	0.251%	0.652%
29	Tanzania	128	29,460,753	0.503%	1.308%
30	Burkina Faso	134	10,891,159	0.186%	0.484%
31	Mozambique	135	18,355,552	0.314%	0.815%
32	Madagascar	136	14,061,627	0.240%	0.624%
33	Seychelles	138	78,142	0.001%	0.003%
34	Niger	139	9,388,859	0.160%	0.417%
35	Algeria	141	29,830,370	0.510%	1.324%
36	Mali	142	9,945,383	0.170%	0.442%
37	Uganda	145	20,604,874	0.352%	0.915%
38	Angola	150	10,623,994	0.182%	0.472%
39	Lesotho	152	2,007,814	0.034%	0.089%
40	Cape Verde	153	462,335	0.008%	0.021%
41	Tunisia	154	9,183,097	0.157%	0.408%
42	Benin	155	5,902,178	0.101%	0.262%
43	Guinea-Bissau	159	1,178,584	0.020%	0.052%
44	Djibouti	161	434,116	0.007%	0.019%
45	Zaire	162	47,440,362	0.811%	2.106%
46	Burundi	163	6,052,614	0.103%	0.269%
47	Nigeria	167	107,129,469	1.831%	4.756%
48	Rwanda	168	7,737,537	0.132%	0.344%
49	Togo	169	4,735,610	0.081%	0.210%
50	Central African Rep.	170	3,342,051	0.057%	0.148%
51	Congo	171	2,583,198	0.044%	0.115%
52	Equatorial Guinea	173	442,516	0.008%	0.020%
53	Libya	176	5,648,359	0.097%	0.251%
54	Sudan	181	32,041,216	0.548%	1.423%
55	Yemen	182	13,972,477	0.239%	0.620%
56	Guinea	183	7,494,913	0.128%	0.333%
57	Iran	188	67,540,002	1.154%	2.999%
58	Eritrea	189	4,141,867	0.071%	0.184%
59	Bhutan	190	1,865,191	0.032%	0.083%
60	Bangladesh	195	125,340,261	2.142%	5.565%
61	Ethiopia	196	58,732,577	1.004%	2.608%
62	Afghanistan	198	23,738,085	0.406%	1.054%
63	Iraq	199	22,219,289	0.380%	0.986%
64	Syria	200	16,137,899	0.276%	0.716%
65	Somalia	202	9,940,232	0.170%	0.441%

HOSTS			INDICATORS			
1997 Number of Hosts	Share of Global Hosts	Share of Regional Hosts	1995-1997 Growth in Hosts	1995-1997 Net Change in Hosts	Hosts Per 100,000 Population	Digital Market Access
170	0.000%	0.076%	*	170	3.9	Ajar
107	0.000%	0.048%	*	107	3.2	Ajar
75	0.000%	0.033%	*	75	0.5	Ajar
62	0.000%	0.028%	*	62	0.2	Ajar
48	0.000%	0.021%	*	48	0.4	Ajar
44	0.000%	0.020%	*	44	0.2	Ajar
41	0.000%	0.018%	*	41	0.3	Ajar
35	0.000%	0.016%	*	35	44.8	Ajar
34	0.000%	0.015%	*	34	0.4	Ajar
31	0.000%	0.014%	39%	15	0.1	Ajar
29	0.000%	0.013%	*	29	0.3	Ajar
26	0.000%	0.012%	410%	25	0.1	Ajar
18	0.000%	0.008%	*	18	0.2	Ajar
16	0.000%	0.007%	*	16	0.8	Ajar
16	0.000%	0.007%	*	16	3.5	Ajar
15	0.000%	0.007%	-52%	(50)	0.2	Ajar
13	0.000%	0.006%	*	13	0.2	Ajar
10	0.000%	0.004%	*	10	0.8	Ajar
9	0.000%	0.004%	*	9	2.1	Ajar
8	0.000%	0.004%	*	8	0.0	Ajar
8	0.000%	0.004%	*	8	0.1	Ajar
6	0.000%	0.003%	*	6	0.0	Ajar
6	0.000%	0.003%	*	6	0.0	Ajar
6	0.000%	0.003%	*	6	0.1	Ajar
6	0.000%	0.003%	*	6	0.2	Ajar
6	0.000%	0.003%	*	6	0.2	Ajar
5	0.000%	0.002%	*	5	1.1	Ajar
4	0.000%	0.002%	*	4	0.0	Ajar
2	0.000%	0.000%	*	2	0.0	Ajar
2	0.000%	0.000%	*	2	0.0	Ajar
2	0.000%	0.000%	0%	0	0.0	Ajar
1	0.000%	0.000%	-93%	(223)	0.0	Ajar
1	0.000%	0.000%	*	1	0.0	Ajar
1	0.000%	0.000%	*	1	0.0	Ajar
0	0.000%	0.000%	*	0	0.0	Closed
0	0.000%	0.000%	*	0	0.0	Closed
0	0.000%	0.000%	*	0	0.0	Closed
0	0.000%	0.000%	*	0	0.0	Closed
0	0.000%	0.000%	*	0	0.0	Closed
0	0.000%	0.000%	*	0	0.0	Closed

RANKINGS			POPULATION		
Regional Rank	Regions/ Countries	Global Rank	1997 Population	Share of Global Population	Share of Regional Population
66	Malawi	203	9,609,081	0.164%	0.427%
67	Chad	204	7,166,023	0.122%	0.318%
68	Sierra Leone	208	5,004,107	0.086%	0.222%
69	Mauritania	209	2,411,317	0.041%	0.107%
70	Oman	210	2,264,590	0.039%	0.101%
71	Liberia	211	2,256,737	0.039%	0.100%
72	West Bank	212	1,495,683	0.026%	0.066%
73	Gambia	213	1,248,085	0.021%	0.055%
74	Gabon	214	1,190,159	0.020%	0.053%
75	Gaza Strip	215	987,869	0.017%	0.044%
76	Reunion	217	692,204	0.012%	0.031%
77	Comoros	219	589,797	0.010%	0.026%
78	Western Sahara	222	228,138	0.004%	0.010%
79	Sao Tome	223	147,865	0.003%	0.007%
80	Mayotte	225	104,715	0.002%	0.005%
81	Saint Helena	232	6,803	0.000%	0.000%

ASIA PACIFIC

REGIONAL COMPOSITE			2,008,599,761	34.322%	100.000%
1	Japan	2	125,716,637	2.148%	6.259%
2	Australia	6	18,438,824	0.315%	0.918%
3	New Zealand	13	3,587,275	0.061%	0.179%
4	South Korea	14	45,948,811	0.785%	2.288%
5	Hong Kong	22	6,412,786	0.110%	0.319%
6	Singapore	25	3,461,929	0.059%	0.172%
7	Taiwan	27	21,655,515	0.370%	1.078%
8	Malaysia	29	20,376,235	0.348%	1.014%
9	China	33	1,221,591,778	20.874%	60.818%
10	Thailand	41	59,450,818	1.016%	2.960%
11	Indonesia	43	209,774,138	3.585%	10.444%
12	Philippines	54	76,103,564	1.300%	3.789%
13	Tonga	83	107,335	0.002%	0.005%
14	Brunei	102	307,616	0.005%	0.015%
15	Macau	103	502,325	0.009%	0.025%
16	Nepal	108	22,641,061	0.387%	1.127%
17	Norfolk Island	110	2,209	0.000%	0.000%
18	French Polynesia	113	229,836	0.004%	0.011%
19	Guam	120	160,595	0.003%	0.008%
20	Papua New Guinea	123	4,496,221	0.077%	0.224%

HOSTS			INDICATORS			
1997 Number of Hosts	Share of Global Hosts	Share of Regional Hosts	1995-1997 Growth in Hosts	1995-1997 Net Change in Hosts	Hosts Per 100,000 Population	Digital Market Access
0	0.000%	0.000%	*	0	0.0	Closed
0	0.000%	0.000%	*	0	0.0	Closed
0	0.000%	0.000%	*	0	0.0	Closed
0	0.000%	0.000%	*	0	0.0	Closed
0	0.000%	0.000%	*	0	0.0	Closed
0	0.000%	0.000%	*	0	0.0	Closed
0	0.000%	0.000%	*	0	0.0	Closed
0	0.000%	0.000%	*	0	0.0	Closed
0	0.000%	0.000%	*	0	0.0	Closed
0	0.000%	0.000%	*	0	0.0	Closed
0	0.000%	0.000%	*	0	0.0	Closed
0	0.000%	0.000%	*	0	0.0	Closed
0	0.000%	0.000%	*	0	0.0	Closed
0	0.000%	0.000%	*	0	0.0	Closed
0	0.000%	0.000%	*	0	0.0	Closed
0	0.000%	0.000%	*	0	0.0	Closed
3,252,284	16.644%	100.000%	100%	2,437,905	161.9	Ajar
1,778,249	9.100%	54.677%	106%	1,358,193	1,414.5	Partially open
845,365	4.326%	25.993%	84%	594,350	4,584.7	Wide open
185,917	0.951%	5.716%	87%	132,485	5,182.7	Wide open
168,436	0.862%	5.179%	119%	133,233	366.6	Ajar
69,224	0.354%	2.128%	78%	47,325	1,079.5	Partially open
60,674	0.311%	1.866%	172%	52,466	1,752.6	Partially open
48,615	0.249%	1.495%	61%	29,947	224.5	Ajar
40,533	0.207%	1.246%	511%	39,446	198.9	Ajar
25,594	0.131%	0.787%	400%	24,571	2.1	Ajar
12,794	0.065%	0.393%	127%	10,313	21.5	Ajar
10,862	0.056%	0.334%	258%	10,014	5.2	Ajar
4,309	0.022%	0.132%	244%	3,944	5.7	Ajar
417	0.002%	0.013%	*	417	388.5	Ajar
236	0.001%	0.007%	*	236	76.7	Ajar
220	0.001%	0.007%	116%	173	43.8	Ajar
165	0.000%	0.005%	195%	146	0.7	Ajar
160	0.000%	0.005%	*	160	7,243.1	Partially open
147	0.000%	0.005%	*	147	64.0	Ajar
91	0.000%	0.003%	125%	73	56.7	Ajar
79	0.000%	0.002%	*	79	1.8	Ajar

RANKINGS			POPULATION		
Regional Rank	Regions/ Countries	Global Rank	1997 Population	Share of Global Population	Share of Regional Population
21	New Caledonia	130	191,003	0.003%	0.010%
22	Maldives	133	280,391	0.005%	0.014%
23	Vanuatu	140	181,358	0.003%	0.009%
24	Mongolia	151	2,538,211	0.043%	0.126%
25	Cambodia	164	11,163,861	0.191%	0.556%
26	Niue	166	2,174	0.000%	0.000%
27	Pitcairn Islands	175	56	0.000%	0.000%
28	Vietnam	177	75,123,880	1.284%	3.740%
29	Myanmar	178	46,821,943	0.800%	2.331%
30	Western Samoa	179	219,509	0.004%	0.011%
31	Marshall Islands	180	60,652	0.001%	0.003%
32	Solomon Islands	185	426,855	0.007%	0.021%
33	American Samoa	186	61,819	0.001%	0.003%
34	Palau	187	17,240	0.000%	0.000%
35	Cook Islands	193	19,776	0.000%	0.000%
36	North Korea	197	24,317,004	0.416%	1.211%
37	Laos	207	5,116,959	0.087%	0.255%
38	Fiji	216	792,441	0.014%	0.039%
39	Micronesia	224	127,616	0.002%	0.006%
40	Kiribati	226	82,449	0.001%	0.004%
41	Northern Mariana Islands	227	53,552	0.000%	0.003%
42	Wallis and Futuna	228	14,817	0.000%	0.000%
43	Nauru	229	10,390	0.000%	0.000%
44	Tuvalu	230	10,297	0.000%	0.000%

HOSTS			INDICATORS			
1997 Number of Hosts	Share of Global Hosts	Share of Regional Hosts	1995-1997 Growth in Hosts	1995-1997 Net Change in Hosts	Hosts Per 100,000 Population	Digital Market Access
59	0.000%	0.002%	*	59	30.9	Ajar
51	0.000%	0.002%	*	51	18.2	Ajar
32	0.000%	0.000%	*	32	17.6	Ajar
17	0.000%	0.000%	*	17	0.7	Ajar
7	0.000%	0.000%	*	7	0.0	Ajar
7	0.000%	0.000%	*	7	322.0	Ajar
5	0.000%	0.000%	*	5	8,928.6	Partially open
3	0.000%	0.000%	*	3	0.0	Ajar
3	0.000%	0.000%	*	3	0.0	Ajar
3	0.000%	0.000%	*	3	1.4	Ajar
3	0.000%	0.000%	*	3	4.9	Ajar
2	0.000%	0.000%	*	2	0.5	Ajar
2	0.000%	0.000%	*	2	3.2	Ajar
2	0.000%	0.000%	*	2	11.6	Ajar
1	0.000%	0.000%	*	1	5.1	Ajar
0	0.000%	0.000%	*	0	0.0	Closed
0	0.000%	0.000%	*	0	0.0	Closed
0	0.000%	0.000%	-100%	(9)	0.0	Closed
0	0.000%	0.000%	*	0	0.0	Closed
0	0.000%	0.000%	*	0	0.0	Closed
0	0.000%	0.000%	*	0	0.0	Closed
0	0.000%	0.000%	*	0	0.0	Closed
0	0.000%	0.000%	*	0	0.0	Closed
0	0.000%	0.000%	*	0	0.0	Closed

ABOUT THE COMPANION WEB SITE

B

The Global Information Network (http://www.ginfo.net) provides visitors with free access to a targeted group of superior Web sites throughout the world, hand-picked for their high quality content and relevance to international business executives. This global consortium of business-to-business sites helps users find partners in distant markets, set up new operations, ship and track cargo, increase sales, and enhance their global business profiles.

Global trade is a robust $4 trillion market, fueled by explosive growth in new technologies, including worldwide Internet usage. Mainstream business applications on the Internet—from trade lead databases to electronic purchasing—are helping companies of all sizes compete worldwide.

For companies already active in global markets, the Internet plays an increasingly integral role in day-to-day transactions and in the timely delivery of mission critical information. Whether it's a tool that's used for tracking cargo across the Pacific or for downloading customs documents from India, exporters and importers rely on the Internet to keep their products moving. For worldwide marketing, sales, and customer service, the Internet offers both global, broad-based reach and the ability to deliver highly targeted, interactive information, customized by language, currency, industry, and particular interest.

The Global Information Network (GIN) is a powerful vehicle for global advertisers, combining the collective reach of a large business-to-business network with the highly targeted profile of users at companies active in global business. By unifying a fragmented market, GIN offers advertisers a scale approach without compromising on quality demographics.

What's on the Site

Upon entering the homepage of The Global Information Network (GIN), shown in Figure B.1, you'll find a wealth of resources and information designed to help you conduct global business operations over the Internet. The network now represents more than 150 top-quality Web sites from around the world that provide information, news, and services to business professionals and global traders. Access to GIN is always free, as it is supported by a number of significant national and international advertisers. The purpose of GIN is to provide a single, comprehensive source of world trade information that can be viewed either geographically or by subject matter (Figure B.2).

Users navigating through the World Regions area of GIN might end up on the North America & Caribbean page, the South America page, or the Europe page (Figures B.3 through B.5). In every case, GIN network affiliates and other significant Web sites from these regions of the world are listed with a copy of their identifying logos and a brief description of the services and resources they provide.

Figure B.1 GIN homepage.

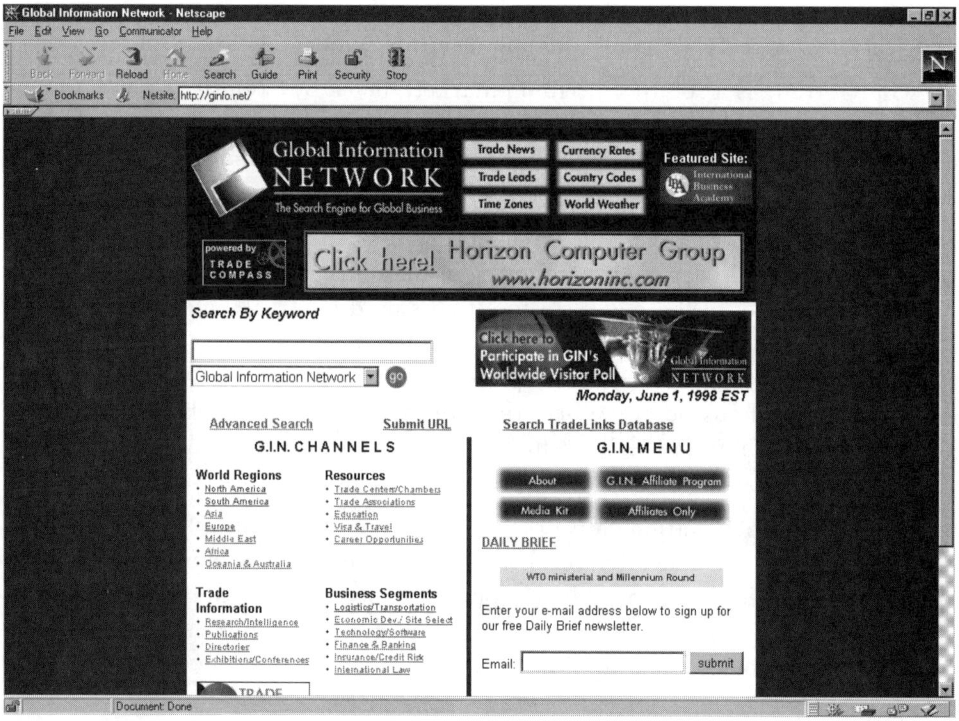

Figure B.2 GIN closeup.

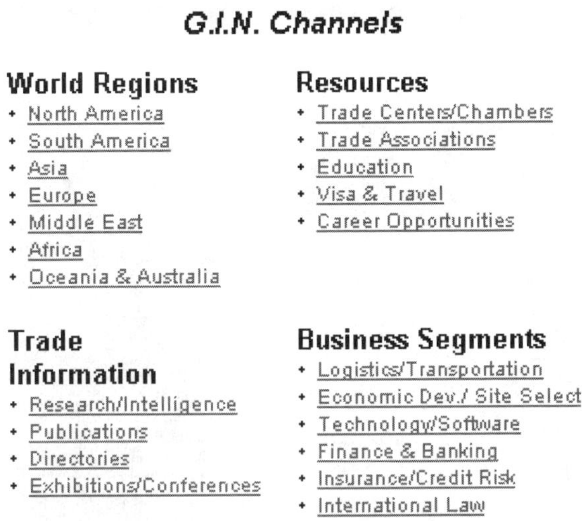

G.I.N. Channels
World Regions
North America
South America
Asia
Europe
Middle East
Africa
Oceania & Australia
Resources
Trade Centers/Chambers
Trade Associations
Education
Visa & Travel
Career Opportunities
Trade Information
Research/Intelligence
Publications
Directories
Exhibitions/Conferences
Business Segments
Logistics/Transportation
Economic Dev./ Site Select
Technology/Software
Finance & Banking
Insurance/Credit Risk
International Law

Figure B.3 North America & Caribbean page.

Global Information Network- North America & Caribbean - Netscape
File Edit View Go Communicator Help
Back Forward Reload Home Search Guide Print Security Stop
Bookmarks Netsite: http://ginfo.net/namerica.html
Global Information NETWORK
The Search Engine for Global Business
Trade News
Currency Rates
Trade Leads
Country Codes
Time Zones
World Weather
Feature Site
International Business Academy
powered by TRADE COMPASS
TradeWinds Publishing
Receive Daily TRADE
Search
About
Home
G.I.N. CHANNELS
NORTH AMERICA & CARIBBEAN
Trade Compass is the leading web site for international business, providing a wide variety of business tools and information to thousands of companies like yours each month.
BC Trade Network (BCTN) is your online gateway to British Columbia exports. BC Trade Network offers a variety of online services all directed at supporting the exporting of British Columbia products.
Mexico Trade Monitor The International Business Site that promotes what Mexico has to offer to the world.
Trade Compass Canada is your link to Canadian trade information and products available no where else.
Carribean Export is designed to help Caribbean exporters and manufacturers increase their exports
World Regions
North America/Caribbean
South America
Asia
Europe
Africa
Middle East
Oceania & Australia
Resources
Trade Centers/Chambers
Trade Associations
Education
Visa & Travel
Career Opportunities
Business Segments
Logistics/Transportation
Econ Development Sites
Technology/Software
Finance/Banking
Insurance/Credit Risk
53% of 11K

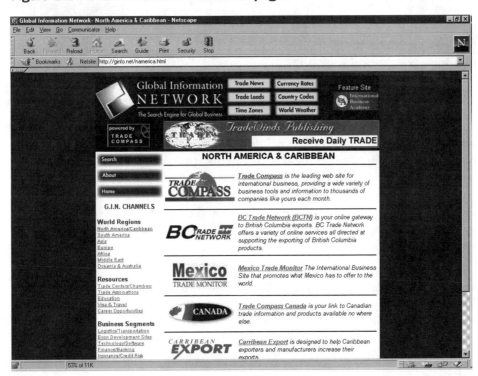

Figure B.4 South America page.

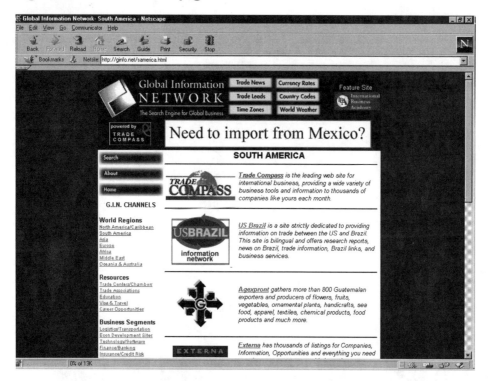

The same informational format is used when navigating through any of GIN's three primary subject areas: Trade Information, Resources, and Business Segments. For instance, under Business Segments, the sub-category Logistics and Transportation provides users with a number of helpful links to prominent Web sites around the world (Figure B.6). Trade Information identifies a number of publications, directories, conferences, exhibitions and content research sources. And, under Resources, various trade associations, centers, educational facilities and career opportunities are listed.

Using an advanced search engine capability powered by AltaVista, GIN allows searches in any of three ways: across the entire network, across a larger Tradelinks Database of 1,600 related Web sites, or across the entire Worldwide Web (Figure B.7). The functionality of the search engine was developed to improve the quality of returns for users when trying to conduct global searches for business-to-business content, especially since larger search engines are more consumer oriented. In this

Figure B.5 Europe page.

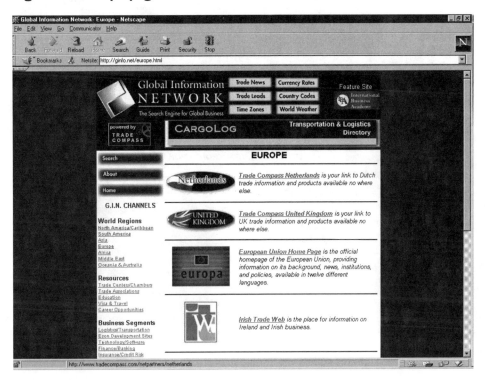

sense, GIN has emerged as the most comprehensive search engine and data source of its kind on the World Wide Web.

GIN's unique Tradelinks database comprises more than 1,600 sites that offer a variety of resources for global business (Figure B.8). These entries are constantly monitored for their quality and relevance to GIN's online community. The Tradelinks database provides a means for visitors to find quality global trade and business sites quickly and efficiently. GIN provides a feature on the homepage by which Web sites can submit their URLs for inclusion in the Tradelinks database.

Another helpful feature on the top of the GIN homepage is a bank of six pushbuttons that link to information that is updated daily, and which world trade professionals frequently want to know (Figure B.9). GIN keeps users up to date each day on Trade News, Trade Leads, Currency Rates, and World Weather. There are also helpful maps showing World Time Zones and all major Country Codes.

Figure B.6 Logistics & Transportation

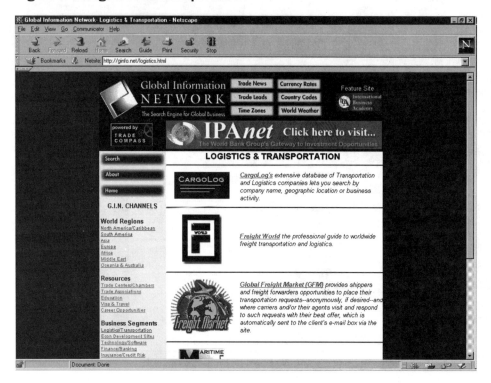

By offering access to large proprietary databases, search functionality to the entire Web, trade leads, time-zone information, country codes, industry-related news, and tips along with a number of other valuable resources, GIN dramatically showcases the Internet's ability to facilitate global commerce and world business.

GIN Provides Global Web Site Promotion

GIN provides an opportunity for many top-quality Web sites to join an elite network of specialized Internet companies, handpicked for their relevance to world trade professionals. Becoming part of this global consortium of targeted business-to-business sites can help attract additional advertising revenue, boost exposure, increase overall site traffic, and enhance a Web site's global business profile.

Right now, many high-quality targeted Web sites have trouble attracting quality advertisers because they don't have the technical capabilities to track ad deliv-

Figure B.7 GIN search page.

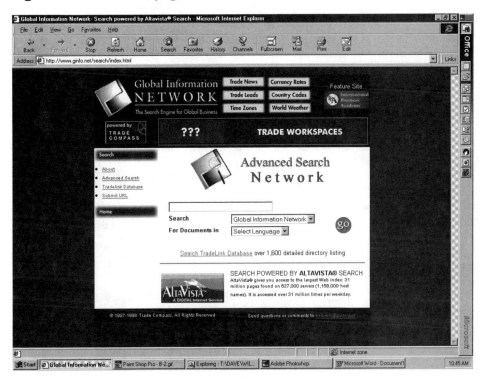

ery, don't have enough traffic, or don't have the personnel resources needed to handle online advertising demand.

Affiliates of GIN do not need to concern themselves with any of these issues. The network tracks and manages all ad delivery statistics, helps build traffic, and actively sells network advertising to well-known industry brands. Network affiliates share in the revenue collected from advertisers on the network, based on a percentage of the overall traffic they contribute during any given ad run. The affiliates are simply asked to continue to maintain the high caliber of their Web sites and to deliver quality traffic to the overall network.

As the Internet grows, it is also becoming harder and harder to navigate the growing number of sites coming online. Some sites struggle to gain prominent positioning on the main search engines, while others undertake the chore of exchanging links with everyone on the Web. GIN has established a single destination for business executives in search of the best in global trade resources.

Figure B.8 Tradelinks page.

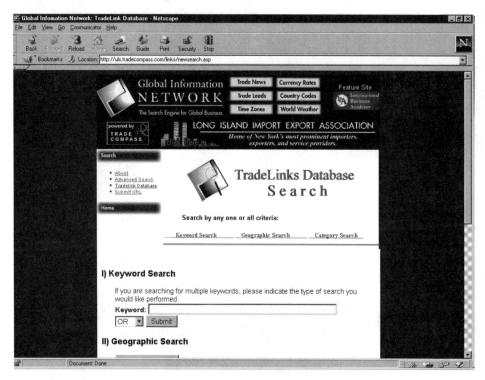

In addition to increased exposure as a network affiliate, all network sites are registered in GIN's advanced search engine. This search engine helps global trade executives find sites in the GIN network that contain the information they need, and this listing is free to all network members.

Minimum Requirements for GIN Affiliates

To become a GIN affiliate, each site in the network must meet the following minimum requirements for Quality, Traffic, and Demographics:

Quality. All GIN Web sites must look professional, be reasonably easy to navigate, contain a substantial amount of original content, and have accurate information.

Traffic. Instead of setting a minimum traffic requirement, we ask that all members take an active role in attracting qualified traffic to their site.

Figure B.9 GIN pushbuttons.

Demographics. Sites must prove, either by the nature of their site's content or by demographic information collected, that a substantial majority of their visitors are involved in global trade, importing, and exporting.

RSAC Rating. Affiliate sites must not exceed the Recreational Software Advisory Council (RSAC) standards for a rating of 0 for violence, sexual content, nudity, or strong language. For further details please visit www.rasc.org.

Any site wishing to become a GIN affiliate can start the process by clicking the link on the GIN homepage labeled "GIN Affiliates Program."

INDEX

Page references in *italic* type indicate illustrations.

150–180, 280–293
HotBot, 185
hoteling, 140
hot fixes, 113
hot links, 234
hot searching, 210
How to Do Business in
  Austria, 191
HTML extraction, in Web site
  localization, 68–69
Hungarian Home Page, 193
Hungary, 159
hyperlinks, copyright issues,
  79–80

I

ICARUS (Irish Community
  AirCargo Realtime Users
  System), 267
Iceland, 154, 158
Import/Export, 202
InAsia, 195, 221
in-country review, of localized
  Web sites, 70
India, 7, 161, 175
India Online, 194
India World, 194
indirect exporting, 248
Individuals, Inc., 137
individual security, 105–109
Indonesia, 7, 161, 162,
  175–176
industry associations, 223–224
Industry Sector Analyses, 22
industry-specific link sites, 215
Informant, 185, 214
information, 133. *See also*
  content; searching
    accessibility, 137, 138–139
    availability, 16
    relevance, 137–138
    sharing with colleagues,
      238
    source, 14–16
    timeliness, 14, 137,
      138–139
    updating, 137, 138

Information Age, 75
Information Content and
  Exchange (ICE) protocol,
  271
information economy, 133
Infoseek, 185
  buying words on, 230
  with Informant, 214
InfoSpace, 199, 237
Inter-American Development
  Bank, 188
internal communications,
  142–143
International Ad Hoc
  Committee, 87
International Advertising
  Resource Center, 229
International Business
  Resources, 27, 210, 215
international buying centers,
  252
International Comparisons,
  199
International Council of
  Management Consulting
  Institutes, 228–229
international financial
  institutions, 223
International Market Insights,
  21–22
International Tax Resources,
  227
International Trade
  Administration, 27, *28,*
  29, 188
International Trade Law
  Firms and Associations, 229
International Trade Law
  Monitor, 201
International Trade Law
  Project, 28
International Trade Leads,
  200, 215
Internet, 1. *See also* electronic
  commerce; global Internet
  markets surveys; global
  Webtrade; World Wide Web
    access and security

policies, 88–95
for buying, 208
global trends, 152–154
growth, 5, 31
inherent conflicts, 9–10
legal factors, see legal
  issues
market access, 149–150
nature of, 115
regional trends, 154–163
toaster urban legend, 97
Internet Advertising Resource
  Guide, 229
Internet Assigned Numbers
  Authority, 83, 85–87
Internet commerce, *see*
  electronic commerce
Internet communities,
  115–117, 253
    business strategy and,
      122–131
    elements of, 117–119
    evolution of, 120–121
    examples, 127–131
    institutional benefits,
      118–119
    social imperative in,
      126–131
    as strategic tool, 127
    success factors, 116
    technology, 119–120
    types of, 121–122
Internet Explorer, 182
Internet hosts, *see* hosts
Internet marketing network,
  236
Internet markets survey, *see*
  global Internet markets
  survey
Internet Network Information
  Center, 83
Internet service providers
  (ISPs), 182
    copyright law and, 76,
      78–79
Internet tip sheet, 237–238
Internet World, 203
interviews, 213

intranets
  checklist, 142–143
  content, 136–139
  defined, 133–134
  effectiveness benefits,
    135–136
  efficiency benefits,
    134–135
  future expectations,
    145–147
  goal setting, 143–145
  need determination,
    141–142
  virtual corporations,
    139–141
introductions, in virtual trade
  missions, 239–244
Irish Trade Web, 191
Israel, 160
Israel's Business Arena, 194
Italy, 158
I-Trade Export Guide, 18

J

Japan, 161–162, 164
Japanese language, 60, 61–64
Japan Information, 196
Japan Ministry of Foreign
  Affairs, 248
jargon, avoiding on virtual
  trade missions, 242
JETRO, 196
JFAX Personal Telecom, 238
joint research and
  development, 250
joint ventures, 249
journals, 220

K

Kazakhstan, 159
Kenya, 160
Kenya Web, 195
keys, 99–100
  escrow, 100–101
keyword ads, 229–230
keyword searches, 211
Kids with Cancer site, 122

Korean language, 60, 61–62
Kuwait, 160–161

L

language differences, in Web
  site localization, 56–58
Latin America, 280–282
  bookmarks, 188–190
  regional trends, 156–157
Latin American Network
  Information Center, 188
Lawrence Cybervillage, 121
lawyers, 229
lawyer subfolder bookmarks,
  201
Lebanon, 160
legal issues
  copyright law, 76–82
  corporate Internet access
    and security policies,
    88–95
  domain names, 83–87
  exporting, 28
  trademark law, 82–83
letter of intent, 255
licensing, 250
  copyright and, 77
  implied, in caching, 80–81
link sites, 214–218
The List, 182
local governments, 222–223
localization, *see* Web site
  localization
look and feel protection, 76
Lycos, 185
  with Informant, 214
Lyris, 236

M

Macedonia, 159
macro viruses, 109
magazines, 219
magazine writers, 220
mailing lists, 236
Malaysia, 161, 179–180
Malaysia Electronic
  Publication, 196

malls, online, 275
Malta External Trade
  Corporation, 192
management consultants,
  228–229
Managing Export Operations
  course, 18–19
Maritime Global Net, 202
market access, 149–150
market identification, 17,
  21–27
Market Potential Indicators
  for Emerging Markets,
  21, *22*
Market Research, 199, 216
market research reports, 216
market surveys, *see* global
  Internet markets survey
McDonald's Corporation,
  domain name, 86
MediaINFO Links, 199–200,
  219
MedSupport FSF, 128
memberships, of prospective
  partners, 247
mergers and acquisitions, 250
metaengines, 214
Mexico, 7, 157, 176–177
Mexico Information Center,
  189
Microsoft Internet Explorer,
  182
Middle East and Africa,
  286–290
  bookmarks, 194–195
  regional trends, 160–161
Middle East/North Africa
  Home Page, 194
Millipore Corporation
  Japanese Web site, 62–64
modems, 182, 277
motor carriers, 227–228

N

National Association of
  Foreign Trade Zones, 225
National Computer Security

Association (NCSA), 114
national governments,
    221–222
National Technology Index,
    216–217
National Trade Data Bank,
    17–18, 20, 21
negotiation, on virtual trade
    missions, 255–258
Net broadcasts, 218
Netcom, copyright case
    involving, 78
Netherlands, 158, 166–167
Netscape, 182
.net TLDs, 84
Network Associates virus
    software, 109
network security, 110–113
Network Solutions (NSI),
    83–87
Network Wizards, 150
    global survey data,
        150–163
news feeds, 137–139
newsgroups, 219
news networks, 219
newspaper ads, 219
NewsReal, 137
New Zealand, 161, 162, 170
New Zealand Embassy, 197
North America, 280–281
    bookmarks, 187–188
    regional trends, 154–156
North American Free Trade
    Agreement (NAFTA), 7
North American Industry
    Classification System, 207
Northern Lights, 185
Norway, 154, 158, 169–170
Norway Online, 192

O

obscene communications,
    92–93
ocean carriers, 228
offensive communications,
    92–93

Office of International Trade,
    29
128-bit keys, 100, 103
online auctions, 254
Online Dictionaries and
    Translators, 229
Online Language
    Dictionaries, 203
online malls, 252
online research, 13–16
online sales, 274–275
online services
    caching by, 80
    chat, 119–120
    copyright law and, 76
online storefronts, 252
online support, 254
Open Buying on the Internet
    (OBI) protocol, 271
Open Trading Protocols
    (OTP), 271
Opportunities for
    Employment, 217
organizations, trade leads,
    220–225
.org TLDs, 84
outsourcing, 140
overseas encryption software,
    101–102

P

PaintShop Pro, 234
Pakistan, 161
Panama: Crossroads of the
    Americas, 189
partnership trade pitches,
    249–250
passwords, 105–107
patch levels, 113
patent databases, 216
Patent Web, 216
periodicals, trade leads,
    218–220
personal computers, 182
    security, 109–110
personal information, 260
Peru Online, 190

Philippine Embassy, 196
Philippines, 161, 162
phone tag, 134–135
physical security, of networks,
    111
pictures, for virtual trade
    mission brochure, 233–234
piggyback marketing, 249
Playboy Enterprises, copyright
    case involving, 78
PointCast, 137
point-to-point data
    transmission, 268
Poland, 7, 159, 178–179
Poland Now, 193
pollster subfolder bookmarks,
    200
pornographic Web sites policy,
    88
press releases, 217
private key cryptography,
    98–99
private keys (public key
    cryptography), 99–101
PR Newswire, 217
procurement agencies, 221
Procurement Assistance
    Jumpstation, 200, 221
Prodigy, 121
product development, intranet
    applications, 136
professionals, trade leads,
    226–230
promotion, virtual trade
    missions, 237
provincial governments, 222
proxy caching, 80
proxy servers, 112
public key cryptography,
    99–102
public keys, 99–100
public libraries, 213

Q

qualifying
    language specialists, 67
    trade partners, 244–248

Queen's Award for Export
   Achievement, 226
Quick Consultant, 18

R

rail carriers, 228
Railroads Worldwide, 228
rainmaker subfolder
   bookmarks, 200
RealAudio, 182, 218
RealVideo, 218
REESWeb, 192
referral networks, 253
referrals, 241
regional governments, 222
regional Internet market
   rankings, 154–163, 280–293
registration, with online
   business directories, 237
reporter subfolder bookmarks,
   199–200
researcher subfolder
   bookmarks, 198–199
research papers, 213
resume databases, 218
retail outlets, 249
Reuters, 137
Revenue Canada Importing
   and Exporting, 187
Riley Guide, 203, 218
Roadrunner Computer
   Systems, domain name, 86
Romania, 159
Romania Business Economics,
   193
Royal Netherlands Embassy, 192
Royal Thai Embassy, 197
Russia, 159, 172–173
Russian Business and Trade
   Connections, 193
Russia Today, 193

S

Salam Iran, 194
sales figures, making available
   on intranets, 138

sales representatives, 249
San Francisco Partnership,
   57–58
Scandinavia, 154, 158
scheduling, intranets for, 135
seaport business development
   managers, 228
search engines
   buying words on, 230
   for trade lead scanning,
      213–214
   trade resource center
      folder, 183–185
searching
   online research, 13–16
   trade leads, 208–213
   trade partner qualifying
      information, 247
Secure Electronic
   Transactions (SET) protocol,
   103–104, 271
secure identification, 105–107
Secure Sockets Layer (SSL)
   protocol, 103
security
   data, 98–105
   individuals, 105–109
   resources, 114
   systems, 110–113
   workstations, 109–110, 113
security technology, 102–105
selling trade pitches, 248–249
Serbia, 160
server security, 111, 113
Service Corps of Retired
   Executives (SCORE), 29
service packs, 113
sexually explicit Web sites, 88
Shareware.com, 182
shipper subfolder bookmarks,
   202–203
Si, Spain, 192
signature file, 235–236
Singapore, 162
Singapore Government, 196
Slovenia, 159
Slovenia Chamber of

Commerce, 193
Small Business Exporters
   Association, 29
Small Business Guide to
   Exporting, 198
smart cards, 108
sourcing trade pitches,
   250–251
South Africa, 7, 160, 173
South African Business
   Directory, 195
South Asian Preferential
   Trade Arrangement
   (SAPTA), 7
Southern Cone Common
   Market, 7
South Korea, 7, 161, 162,
   170–171
Spain, 158, 172, 192
spam, 241
Spanish language, 57
sponsored databases, 254
sponsors, of intranets, 134
Standard Industrial
   Classification (SIC) codes,
   20, 207
Standard International Trade
   Classification (SITC) codes,
   20
state governments, 222
STAT-USA, 16
STAT-USA Export and
   International Trade, 199
stock trading, 138
storefronts, online, 275
.store (proposed TLD), 87
Strategis, 187
Stronghold, 103
subject-specific link sites, 215
subscription-based services,
   16, 254
suppliers, 208
support-based Internet
   communities, 122
surge protectors, 111
Survey of Luxembourg, 191
surveys, 213

V

value-added networks (VANs),
265, 269
  Web-based EDI, 272–273
venture capital firms, 226–227
VeriSign, 102, 107
virtual billboards, 251
virtual business matchmakers,
253
virtual communities, *see*
  Internet communities
virtual consultants, 253
virtual corporations, 139–141
Virtual Customs Online, 202
Virtual International Search
  Engines, 214
virtual offices, 238
virtual private networking
  (VPN), 112–113, 274
virtual reference checks, 246
virtual seminars, 254
virtual trade missions, 231
  follow-up, 239
  introducing yourself,
    239–244
  managing new business
    relationships, 258–261
  negotiating, 255–258
  partnership pitches,
    249–250
  preparing for, 232–238
  qualifying potential
    partners, 244–248
  selling pitches, 248–249
  sourcing pitches, 250–251
  web-based pitches,
    251–254
virtual trade shows, 253
virtual trade team, 258
virtual trade teams folder,
  trade resource center,
  197–203
virtual universities, 18–19
viruses, *see* computer viruses

W

warm searching, 210
Web, *see* World Wide Web
Web-based EDI, 269–273
Web-based standards, 263–264
web-based trade pitches,
  251–254
Webcasting, 254
Web cookies, 104–105
Webcrawler, 185
Web/Internet resource
  executive (WIRE), 181–182
Web Marketing Info Center,
  203
Webmaster, 76
Webmaster subfolder
  bookmarks, 203
Website Banner Advertising,
  229, 252
Web site globalization, 97–98.
  See also security
Web site localization, 55–56
  agency selection, 64–68
  cultural differences, 58–59
  language differences,
    56–58
  process, 68–73
  typesetting issues, 59–64
Webzines, 254
Welcome to Italy, 191
Welcome to Kyrgyzstan, 193
Welcome to Portugal, 192
Welcome to South Africa, 195
Welcome to Vietnam, 197
The Well, 120
Western Europe, 282–284
  bookmarks, 190–192
  regional trends, 157–158
Whowhere, 237
wide area networks (WANs),
  112–113, 142
wide-open markets, 153
wireless communications, 264,
  277
word processor, using while

browsing, 210
worker empowerment, 146
workstation security, 109–110,
  113
WorldClass, 199, 210, 215
World Customs Organization,
  202
The World Factbook, 26, 198
World Intellectual Property
  Organization, 6, 81–82
World Trade Analyzer, 20
World Trade Database, 196
World Trade Organization, 6
World Trade Organization
  negotiations, 260
Worldwide Corporate Tax
  Guide, 28
World Wide Web, 1. *See also*
  electronic commerce; global
  Webtrade; Internet
    datawebs, 10–11
    frustrations, 211
    growth, 31
    inherent conflicts, 9–10
    legal factors, see legal
      issues
    online sales, 275–276
    searching for trade partner
      qualifying information,
      247–248
WWW Virtual Library, 215

Y

Yahoo, 185, 230

Z

Ziff Davis Net University,
  129–130